I0793318

IMAGES
*of America*

# HAMPTON COUNTY

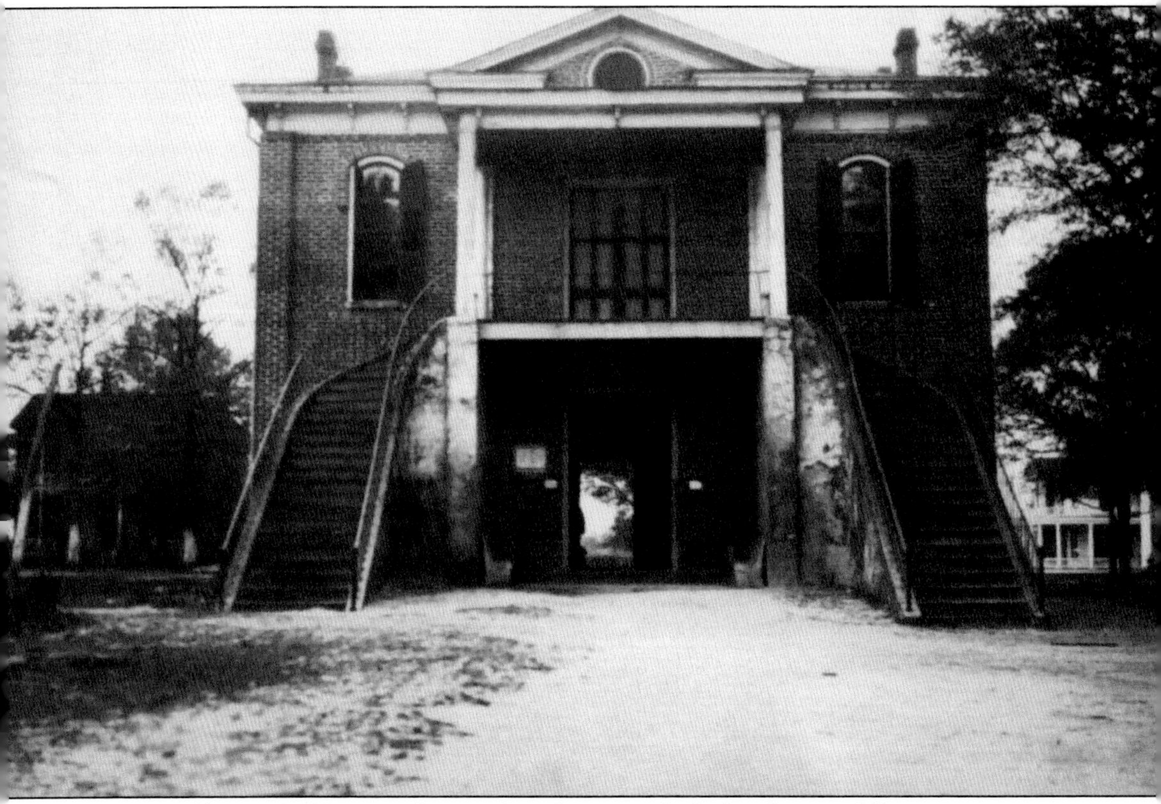

Pictured here is the Hampton County Courthouse as it looked in the years following its construction in 1878, shortly after the county was carved from the Beaufort District. The recently renovated and modernized courthouse still overlooks historic Lee Avenue and remains the legal and symbolic heart and soul of Hampton County. (Courtesy of the *Hampton County Guardian* archives.)

**On the Cover:** Piles of ice-cold, juicy watermelons, families with children, and lots of smiles can be found at the Hampton County Watermelon Festival, which began in 1939. In this 1960s-era photograph, a lovely elementary school teacher, Ellen Phillips, poses for a photograph during the watermelon festival, surrounded by curious youngsters. In the background is a truck from a festival sponsor, C.B. Herndon trucking. (Courtesy of Libby Smith.)

IMAGES
*of America*

# HAMPTON COUNTY

Michael DeWitt Jr.

ARCADIA
PUBLISHING

ISBN 978-1-4671-1408-0

Published by Arcadia Publishing
Charleston, South Carolina

Printed in the United States of America

Library of Congress Control Number: 2014957993

For all general information, please contact Arcadia Publishing:
Telephone 843-853-2070
Fax 843-853-0044
E-mail sales@arcadiapublishing.com
For customer service and orders:
Toll-Free 1-888-313-2665

Visit us on the Internet at www.arcadiapublishing.com

*This book is dedicated to my children and your children that they may discover their past and build a better tomorrow.*

# Contents

# ACKNOWLEDGMENTS

The author wishes to acknowledge, with the utmost gratitude and respect, the keepers of our history and the true historians of Hampton County: the volunteers and curators at the Hampton County Historical Society, the Hampton Museum and Visitors' Center, and the Hampton Old Colored School Museum; Marie Ellis and the late Mildred Rivers, who taught me that history was truly alive in all of us and a museum was more than just a place to store old things; the late Dwight Moore, a man who loved photographing Hampton County, its happenings, and its people; and Jeff Hunt, who had the wisdom and desire to preserve Moore's work and the generosity to share it. My sincere gratitude also goes to the many people who took the time to locate and submit their cherished photographs and entrust them to me. And a deeply felt, personal thank-you is due to the two ladies who come to my aid the most: my devoted and patient wife, Valerie, for motivating me and inspiring me to stay focused and organized, and my faithful partner in business and journalism, the talented and artistic Kim Doctor.

The majority of the images in this volume appear courtesy of the *Hampton County Guardian* archives (HCG), the Hampton Museum and Visitors' Center (HMVC), the Brunson Museum and Visitors' Center (BMVC), and the collection of the late Dwight Moore, courtesy of Jeff Hunt (DM).

# INTRODUCTION

From Indian uprisings through the Civil War and Reconstruction to the harrowing days of the Cold War–era space race, Hampton County is a place where history, natural beauty, and Southern charm meet and get along quite nicely.

That history lives in its place names, rivers, and landmarks and is preserved on county road signs and chamber of commerce maps, featuring names of once-great tribes like Salkehatchie, Coosawhatchie, Yemassee, and Savannah. Here, Indian warriors attacked settlers amid echoing war drums, British Redcoats wrought widespread destruction, Revolutionary guerilla bands taunted and attacked Loyalists and the king's army and then fled to the safety of the densely wooded Savannah River basin, Union solders burned churches, homes, and dreams during Sherman's devastating March to the Sea, and Yankee carpetbaggers descended to prey on vanquished Confederates.

French corsairs and Spanish galleons came and went, leaving little more than a few ruins and artifacts in their quickly erased footprints amid the sands of history, but the English established a lasting foothold. In 1707, the nearby coastal settlement of Beaufort was founded and the Beaufort District contained modern-day Beaufort and Hampton Counties. After the Civil War and the chaos of Reconstruction, soon-to-be governor Gen. Wade Hampton and his Red Shirts followers restored their brand of Southern order. In 1877, locals were granted permission to establish a separate Hampton County in General Hampton's honor. In 1878, the Hampton County Courthouse was completed and the county seat established in what would later become the town of Hampton. Governor Hampton even journeyed down from the state capital of Columbia to personally lay the courthouse cornerstone.

In the late 1800s and early 1900s, the Hampton County Courthouse, the county's physical and symbolic center of law, order, and justice, was often the scene of many violent and drunken political rallies, the occasional court-ordered hanging, and even a murder by stabbing on the courthouse steps on Election Day in 1880. But with a wink followed by a stern look, some local historians will insist that out of politeness folks should not talk about such dark historic events.

The brick and mortar and pine of the courthouse has crumbled, been replaced, and at least thrice been remodeled over the decades, with the most recent renovation funded by a penny sales tax approved by Hampton County voters. The Hampton County Courthouse visitors see today is an aesthetically pleasing Lowcountry landmark that combines rustic architecture and historical décor with state-of-the-art security and computer software systems.

Hampton County, with its abundant waterways, fertile forests, and rural settings, became a farmers' and sportsmen's paradise for freshwater fishing as well as quail, dove, and duck hunting, sundry small game, and majestic whitetail deer, but then again natives have known that for hundreds of years. Over the centuries, plantations that once used slave labor to produce cotton and other crops are now either private hunting retreats, commercial hunting lodges, or have been sold or donated to the state for preservation in wildlife easements and Department of Natural Resources–operated game management areas. Word got out about the area's natural resources, of course, and today the outdoor recreation and tourism industry commands a sizable portion of the local economy, with countless hunters making an annual pilgrimage from as far away as the Florida peninsula or the frigid New England areas to enjoy one of the longest and most productive deer seasons in the Southeast.

Isolated by rural miles and the agrarian lifestyle, families formed small, close-knit communities throughout the county—seemingly at almost every crossroads or rail depot—and built a plethora of churches and schools. Reportedly, the oldest documented church is Lawtonville Baptist, organized in 1775 in the Lawtonville community, near the Estill area. For many hardworking residents, church was an important institution that offered not only salvation for the soul but a welcome respite from the labors of the farm and an equally treasured opportunity to gather with family, friends, and neighbors for anything from sermons and revivals to dinners on the grounds and softball games.

But from time to time, folks liked to gather for bigger events such as countywide field days, which often drew people from every village in the county. In 1939, a band of volunteers decided to hold a festival in honor of the sweet watermelon, for decades the area's largest crop and export, and thus the Hampton County Watermelon Festival was born. The watermelon festival has grown to become the oldest continuing festival in South Carolina, with reportedly the longest parade route of any event in the state. The festival, which includes parades for adults and children alike, family fun days, the best of local Southern cuisine, a Battle of the Towns, dancing in the street, mud racing and more, continues to draw visitors and home folks alike from around the Southeast and beyond. It has become an annual reunion for many family members and old friends.

Scores of miles away from the attractions of the nearest cities, Hampton County residents yearned for entertainment and culture of their own. At onetime, there were several small movie theaters around the county, primarily in the towns of Hampton and Varnville, which were popular in the early- and mid-1900s. But only one theater survived: the Palmetto Theater on Lee Avenue, Hampton's historic main street. Built in 1946, the theater closed as a motion picture venue in the late 1980s and lay dormant for years before being purchased in 1989 by the newly created Hampton County Arts Council and subsequently restored. Since its restoration, the Palmetto has been reborn as a performing arts center, live concert venue, and community hub. In 2009, the council, with the generous aid of the Stanley family that originally co-owned the Palmetto Theater, was able to obtain the vacant retail property next door and created the T.G. and Ailie Stanley Arts Center to expand its offerings.

In the early 1940s, Plywoods-Plastics Corporation (PPC) brought a manufacturing facility into the town of Hampton, bringing with it hundreds of jobs, and life in Hampton County and surrounding areas changed drastically for many. PPC was later purchased by Westinghouse, which operated its Micarta Division here for decades. During its heyday, the Westinghouse plant employed anywhere from 1,000 to 1,500 people and manufactured everything from plywood and military helmets during World War II to lightweight heat shields for American nuclear ballistic missiles. But the economic winds of change are always blowing, and Westinghouse sold the plant to International Paper (IP) in 1995 and then IP later sold it to Panolam Industries/Nevamar. In July 2014, Panolam officials announced they were closing the factory and laying off all employees by the end of 2014. An important era of progress had come to an end.

Despite Hampton County's many changes over the years, perhaps its most beloved and most lasting industry will always be its industrious people and the hometown small business and tourism industries. Folks still come from miles around to enjoy Hampton County's history, great hunting and fishing, warm Southern hospitality, beautiful scenery, and, of course, lots of ice-cold watermelon.

# *One*

# The Spirit of Hampton County

Small, rural communities dot the American landscape like stars in the Southern sky. Communities around the South shared many of the same wonderful qualities and many of the same challenges. So what made—and still makes—Hampton County special? It is the hardworking, fun-loving, caring, and generous people. In the personalities, pastimes, and stories of these colorful characters, one can truly find the spirit of Hampton County.

That spirit could be found in the hearts of the farmers, who toiled away through hard and simple lives yet considered themselves blessed; in the folks who worked the fields and mills and factories six days a week just to enjoy a Sunday of fishing or splashing in the local swimming hole after church; and in the volunteer firefighters who manned trucks and hoses to come to the aid of their neighbors. The Hampton County spirit especially shines through in times of need, such as when a friend or neighbor takes sick or suffers a devastating loss, and friends and strangers alike rally to their aid.

Hampton County's spirit of fun, love, and giving was most evident in its devotion to causes like the American Cancer Society's Relay For Life, an event that combines fun community activities with charitable giving. In recent years, this devotion led Hampton County to become the event's top fundraising county per capita in the state of South Carolina and one of the top 10 in the nation.

And this history of giving remains just as powerful today.

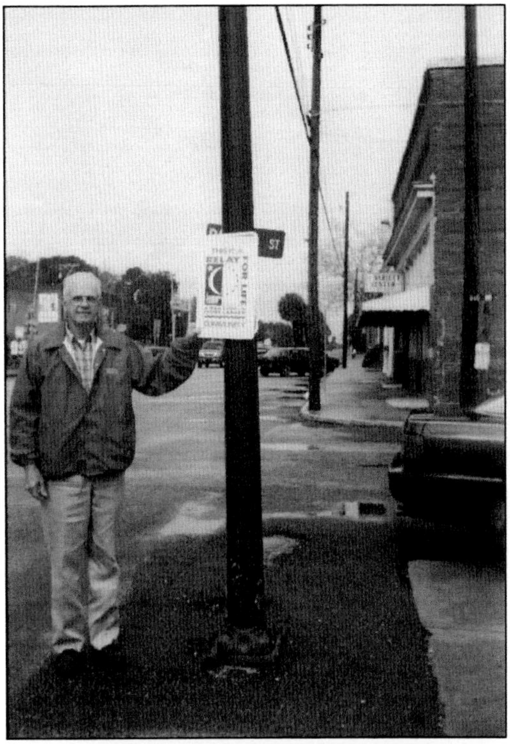

Hampton County joined the American Cancer Society's international Relay For Life effort in 1994, and within five years it had truly become a countywide endeavor. Hundreds of locals enjoyed a good time while supporting the fight against cancer. In the late 1990s, Varnville mayor Don DeLoach (pictured) and Hampton mayor John Rhoden proudly erected signs proclaiming their towns as Relay Communities. (Courtesy of Catherine Whittington.)

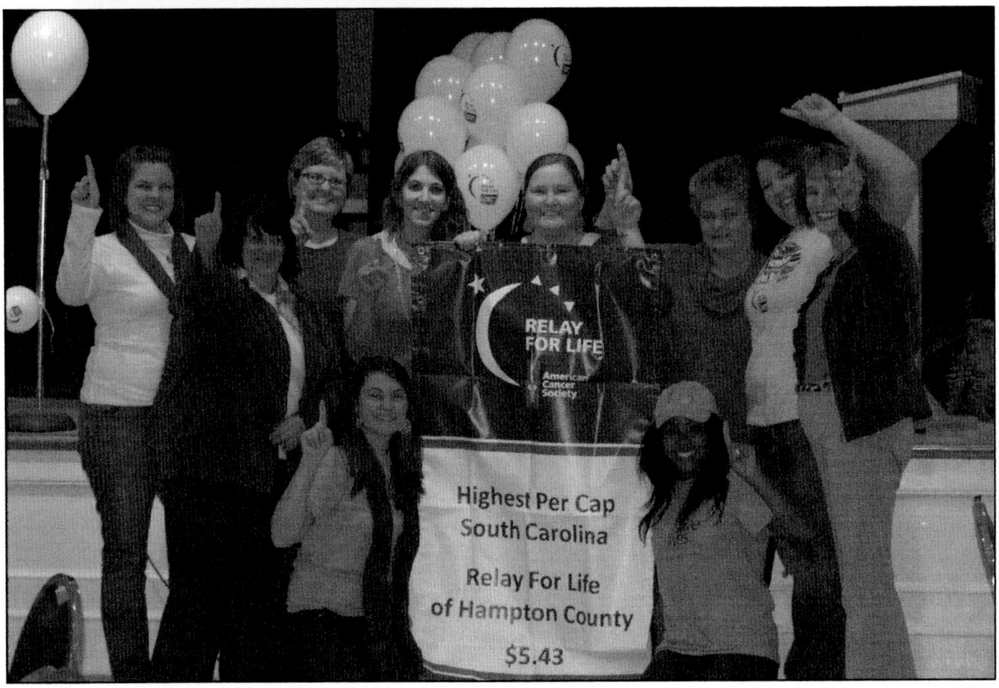


The first Relay For Life in Hampton County was held at Lake Warren State Park in 1994, and by the American Cancer Society's 2011–2012 fiscal fundraising year, the local effort had grown to become the top per capita fundraising county in South Carolina and no. 10 in the entire nation. (Courtesy of HCG.)

In 1952, 64-year-old W.L. Woods became custodian of the Hampton County Jail and served as one of the few female jailers in the nation for several years. It was reported that she ran her jail with a firm but motherly touch, feeding the prisoners well, keeping flowers, vegetables, and chickens in the prison yard, and counseling the wayward young offenders. (Courtesy of HCG.)

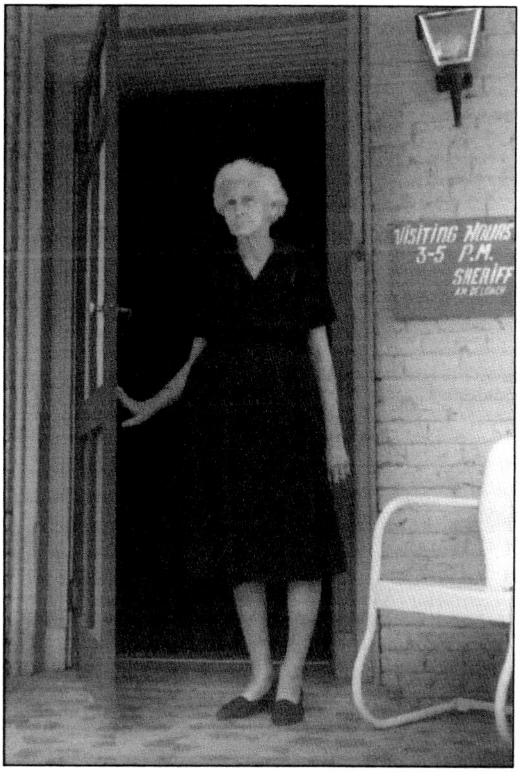


Loan and Exchange Bank president R.O. Bowden (left) made national headlines and the television news when he invited notorious bank robber James "Big Jim" Morton into his bank to discuss security in October 1950. Bowden was a colorful character and many stories about him are preserved in the Salkehatchie Stew oral history project, including the time he buried his gold under horse manure to keep it from the federal regulators. (Courtesy of HCG.)

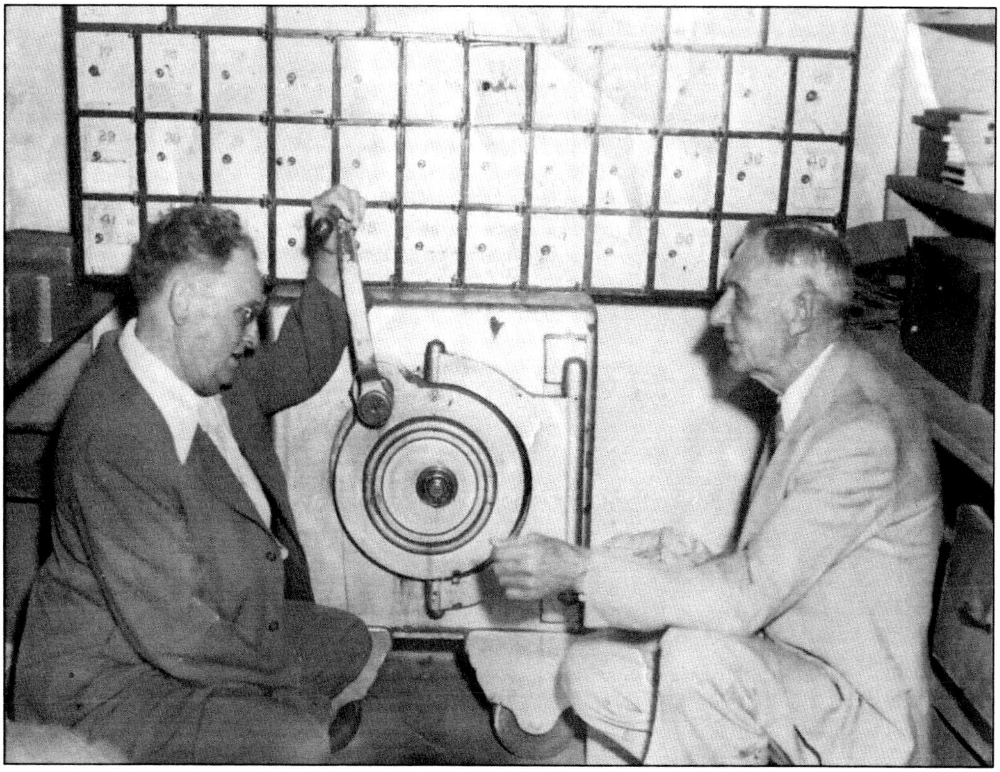

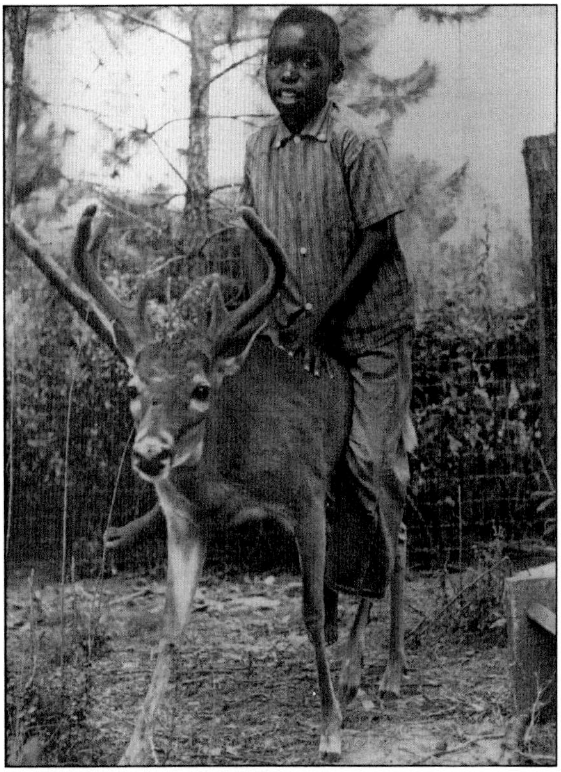

In this photograph taken on June 19, 1959, Garnett-area youngster Leroy Johnston playfully rides his pet deer Bambi. This photograph perfectly illustrates the close relationship the people of Hampton County have with nature and the environment: Wildlife not only provided food and recreation for rural residents but companionship as well. (Courtesy of DM.)

In this 1955 photograph, Larry Lee and an unidentified friend, shotguns and bridled pony ready, prepare for a day of hunting with smiling faces. Hunting in the Lowcountry could mean lying in wait for a big whitetail buck, stalking rabbits, squirrels, or other small game, or searching the sky for doves—but a trusty 12-gauge shotgun was handy for all hunters. (Courtesy of DM.)

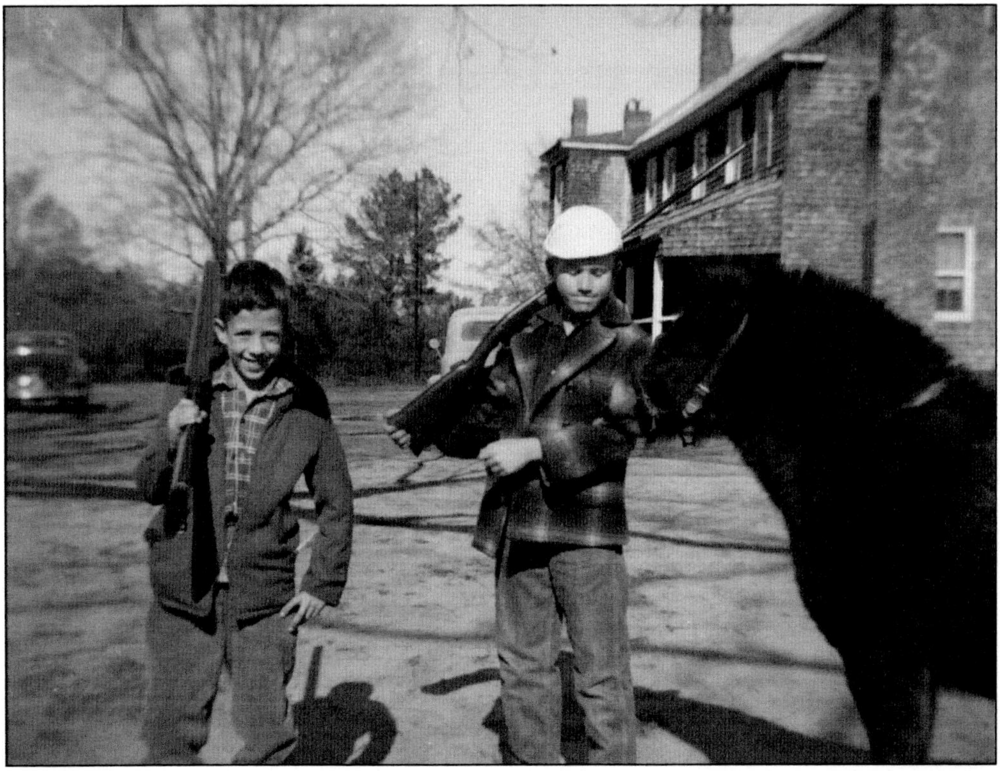

In this June 5, 1958, photograph, E.W. Nail smiles broadly as he proudly displays a stringer of 12 fish, reportedly the first caught from Dunn's Pond on Hamilton Ridge plantation. Ponds like this provided more than just a good fried bream meal for local fishermen: They were a great source of relaxation, recreation, and quality family time for all ages. (Courtesy of DM.)

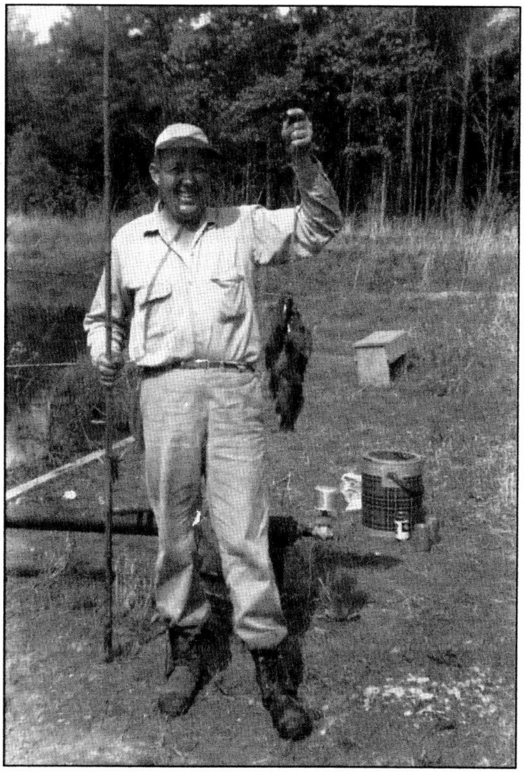

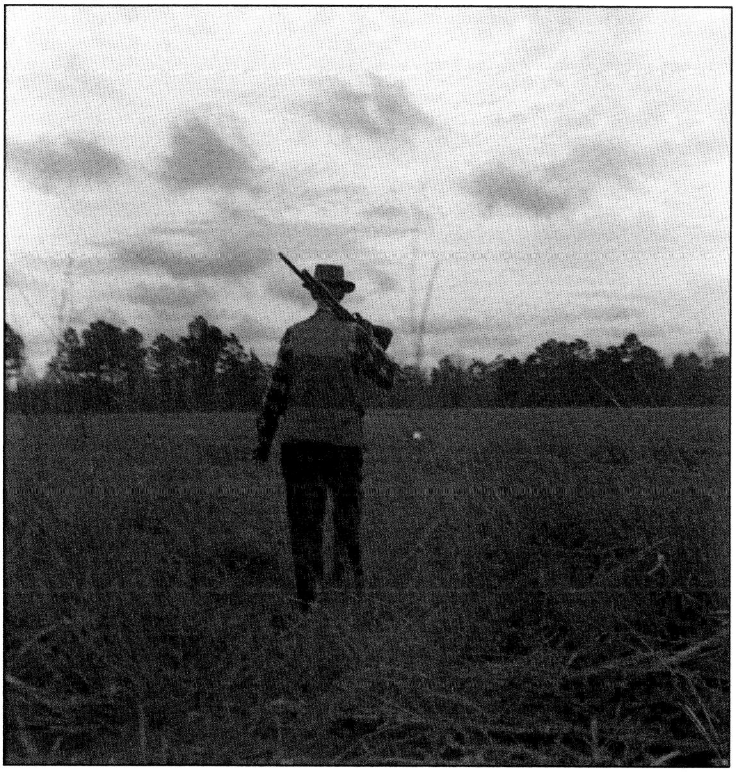

Trusty shotgun in hand, on March 1, 1961, Flynt Moore strolls off through waist-high brush, likely aiming for birds or small game. One of the greatest Southern outdoor writers, Havilah Babcock, often wrote that he would rather hunt birds in the South Carolina Lowcountry than anywhere else in the world. (Courtesy of DM.)

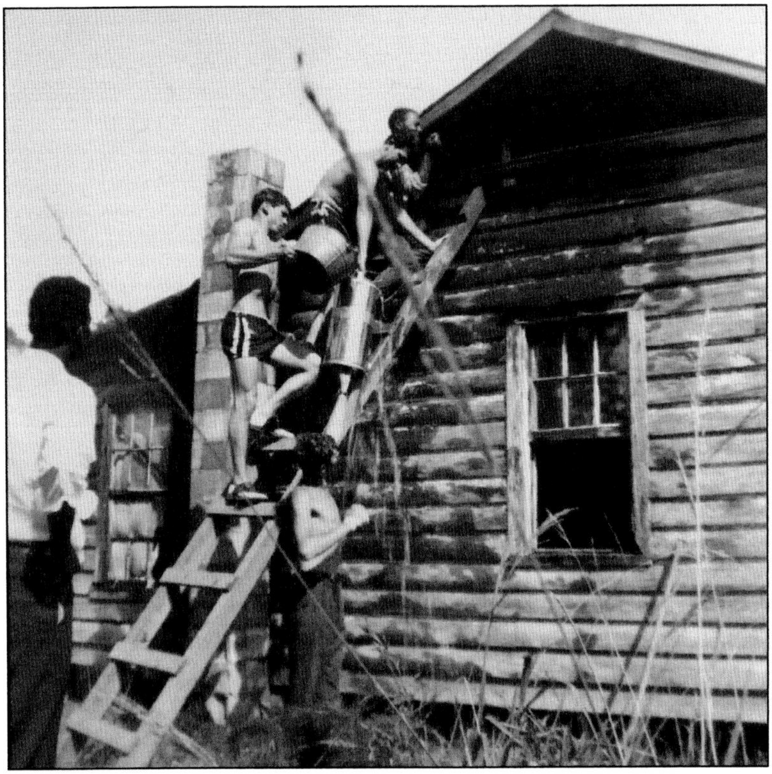

The first volunteer fire departments were the bucket brigades, as evidenced during this Garnett house fire photographed on August 2, 1965. As devastating as they were, tragedies like this tended to bring communities together—black and white, young and old, rich and poor—to rush to the aid of their neighbors. (Courtesy of DM.)

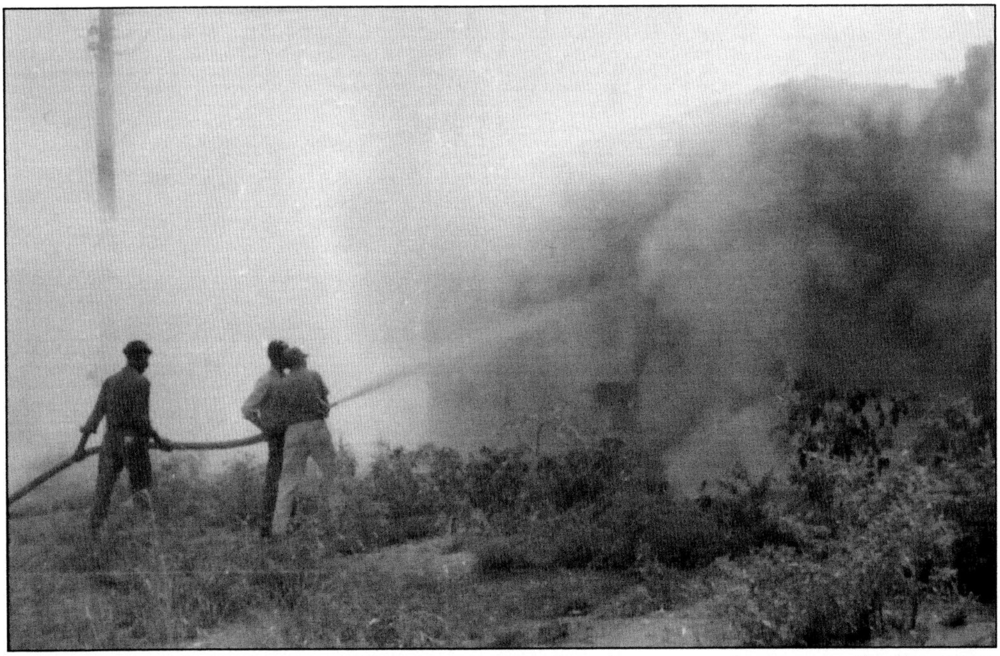

A major fire struck the Harper and Bowers agricultural product storage facility near Estill in 1966. While residential fires often displaced entire families, blazes at agricultural and industrial sites often resulted in multiple families in more than one community left without jobs and income for lengthy periods of time. (Courtesy of DM.)

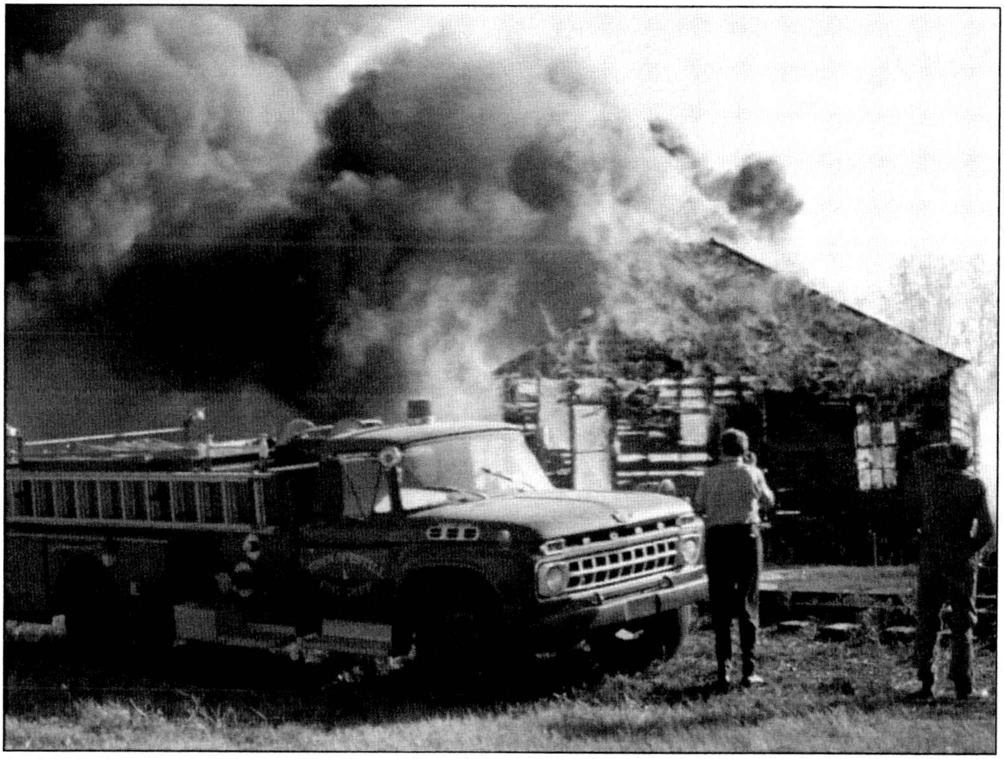

In 1974, this Garnett home was completely destroyed by fire before the Estill Fire Department could arrive. This was often the price of living in a rural area, miles away from towns like Estill that had organized volunteer fire departments. Garnett, located in the southwest corner of the county near the Georgia border, was the most isolated community in Hampton County. (Courtesy of DM.)

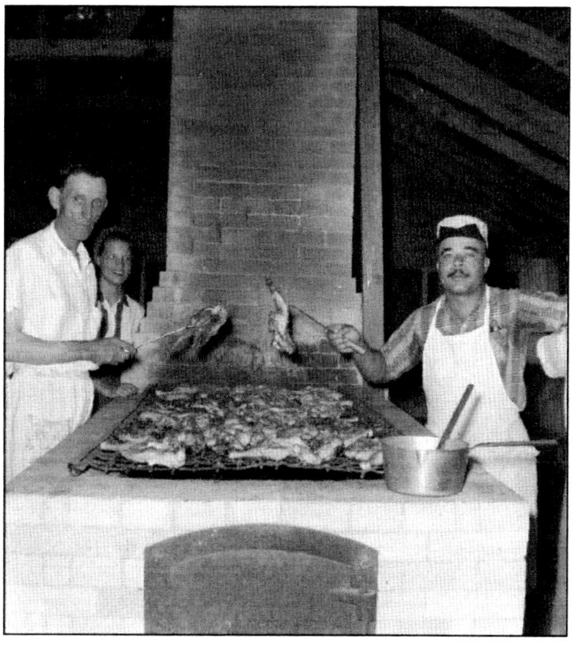

H.F. Arledge (left), Virginia Rushing (center), and Jake ? tend to an old-fashioned pit barbecue on May 25, 1958. Barbecue was more than a smoky, sweet Southern staple; it was often a source of fellowship and fundraising for local fire departments, churches, or even caring neighbors looking to raise money for a friend battling cancer or other problems. (Courtesy of DM.)

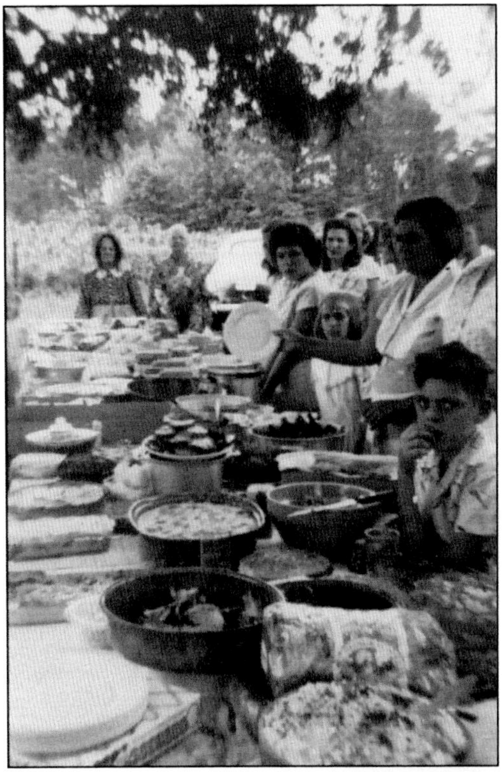

Tables placed end to end under a shady, ancient oak tree can barely contain all of the dishes prepared for a DeWitt family get-together in this 1950s-era photograph. The tables, handmade by a family carpenter, are full of fresh-from-the-farm produce, fried chicken, preserves, homemade bread, and pretty much any covered dish one can imagine. And guests or even strangers were always welcome. (Courtesy of Ann Long.)

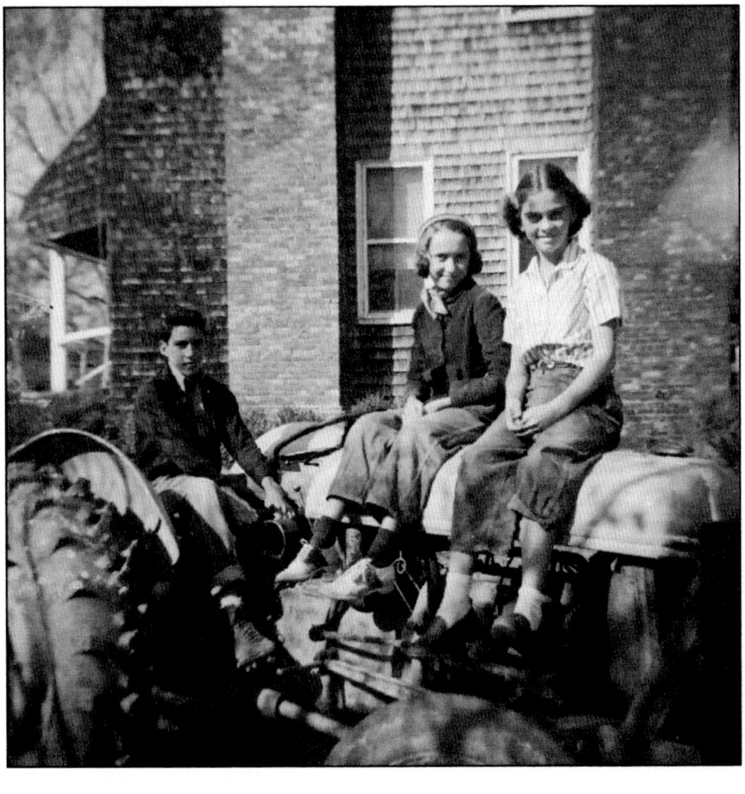

On the farm, work and play were often found in the same activity, as displayed in this June 5, 1958, photograph of Diane Jackson, Sonny Mobley, and Jane Moore. Friends and family often joined in the work and fun at harvesttime and there was sure to be plenty of fresh produce for all. (Courtesy of DM.)

Friends Eugene Pinckney (left) and Louis Hunt were photographed together on June 10, 1968. The photographer does not make note of the reason for the occasion, but this image perfectly illustrates the fact that, despite the differences between these Southern men, they are surprisingly similar in many ways—perhaps a moral for future generations to remember. (Courtesy of DM.)

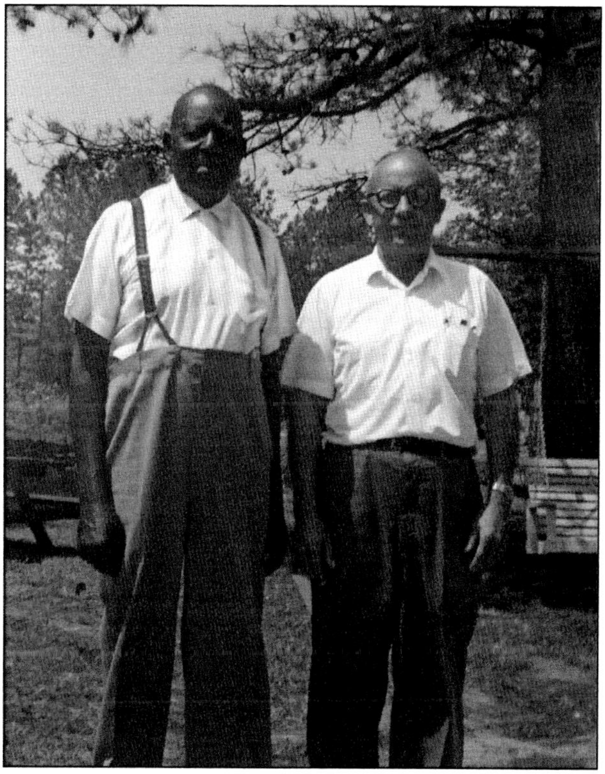

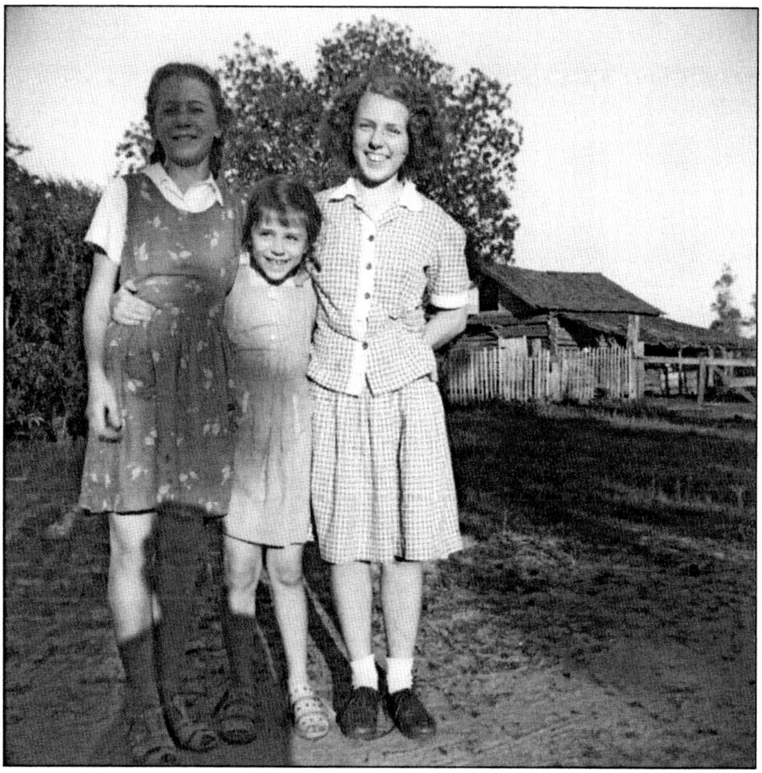

Janie Ellen was photographed with Rita and Miriam Kittles on June 10, 1959. Their clothes appear simple, likely made from feed sacks as was the local custom, and their abode humble, but the smiles on their faces testify to the fact that it was friendship and family, not wealth, that brought happiness. (Courtesy of DM.)

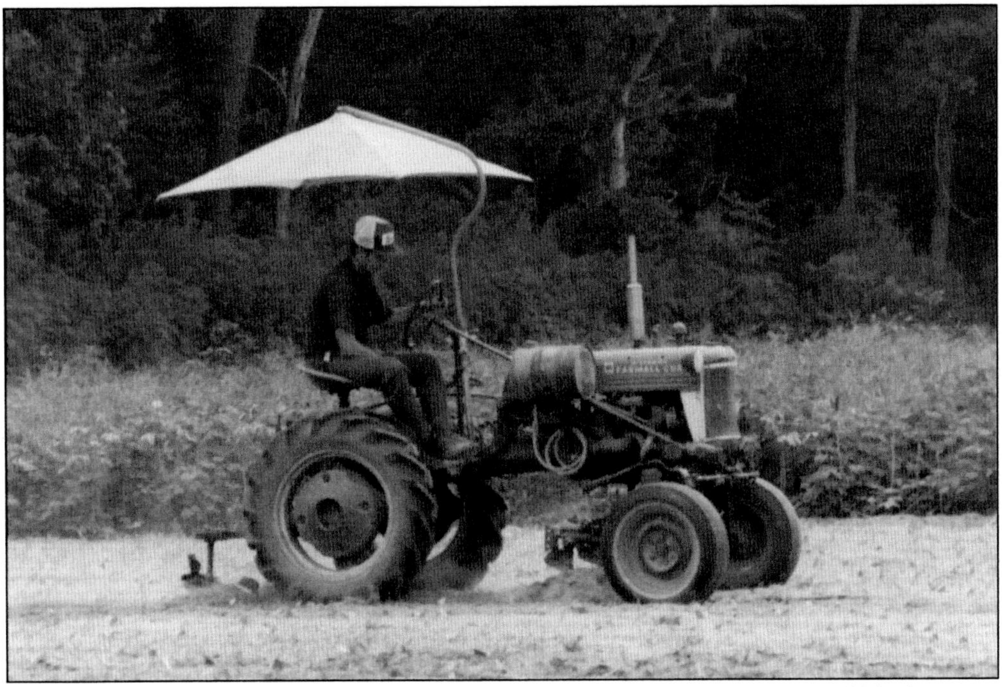

Farming was not just a business for rural Hampton County folks, it was a way of life then as it is for many now. In the 1980 photograph above, David McKenzie gets a lot of mileage out of his 1940s-model tractor while plowing a field on his farm in Shirley. In the 1950s-era photograph below, Varnville-area farmer Quillie McAlhaney takes a break from the day's chores to take his children, Hiram (left) and Marsha for a ride. (Above, courtesy of Cecilia Baker McKenzie; below, courtesy of Ann DeWitt Long.)

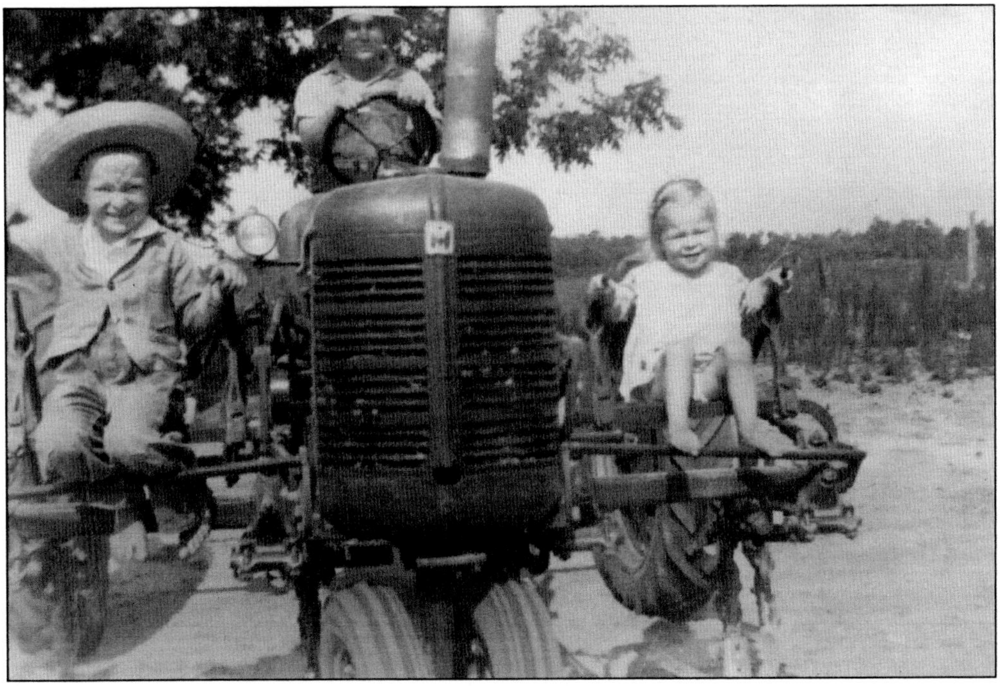

Those born and raised in rural Hampton County developed a close relationship with nature in all its many forms, and that is evident in the farming and hunting lifestyles. Wild game and livestock kept the family fed, but they were also appreciated and often cared for in turn. In the December 1962 photograph on the right, James DeWitt and his eldest son, Michael, skin a freshly killed deer in front of a log smokehouse that was likely used to help preserve some of the meat. In the 1961 photograph below, a young Hampton County farmer bottle-feeds a hungry and feisty calf on his family's farm. (Both, courtesy of Ann DeWitt Long.)

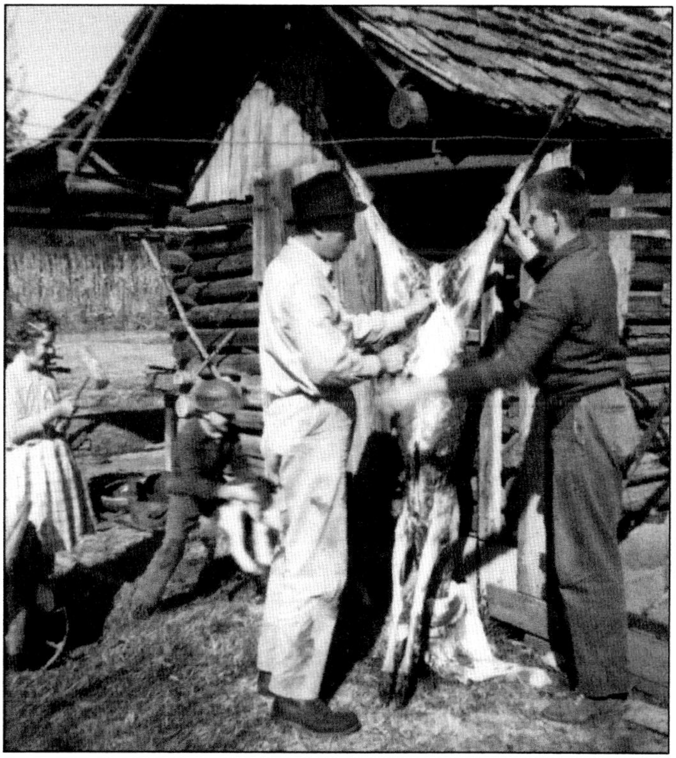

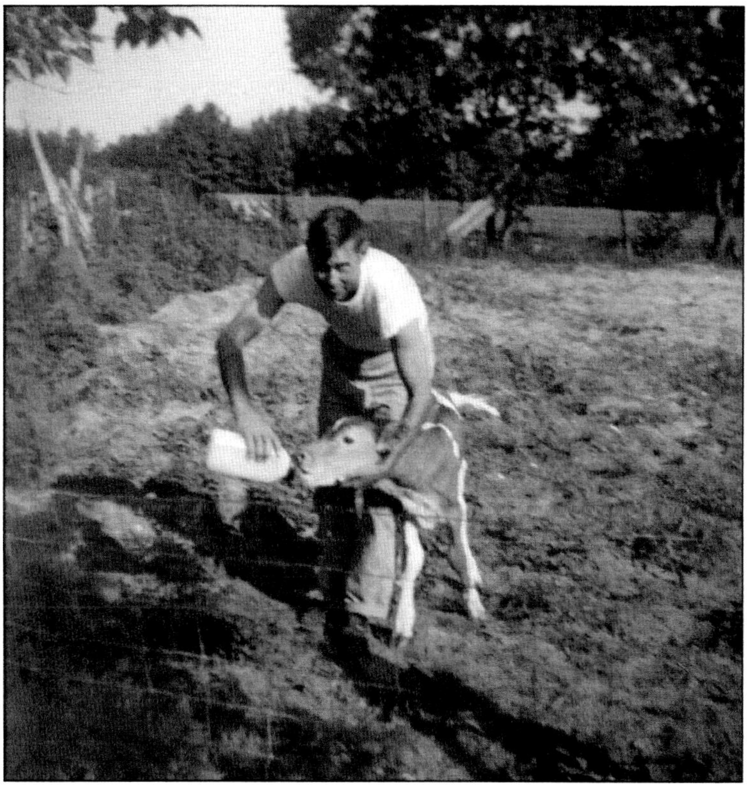

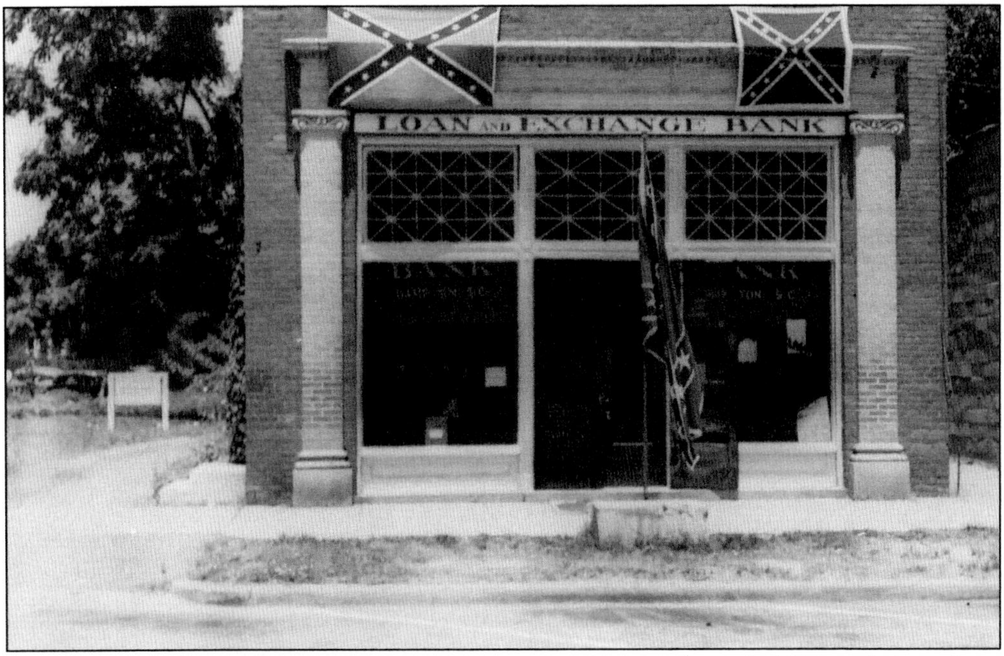


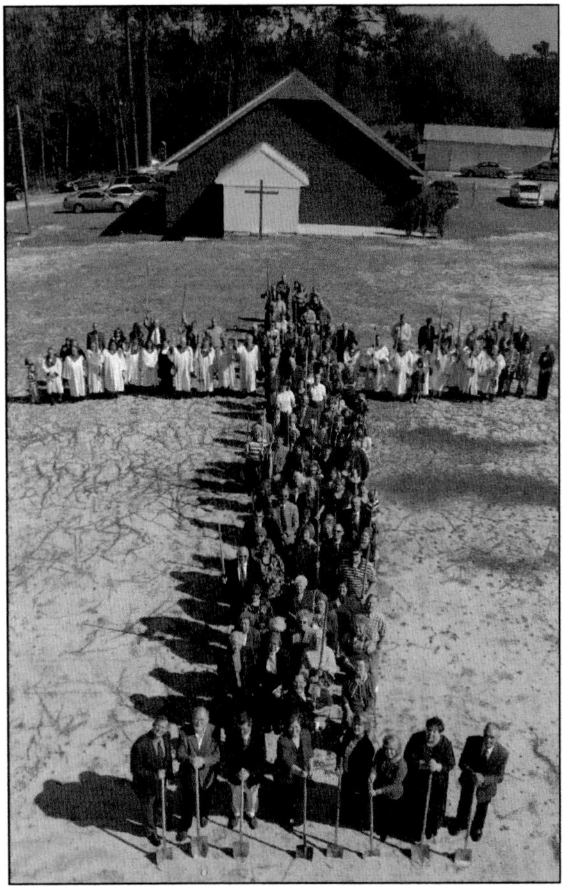

During the early 1900s and through the Great Depression, R.O. Bowden was president of the Loan and Exchange Bank on Lee Avenue, Hampton, and was a well-known but eccentric character who became the source of many local legends, including once reportedly (according to his family) burying his gold beneath his horse stable to keep the federal regulators at bay. Later, Bowden also adorned his bank with Confederate flags and for years refused to take them down. (Courtesy of HMVC.)

Like a phoenix of faith, Sandy Run Baptist Church soared from the ashes. The sanctuary, built in 1904, was destroyed by fire on Sunday, November 4, 2007, but Sandy Run worshipers gathered nonetheless, their church smoldering in the background, one surviving piano still dripping from county fire hoses, to hold Sunday worship and begin rebuilding. This symbolic ground-breaking ceremony was held in March 2009. The church was rebuilt later that year. (Courtesy of HCG.)

# *Two*

# Hampton County at a Glance

Hampton County has not grown much over the years. The most recent census tally looks very much like it did in 1920. One could argue, to use a cliché, that the more things have changed in Hampton County, the more they have stayed the same. Perhaps, to many folks, that is part of the county's charm.

Hampton County's roots and history begin to some large degree with the construction of the Hampton County Courthouse and the establishment of the county seat in 1878. Since that date, the courthouse, while undergoing many changes and renovations, has been a constant fixture in the Hampton landscape, both the physical and symbolic heart and soul of the county. It still stands today, grander than ever, after voters recently approved a penny sales tax referendum to give it a much-needed face-lift.

"Main Street" has always been a business and residential hub in the largest towns of Hampton, Varnville, and Estill and this remains true today. And like the courthouse, Hampton's historic downtown Lee Avenue and other main thoroughfares in the county are now getting the renovations needed to preserve their beauty and charm for future generations.

Commerce is important to any community, and in the pre-industrial days that meant trading with trusted local merchants like the Rivers family in Hampton and the Baker family in Estill. Large industry came in the early 1940s in the form of Plywoods-Plastics (later Westinghouse and then Nevamar), and that manufacturing giant became a game changer for thousands of blue-collar families around the area. Following on its coattails came many spin-off companies, the construction of a new county hospital, and even the construction of a massive lake and the formation of Lake Warren State Park. Things were really looking up for a growing Hampton County.

But Nevamar officials announced plans in 2014 to shutter this key factory for good, leaving county economic development officials with the ongoing challenge of finding and recruiting new industries and new jobs, but also leaving Hampton County ripe for investment and once again hungry for growth and the renewed promise of a bright tomorrow.

The more things change, the more they stay the same. But one thing has remained constant here: the hopeful, hardworking spirit of down-home Hampton County.

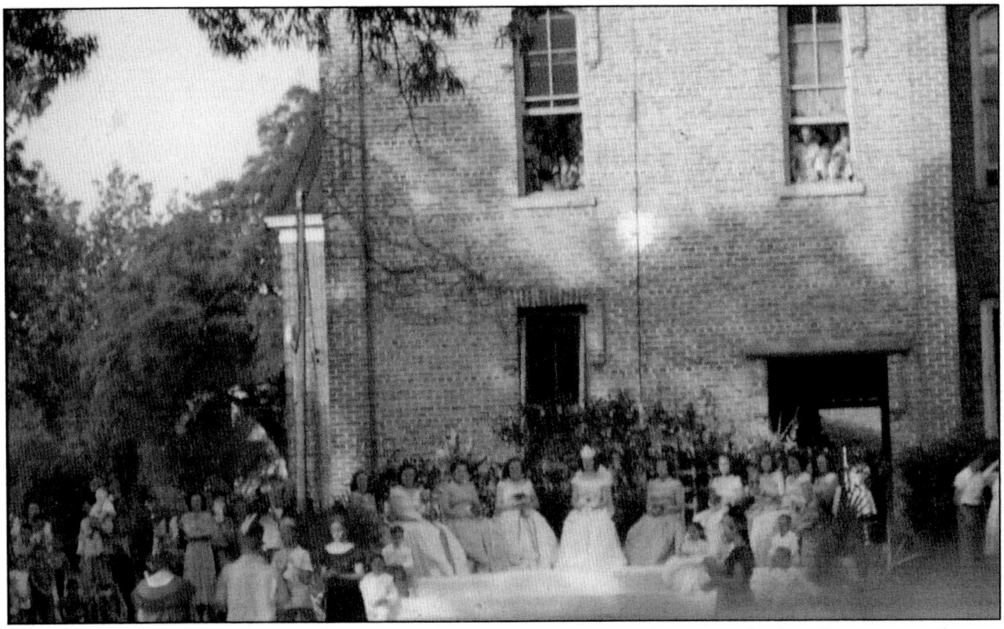

This early 1950s photograph shows the Hampton County Courthouse packed with citizenry during a community celebration. Besides its official use as the county's administrative center and host of criminal, civil, family, and probate courts, the courthouse has also been a popular community hub. The Hampton County Courthouse has been the site for countless political rallies, watermelon festivals, and May festivals for more than 130 years. (Courtesy of HCG.)

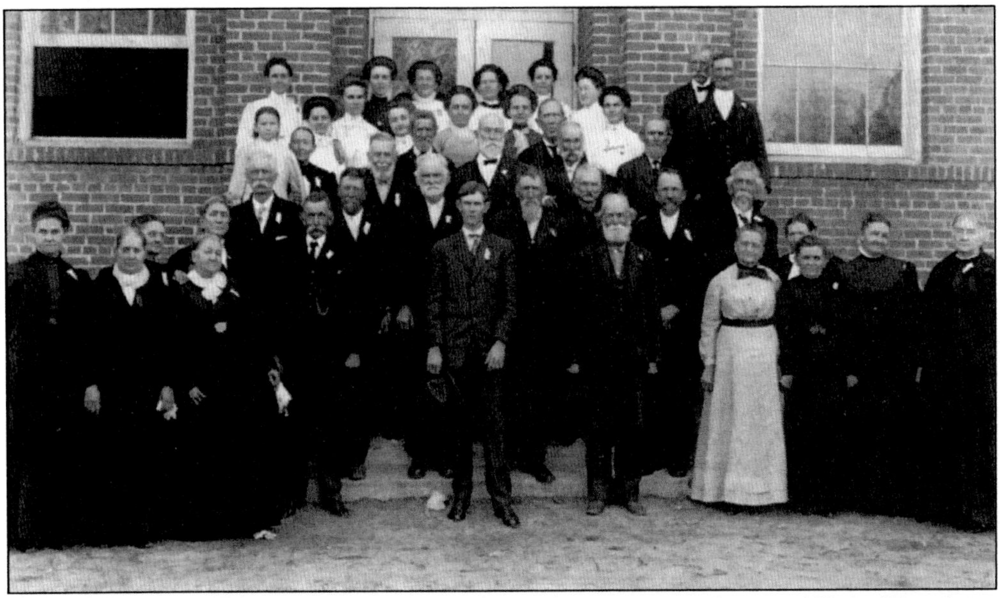

Pictured here is a gathering of Confederate veterans, their wives or widows, and United Daughters of the Confederacy members at Brunson High School, around 1908–1910. Hampton County itself was founded during Reconstruction amid the ruins of the Civil War. Family names represented in the photograph are Brunson, Hogarth, Bowers, Miley, Gooding, Folk, Terry, Chisolm, Kearse, Peeples, Lightsey, Priester, Price, Bassett, Holladay, Tuten, Addison, Langford, and Griner. (Courtesy of HCG.)

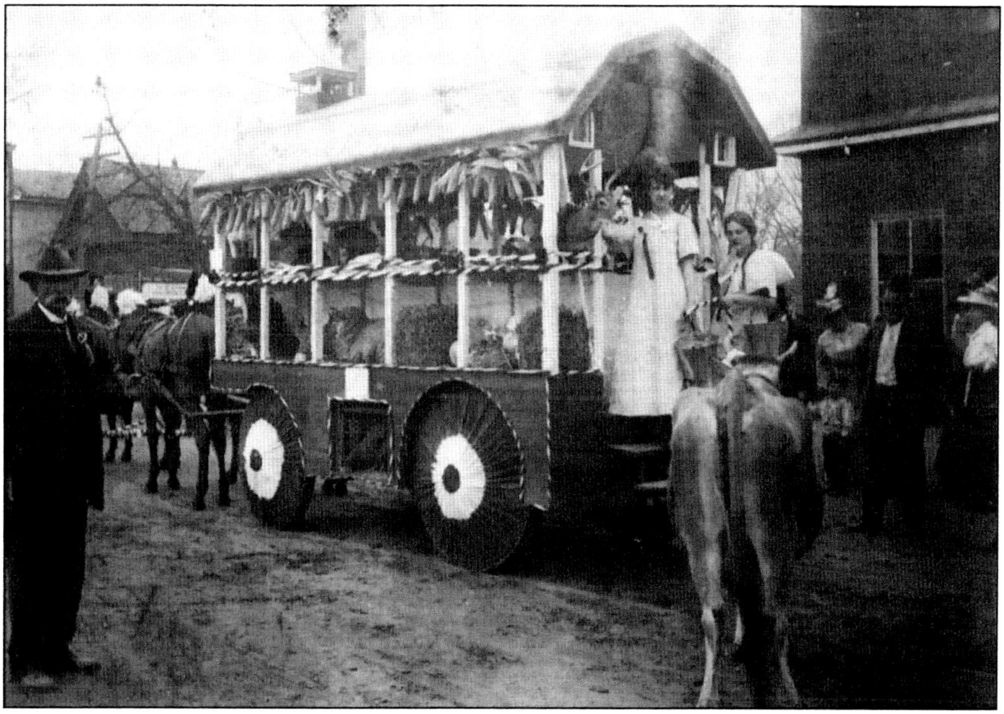

Eula Lawton and Helen Schirer rode 20 miles from Garnett to Hampton in this wagon pulled by a team of mules, but the journey was worth it. The country ladies won first prize for a farm exhibit at the 1912 Hampton County Fair. County fairs not only helped local farmers celebrate the finest of country life on the farm, they were also a good time to trade livestock and goods. (Courtesy of HCG.)

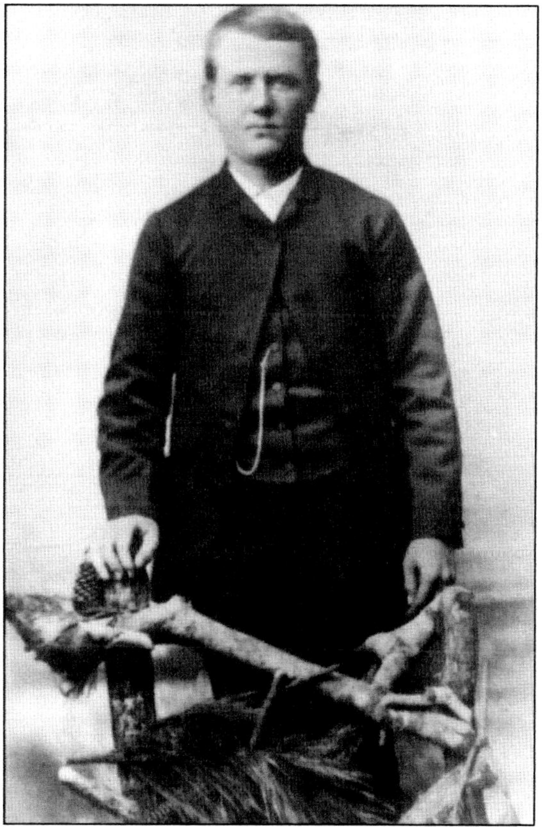

George Washington Fennell was one of the last lamplighters in the town of Hampton. His job was to light the gas lanterns on "Main Street," which is formally named Lee Avenue. Fennell would not recognize the street today, with its stylish, energy-saving electrical light poles, palmetto trees, and concrete curbs. (Courtesy of HCG.)

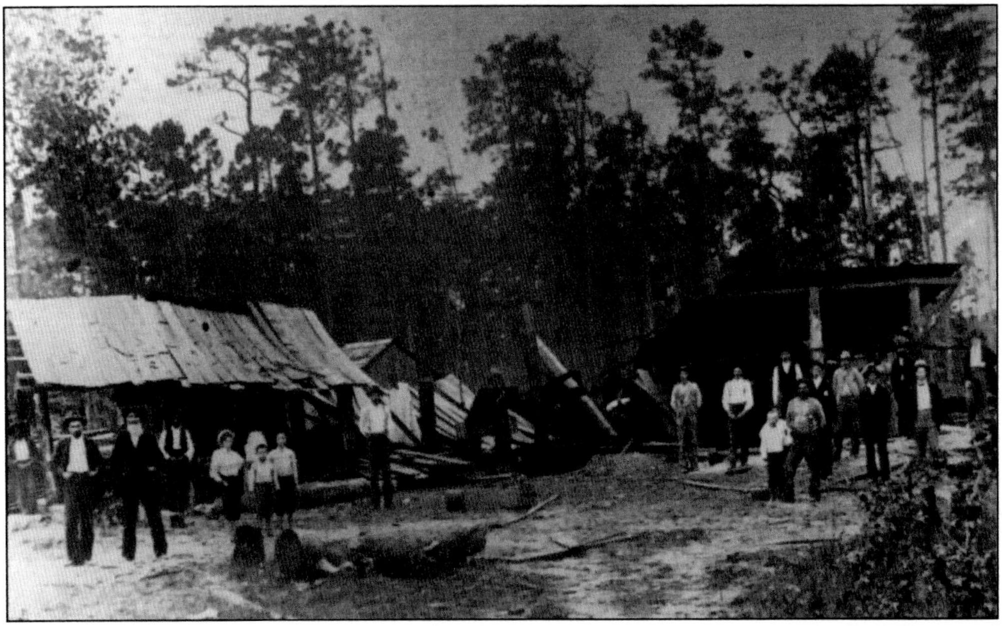

The Bonneau Sawmill was one of several operating in Hampton County in the late 1800s and early 1900s. Two local towns, Varnville and Miley, were founded to a large extent by the sawmilling industry that took advantage of the abundant pine and hardwood forests nearby and the rail lines that crossed the county. In fact, a recent history of the town of Varnville is entitled *Railroads and Sawmills*. (Courtesy of HCG.)

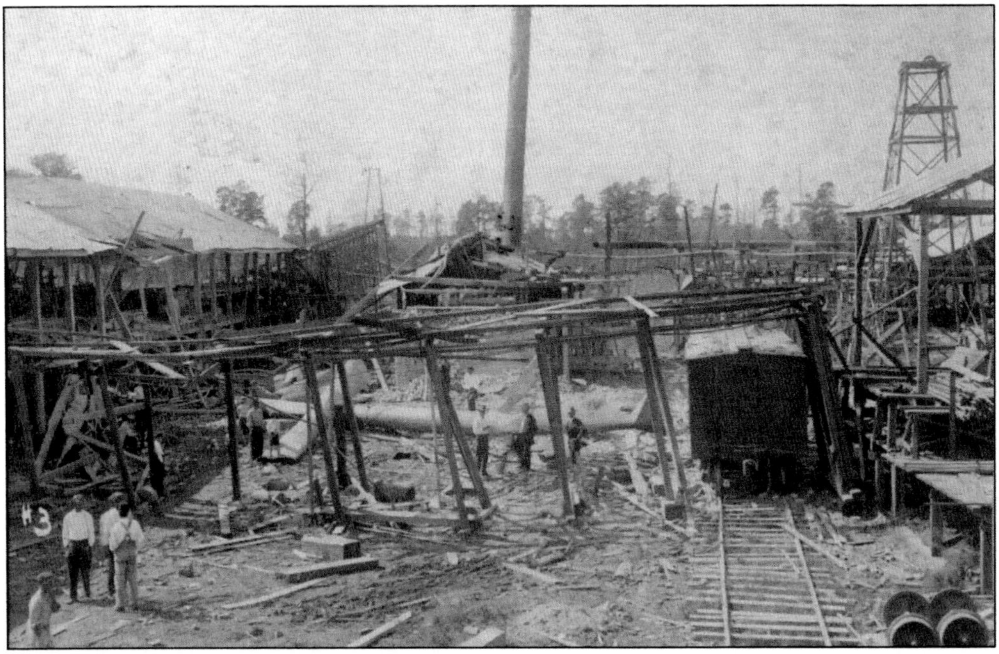


Pictured here in the mid-1930s, a boiler explosion at the Lightsey Brothers Mill in Miley during the early 1930s closed down operations for more than a year. The mill, the town of Miley, and even a railroad were founded by W. Fred Lightsey and Henry W. Lightsey, and at its peak the operation felled 15 million board feet a year and employed 290 men. (Courtesy of HCG.)

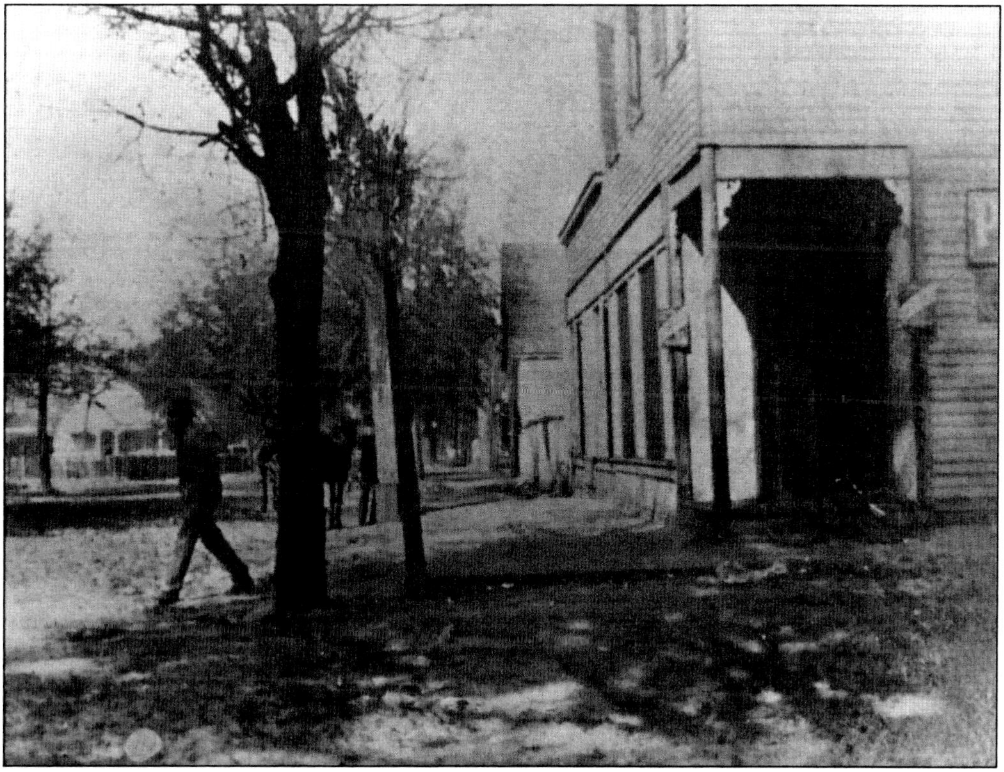

Downtown Hampton's Lee Avenue—better known as Main Street—is pictured as it appeared in 1915. During the late 1800s and early 1900s, the major Hampton County towns of Hampton, Varnville, Estill, Brunson, and Yemassee grew around railroads to become residential hubs as well as centers of business and commerce. (Courtesy of HCG.)

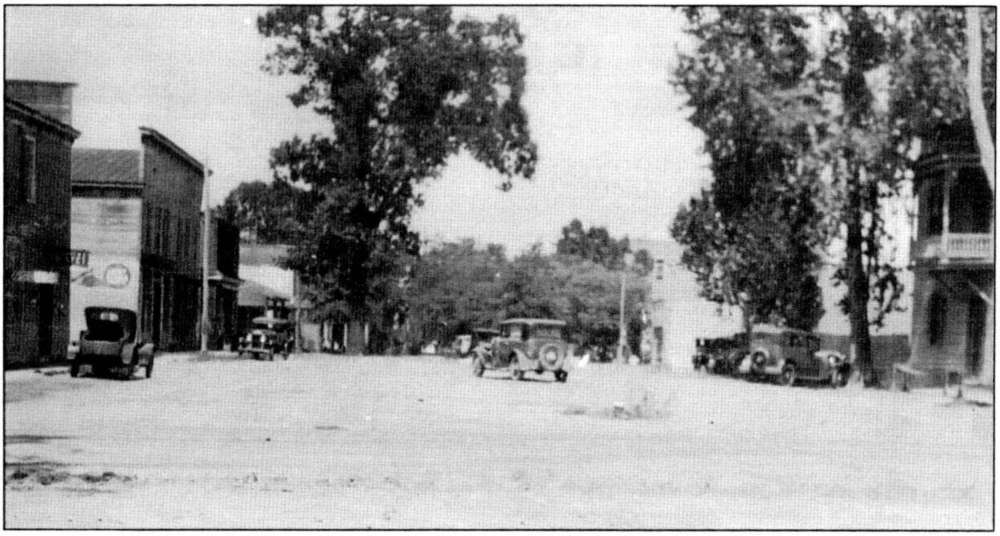

Pictured here is a wide angle view of unpaved Lee Avenue, Hampton, in the 1920s. In the age of the Ford, Hampton's main thoroughfare was approaching its heyday and becoming filled with general stores, dry goods stores, department stores, five-and-dimes, and even hotels. Many years and face-lifts later, the strip remains a center of commerce. (Courtesy of HCG.)

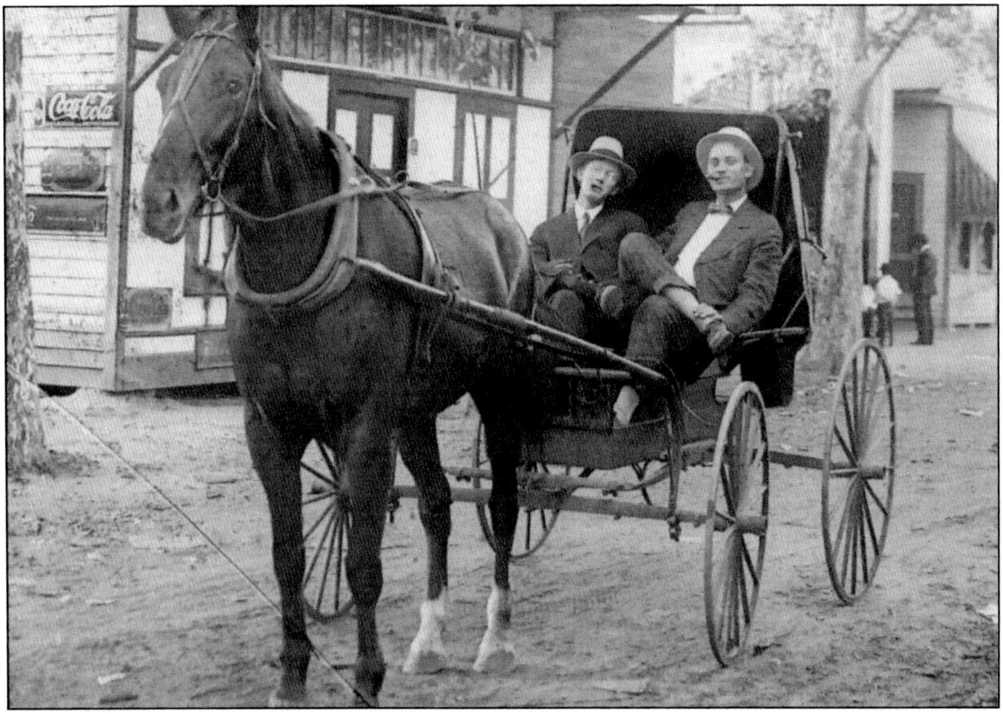

G. Tillman Crews (left), a Hampton horse dealer, and Frank Rivers, mayor of Hampton, take a buggy ride through town in 1909. The Crews, Rivers, and Peeples families were involved in many business ventures in town, from retail merchandise to funeral homes, and were dominant forces in shaping Hampton's history. (Courtesy of HCG.)

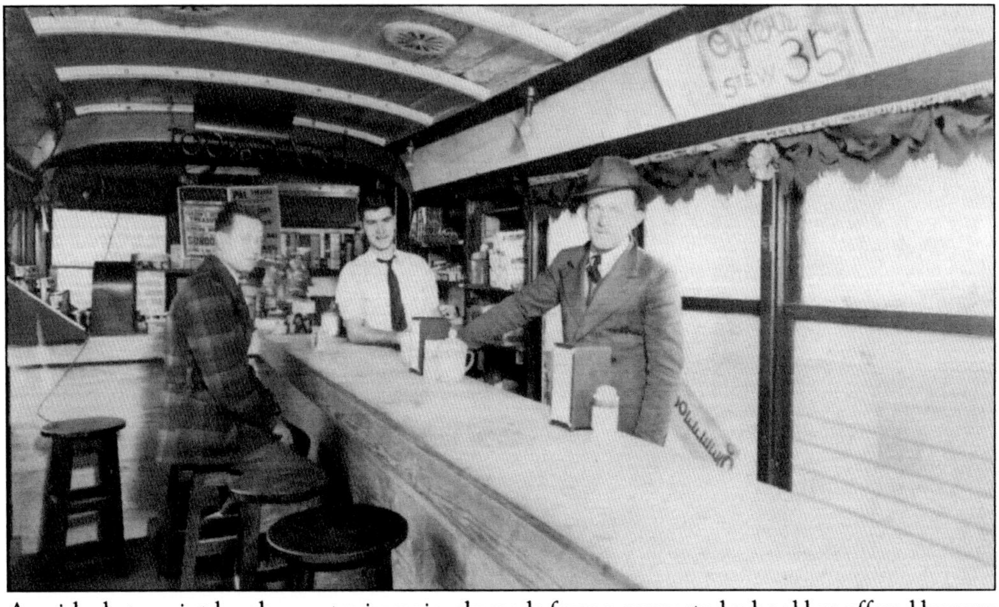

A quirky but quaint lunch counter ingeniously made from a converted school bus offered hungry customers fresh, seasonal, local fare and became quite popular during the 1930s on Hampton's main street. Note the handmade sign advertising oyster stew for 35¢. Pictured are Richard Cain, Martin Ginn, and an unidentified customer. (Courtesy of HCG.)

Pictured here are holiday travelers at the bustling Yemassee Train Depot on Memorial Day 1895. Railroad towns were more than a means of transportation for the sawmills and farmers looking for markets. The depots at Yemassee, Brunson, Hampton, Estill, and smaller communities connected travelers to other towns in the county as well as to the cities of Savannah, Georgia, and Columbia, South Carolina. (Courtesy of HCG.)

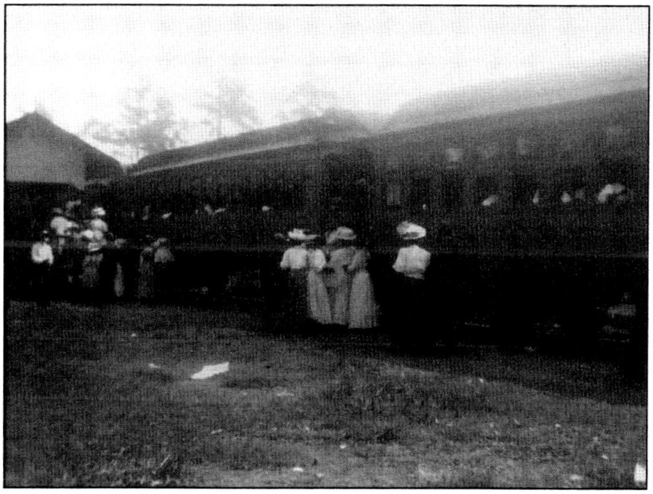

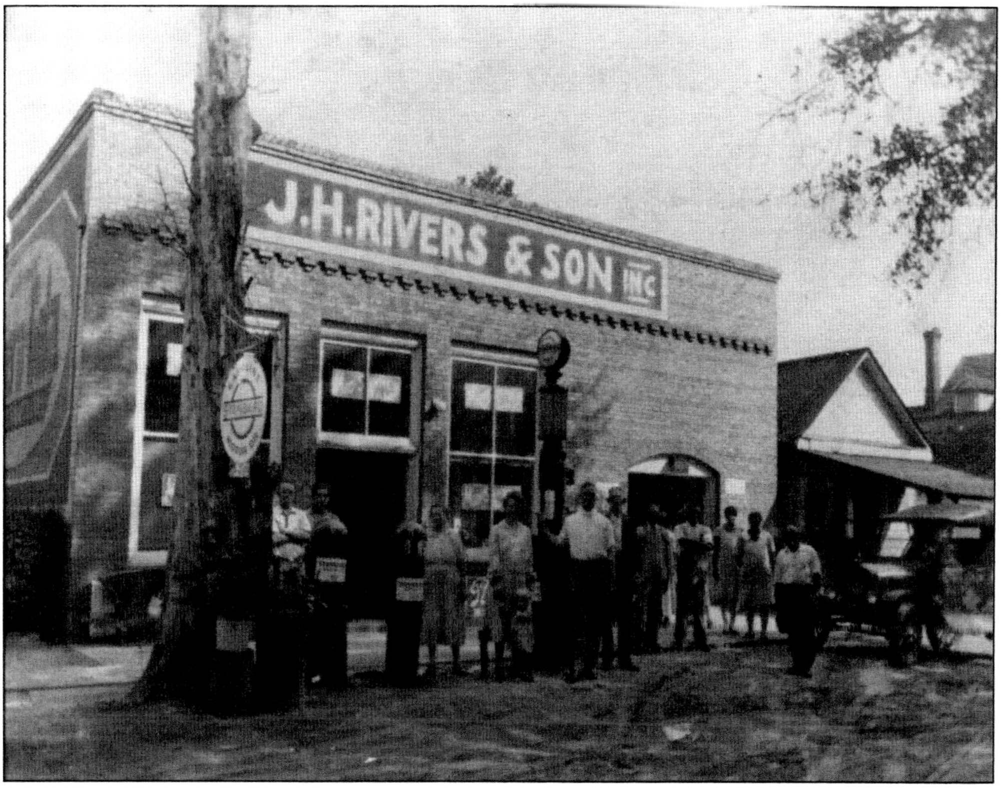


Pictured here is J.H. Rivers and Son, Inc., on Lee Avenue, as it appeared in 1909. From left to right are Willie J. Sauls, Bob Clifton, Mrs. J.B. Rivers, Nancy Pulaski, Ethel Ann Mauldin (child), Frank Rivers Sr., John B. Rivers, Sam Jennings, Poss Rodd, Cora M. Daniels, Canola Adams, and Barney Bennett, the owner of the car and the business next door. (Courtesy of HCG.)

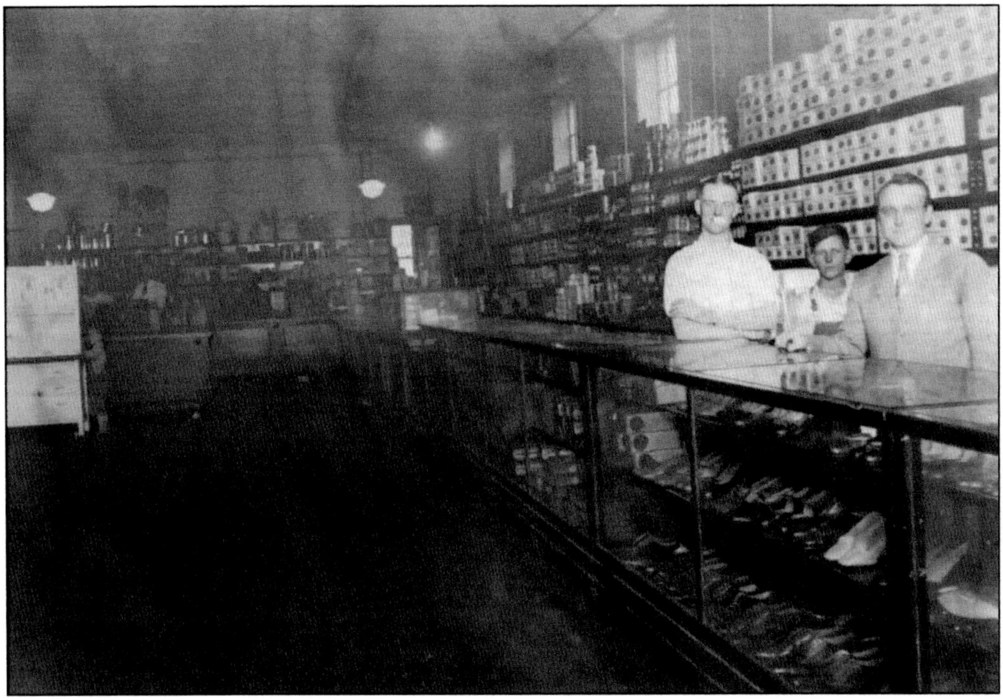

Pictured here is the interior of Ben Hoover's general merchandise store in Hampton, about 1920. Many retail establishments in that era sold a wide variety of merchandise to their loyal customers. Note that the shelves contain everything from men's and women's shoes to pots, buckets, and canned goods—truly a one-stop shop for rural Hampton County folks. (Courtesy of HCG.)

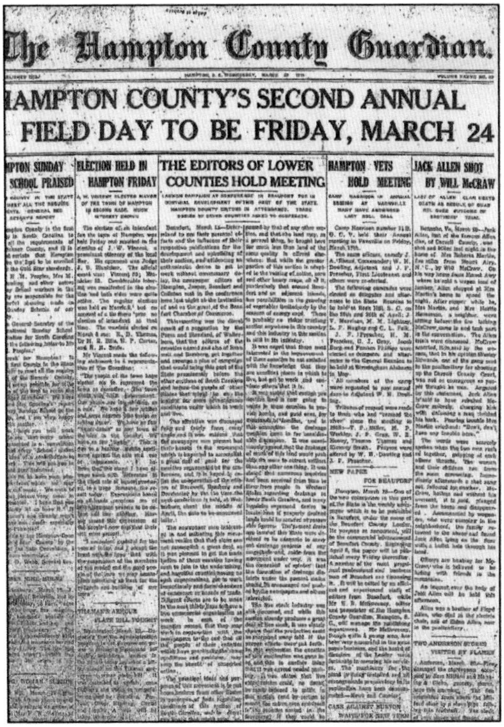

The Hampton County Guardian.

HAMPTON COUNTY'S SECOND ANNUAL FIELD DAY TO BE FRIDAY, MARCH 24

HAMPTON SUNDAY SCHOOL PRAISED

ELECTION HELD IN HAMPTON FRIDAY

THE EDITORS OF LOWER COUNTIES HOLD MEETING

HAMPTON VETS HOLD MEETING

JACK ALLEN SHOT BY WILL McCRAW

The front page of a 1916 edition of the *Hampton County Guardian* looks far different from today's colorful news layouts. The *Guardian* was founded in 1879 by Miles B. McSweeney, the only Hampton County man ever to serve as South Carolina governor. For more than 135 years, the paper has kept citizens informed while helping local businesses advertise their goods and services, and it remains an award-winning community newspaper. (Courtesy of HCG.)

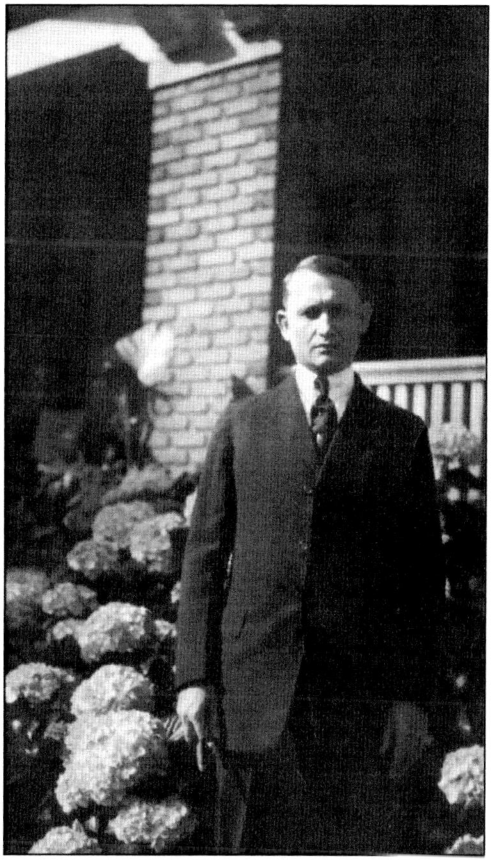

A political and legal legend was born during the elections of 1920. Randolph Murdaugh Sr. was elected solicitor that year and maintained the office until his death in 1940. His son and grandson would go on to serve as solicitors, making a Murdaugh in the solicitor's office a three-generation tradition. (Courtesy of HCG.)

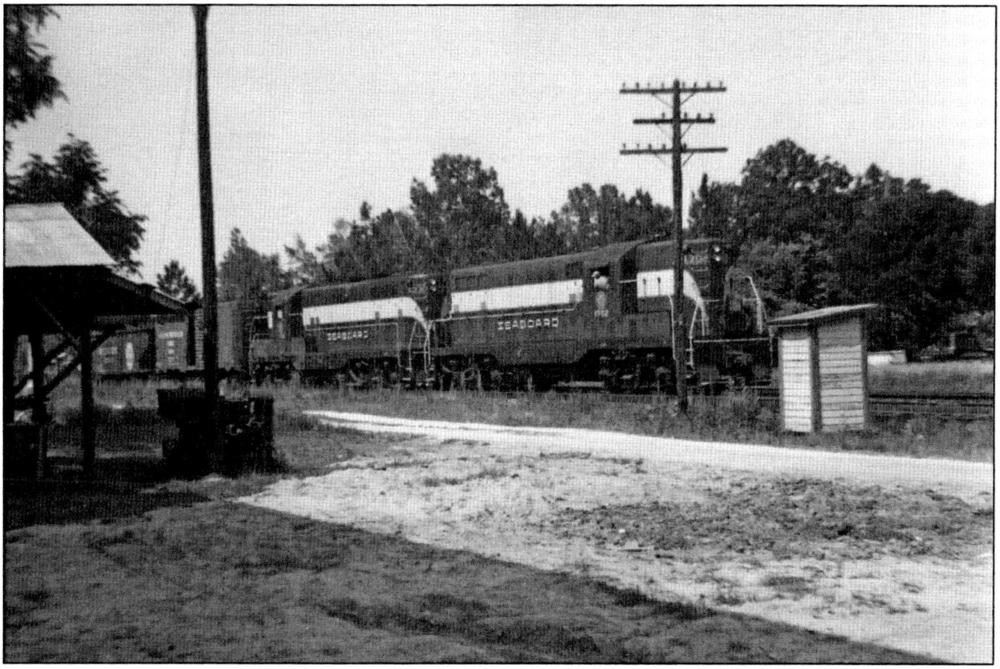

A freight train chugs through Hampton County in June 1957. The county has had interesting relationship with trains and the railroads, providing both livelihood and dangers. Solicitor Randolph Murdaugh Sr. was killed in a train accident, and the law firm he helped establish made a regional name for itself in part by taking on the big railroad companies on behalf of those killed or injured in train wrecks. (Courtesy of DM.)

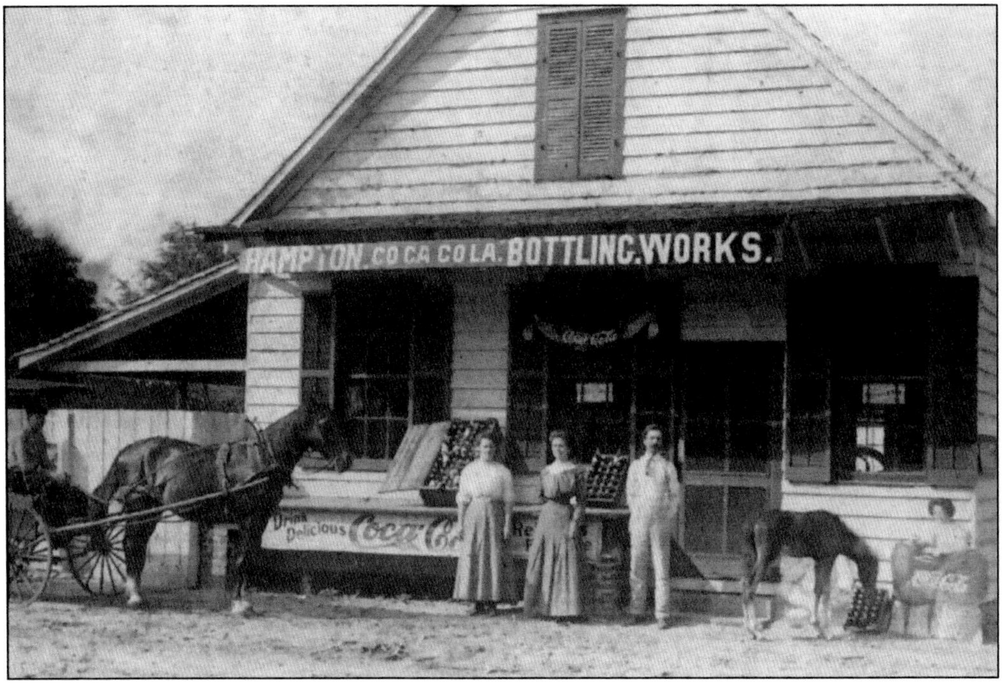


In 1908, Hampton Bottling Works was founded in Hampton. The image above shows the early plant on US Highway 278, which was located across from the present location of Hampton United Methodist Church. The photograph was likely taken around 1914 per the advertisement pictured. In the 1920s, Henry and Virginia Hatcher Lightsey purchased the Coca-Cola Bottling Company in Hampton and later moved the business to where the building now stands at 100 Lightsey Street. The photograph below was taken in the early 1930s, and the car in front of the plant is a 1934 Chevrolet. In 1937, a second story was added, and the building was in service until a fire damaged the structure in 1950, requiring further renovations. The business remained under the Hatcher family's ownership until they sold it in 1985. (Both, courtesy of Jerry Hatcher.)

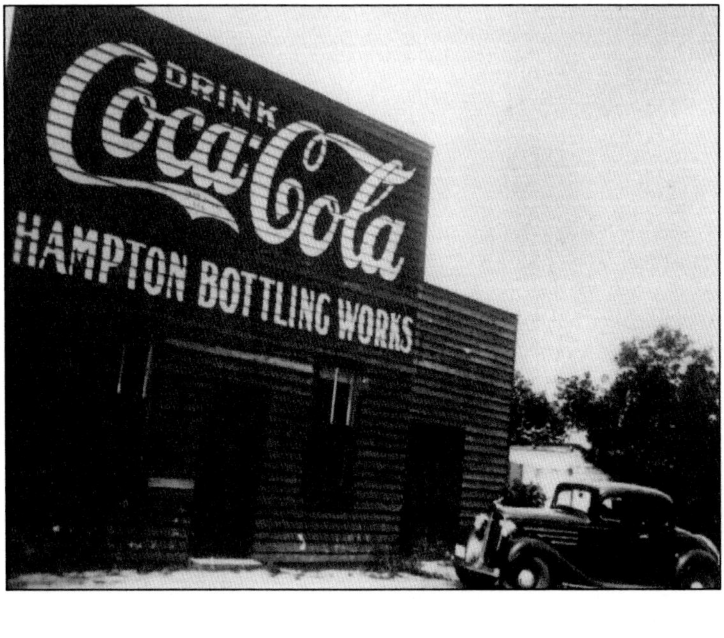

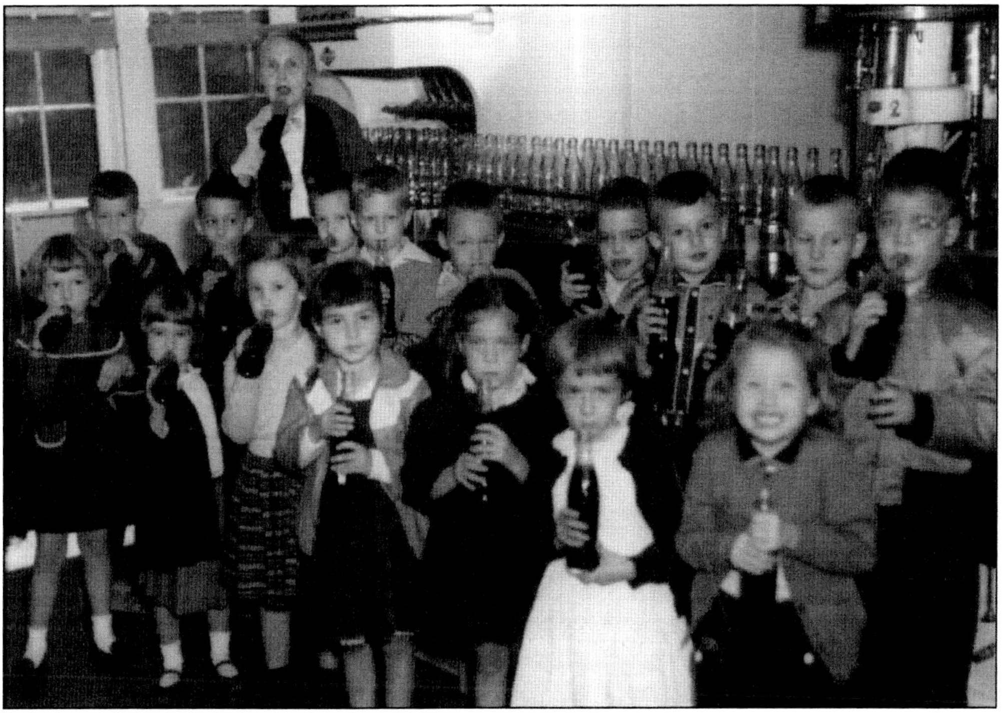

Many from Hampton and surrounding areas will remember fondly their field trips to the Coca-Cola plant while in kindergarten or elementary school. Pictured above is Annie Anderson, mother of longtime *Guardian* editor Martha Bee Anderson, and her 1954–1955 kindergarten class. One of the youth pictured is Jerry A. Hatcher, who would later become president of Hampton Bottling Works after it was sold to Sunbelt Coca-Cola in 1985. Pictured below is a 1965 Ford Coca-Cola route truck in front of the plant in 1966. The year 1965 was noteworthy for the plant because it was the first time a fleet of vehicles had been purchased. The company bought four new trucks and a van for the bargain price of $12,655, and all were painted to Coca-Cola Company specifications. (Both, courtesy of Jerry Hatcher.)

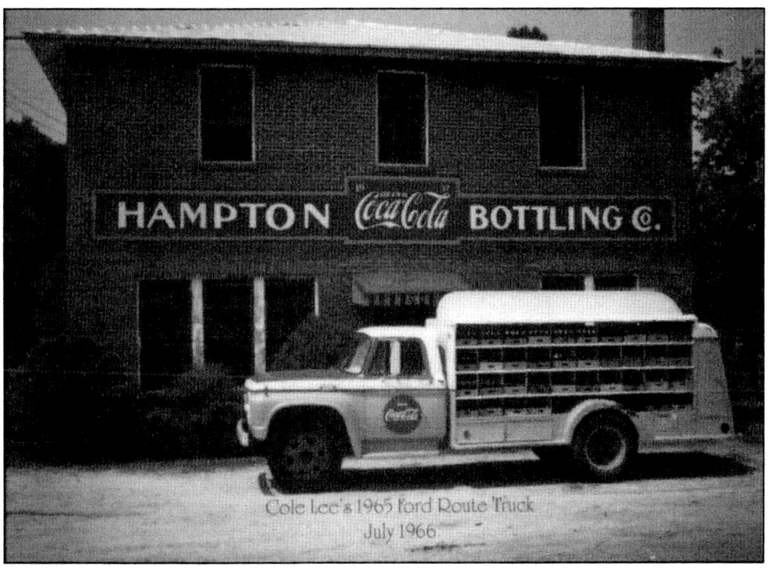

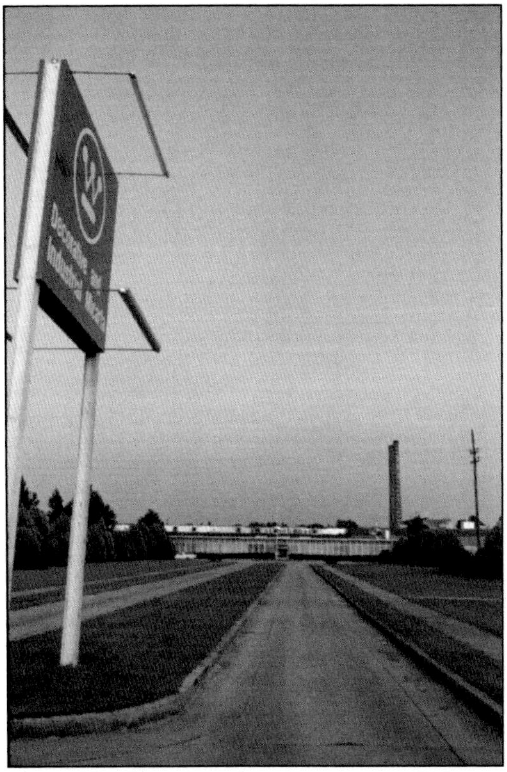

In 1942, big industry came to Hampton County in the form of the Plywoods-Plastics Corporation. PPC provided hundreds of jobs for locals and even drew people from up North as company executives moved in. Shortly after Westinghouse Electric Corporation purchased the plant to establish its Micarta Division here in 1951, the facility had grown to employ up to 1,500 people from around the Lowcountry. (Courtesy of HMVC.)

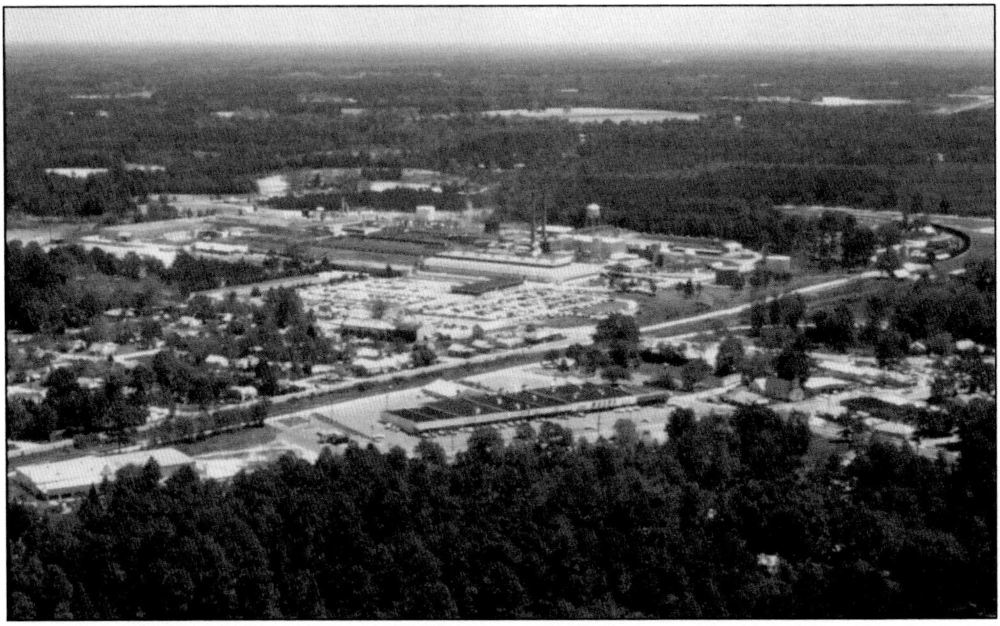

The massive Westinghouse facility, pictured here in an aerial view, sold out in 1995 to International Paper Company, which then sold the facility to Kohlberg Kravis Roberts & Co. in 2002. It operated as Nevamar and remained the county's largest industrial employer. But, in July 2014, company officials announced they would be closing the Hampton site by the end of the year. A local economic institution was coming to an end. (Courtesy of HMVC.)

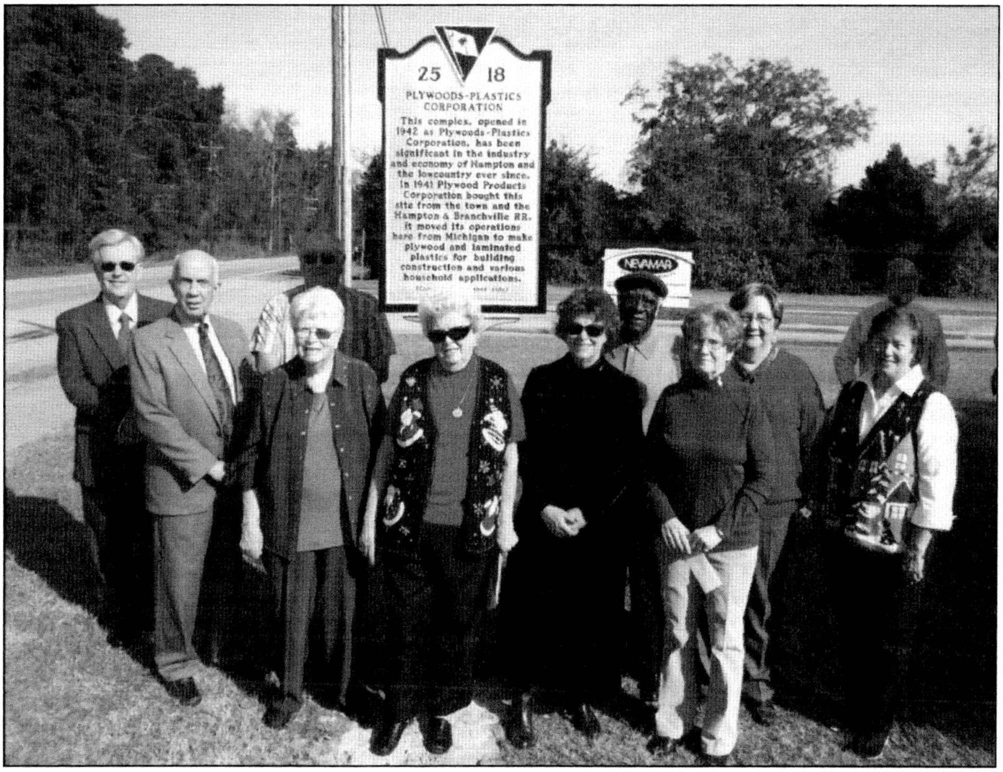


On December 5, 2012, a historical marker was officially dedicated at the Nevamar site to acknowledge the factory's place in Hampton County history. Those attending the event included the driving force behind the historical preservation campaign, Hampton Museum and Visitors' Center curator Marie Ellis (fifth from left), HMVC volunteers, town officials, and factory executives. (Courtesy of HCG.)

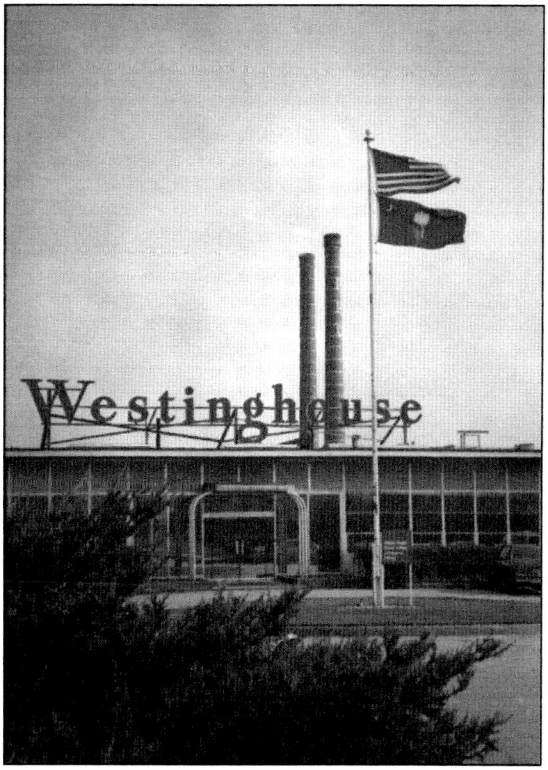


The American flag flew high over Westinghouse and generations of Hampton County's hardworking men and women from 1951 to 1995. This image tells the story of proud, blue-collar Americans and a factory that made a huge impact both locally and around the globe. At one point, the plant produced military helmets, components for US Navy vessels, and heat shields for NASA. (Courtesy of HMVC.)

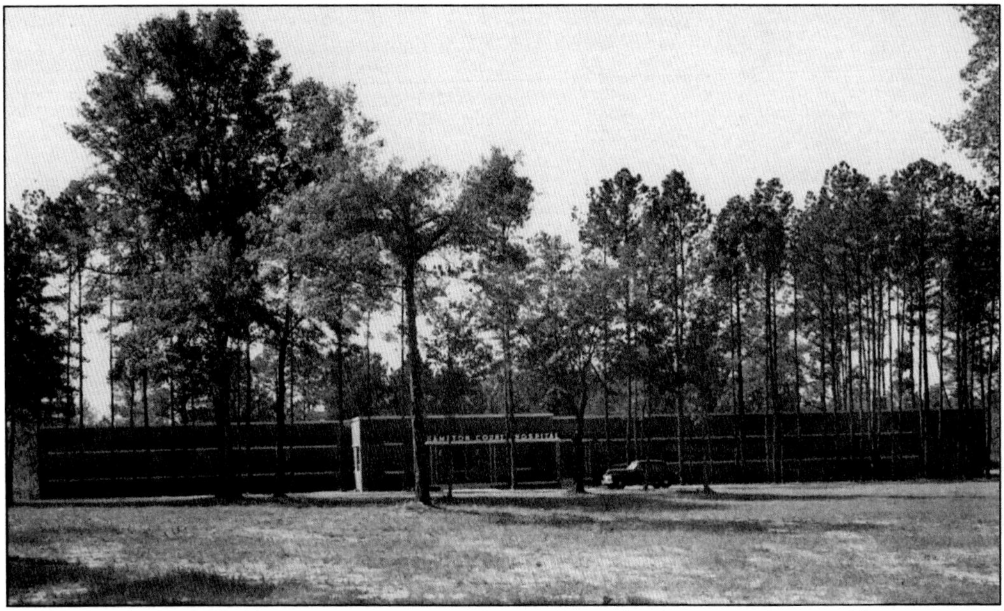

Hampton General Hospital, a county-owned hospital, was built at a total cost of $283,000 and dedicated on November 1, 1950. The 14-acre property was given by Elizabeth M. Rentz in memory of her late husband, William H. Rentz, of Varnville. The new hospital was hailed in every corner of the county, and the *Guardian* newspaper reported that "a dream has materialized in Hampton County." (Courtesy of HRMC.)

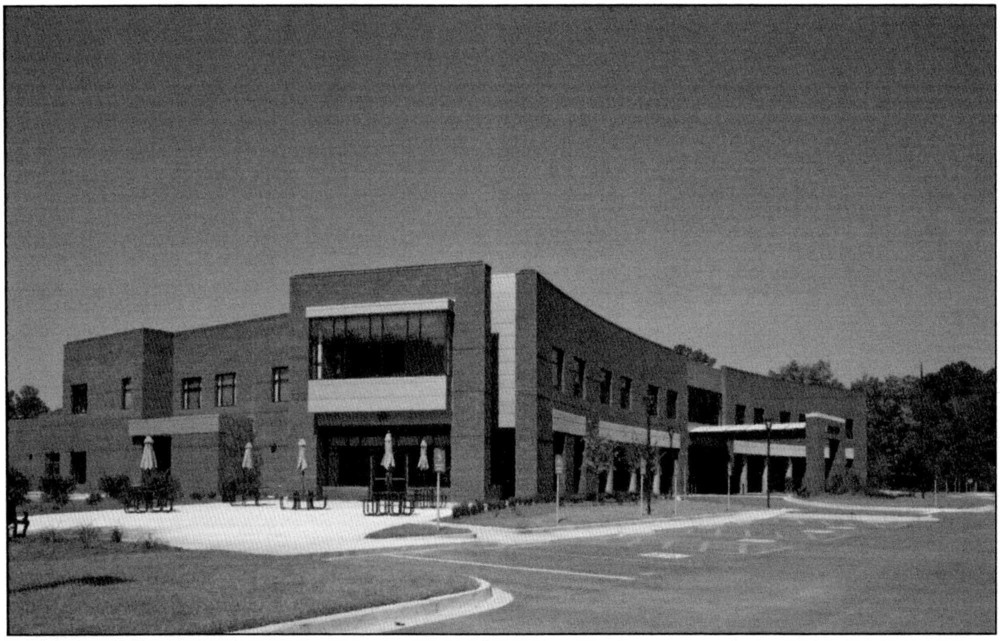

In 1995, Hampton County Council converted Hampton General to a private, not-for-profit hospital and renamed it Hampton Regional Medical Center. In 2008, the hospital moved into its new building, and the old facility was demolished. Since then, HRMC has become an award-winning rural healthcare system affiliated with Roper St. Francis in Charleston, and it was named one of the Top 100 Hospitals in the United States by Cleverley & Associates. (Courtesy of HRMC.)

George Warren served as a state senator representing Hampton and surrounding counties in several terms from 1938 to 1950. He also served as chairman of the South Carolina Wildlife Commission. During that tenure, Warren was instrumental in getting Lake Warren constructed in Hampton County, a project reportedly conceived in the late 1950s by Warren and a friend, local farmer Murray DeLoach, and completed in 1967. (Courtesy of HCG.)

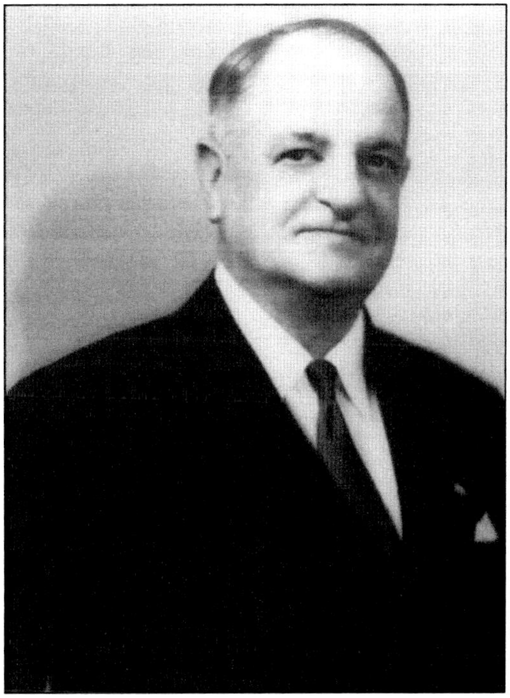

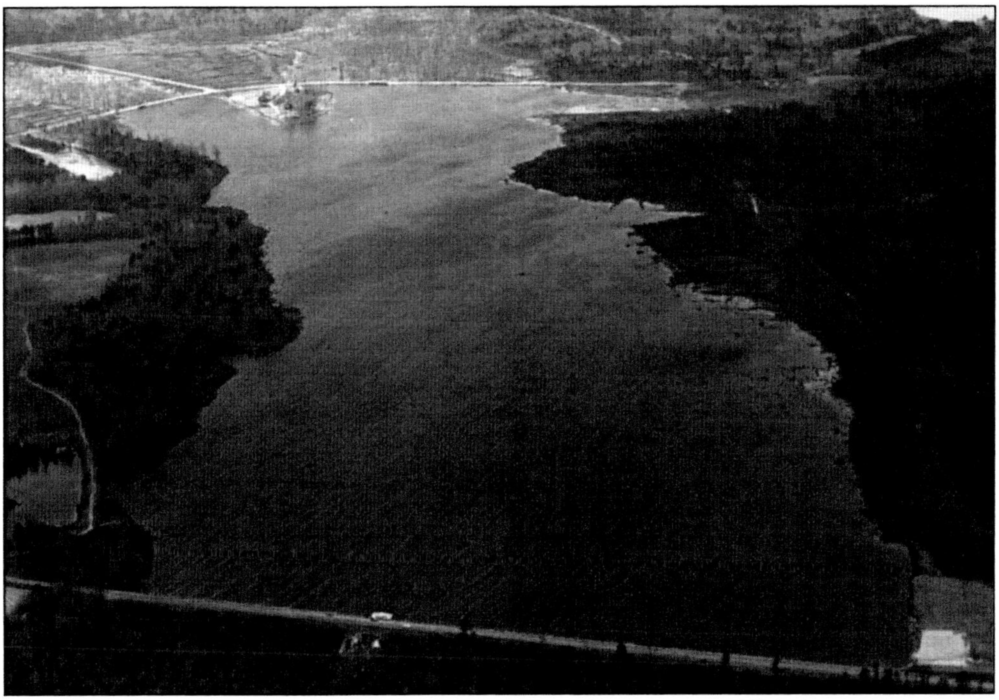

This aerial view details the 200-acre Lake Warren. According to state wildlife department records, the dam and spillway were completed in 1967, and the lake opened for fishing in 1970. Land for 440-acre Lake Warren State Park was obtained in 1980, and South Carolina Parks, Recreation, & Tourism held an official land acquisition ceremony on July 9 of that year. This was Hampton County's first and only major fishing and recreation lake. (Courtesy of HCG.)

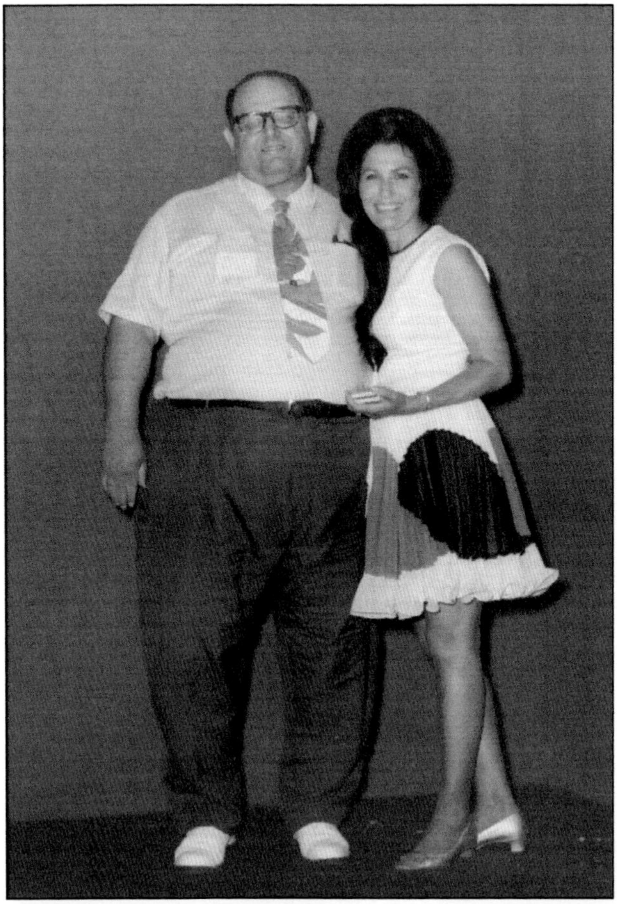

Cranel B. Herndon was a man of many businesses, including a trucking company and Low Country Arena, but he did not stop there. In 1970–1971, the Hampton County businessman opened Low Country Music, Inc. in Varnville, which included the United Low Country Publishing Company and United Low Country Record Company. Between his Low Country Arena music venue and the new recording studio, Herndon was seemingly bringing country music stars like Loretta Lynn (pictured at left with him) and Conway Twitty to Varnville on a weekly basis. In 1975, he started the United Music World Recording Studio in Columbia, South Carolina. The "Big Man with a Big Heart" who went, as a newspaper reported, "from trucking to recording" was later honored with his own exhibits in the Hampton Museum and Visitors' Center in Hampton by curator Marie Ellis (below). (Both, courtesy of Libby Smith.)

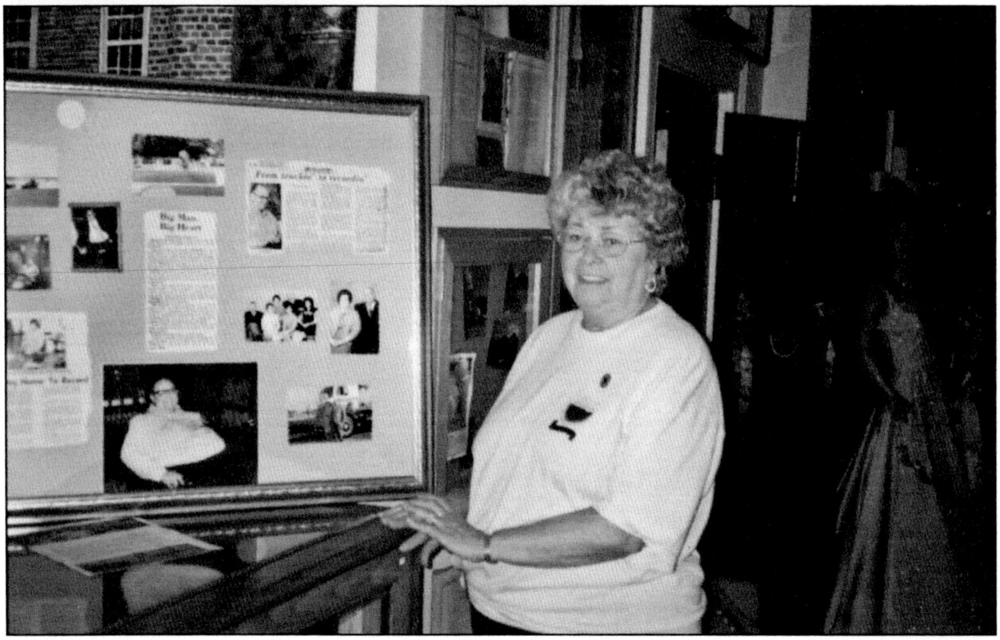

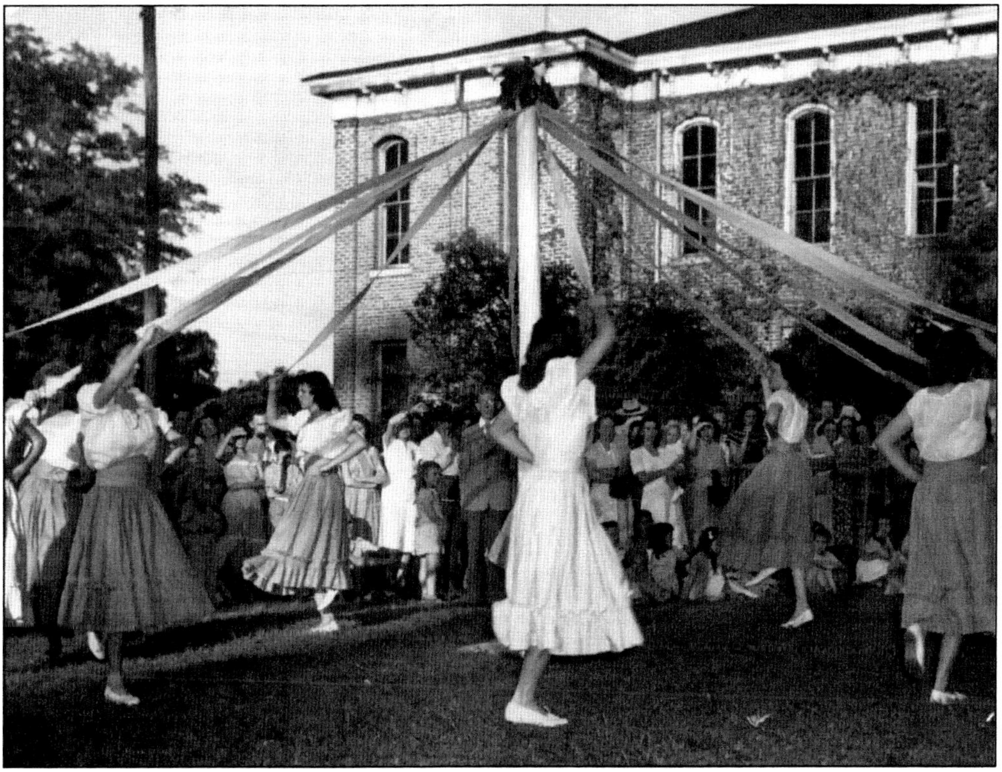

Captured in this photograph is a May Day celebration at the Hampton County Courthouse in 1953. Since its construction in 1878, the courthouse has become more than a center for law, justice, and politics. The courthouse grounds have played host to untold scores of festivals, community celebrations, and even weddings, but today it is most fondly remembered as being the physical center of the Hampton County Watermelon Festival. (Courtesy of HCG.)

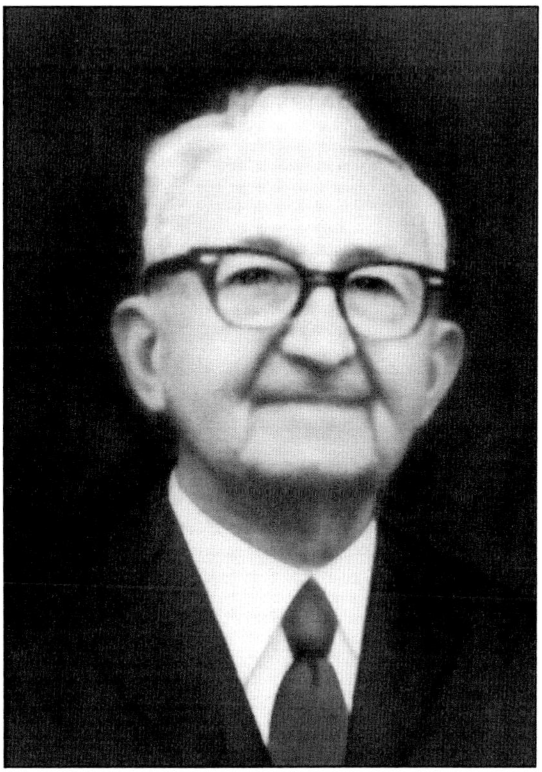

Ben Tillman DeLoach became Hampton County's clerk of circuit court around 1919 and served for more than 56 years, one of the longest-serving elected county officials ever. He was born in the Nixville community on April 28, 1894, and died on September 10, 1973. In 1977, Hampton County named its primary county building, the B.T. DeLoach Building, in his honor. (Courtesy of HCG.)

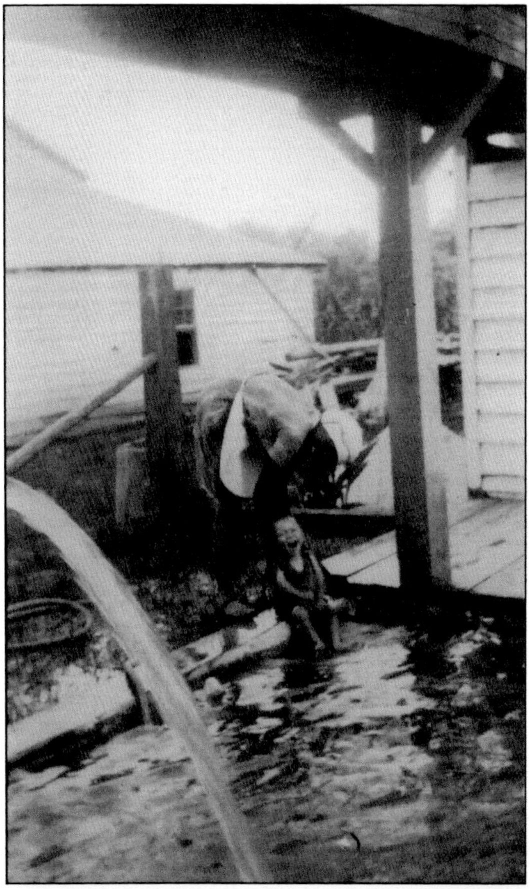

Davis Swimming Pool, located near Estill, was founded in 1916 by Charles Davis Sr. and his father, Wilbur E. Davis. The photograph at left is dated around 1940, and pictured is Charles Davis Jr., who later took ownership of the pool. Davis Jr. recalls how folks used to hop a train in Estill and points beyond just for a swim, and his father allowed World War II prisoners of war, who were used for farm labor, to take a dip after work was done. The pool was a popular cooling off spot for people of all ages, as demonstrated in the 1960s-era photograph below, until it closed in 1996. The Davis pool also offered dances, games, and barbecues. On the eve of its 100th anniversary, efforts are underway to place this structure in the National Register of Historic Places. (Both, courtesy of Charles Davis Jr.)

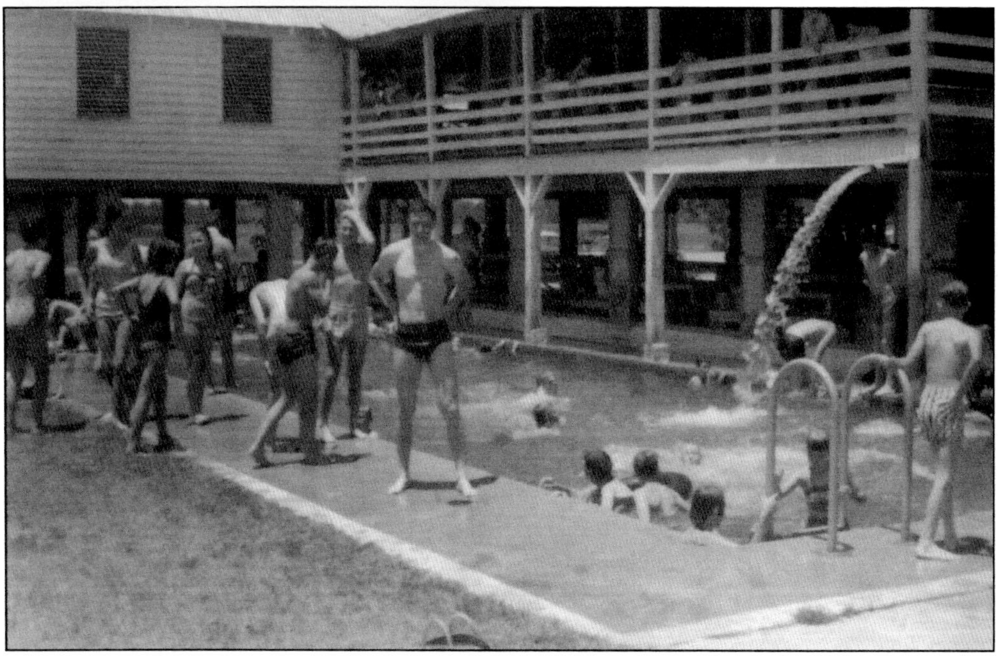

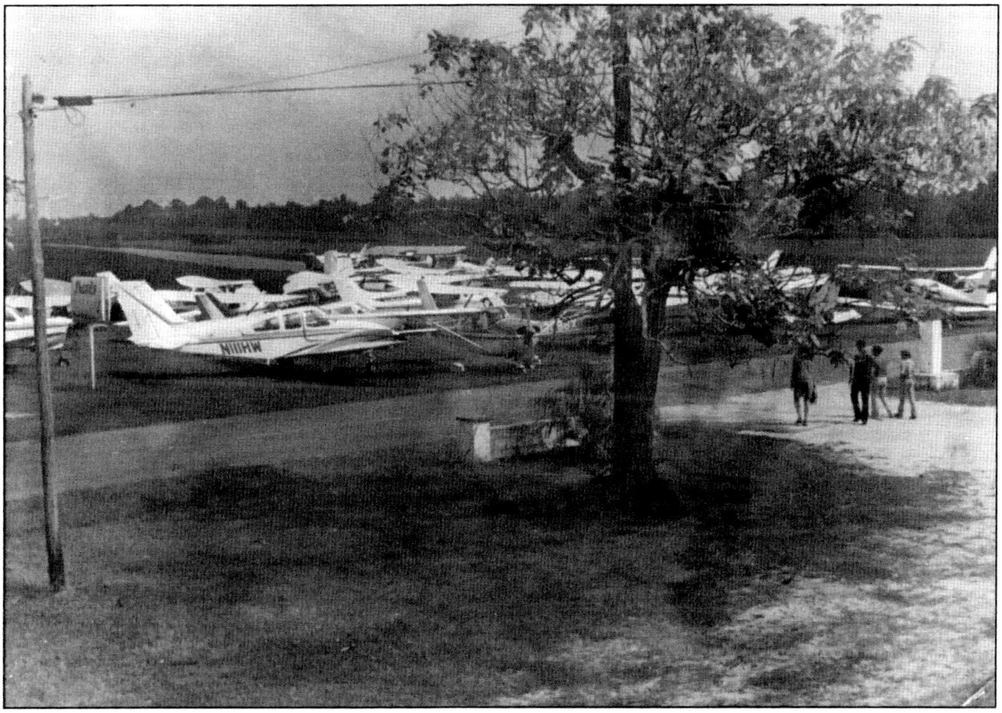

The Davis Swimming Pool was much more than a pool: The Davis family also ran a farm, a go-kart racing track, and even an airport, as demonstrated in the 1969 photograph above. Owner Charles Davis Jr. was a pilot, and for more than 30 years his airport was a frequent stop for the Carolina Breakfast Club, an aviators' club dating back to 1938 that jaunted around the state looking for a good meal, fellowship, and adventure. Politicians from around the state sometimes flew in for barbecues and political rallies, and Sen. Strom Thurmond flew in to deliver a speech to celebrate the 50th anniversary of Davis Pool in 1966. At right, Thurmond (left) is pictured with Charles Davis Sr. (Both, courtesy of Charles Davis Jr.)

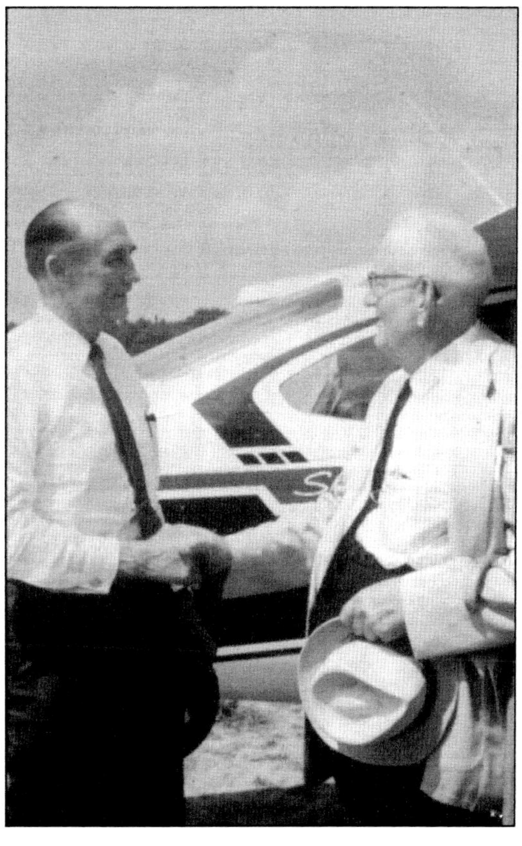

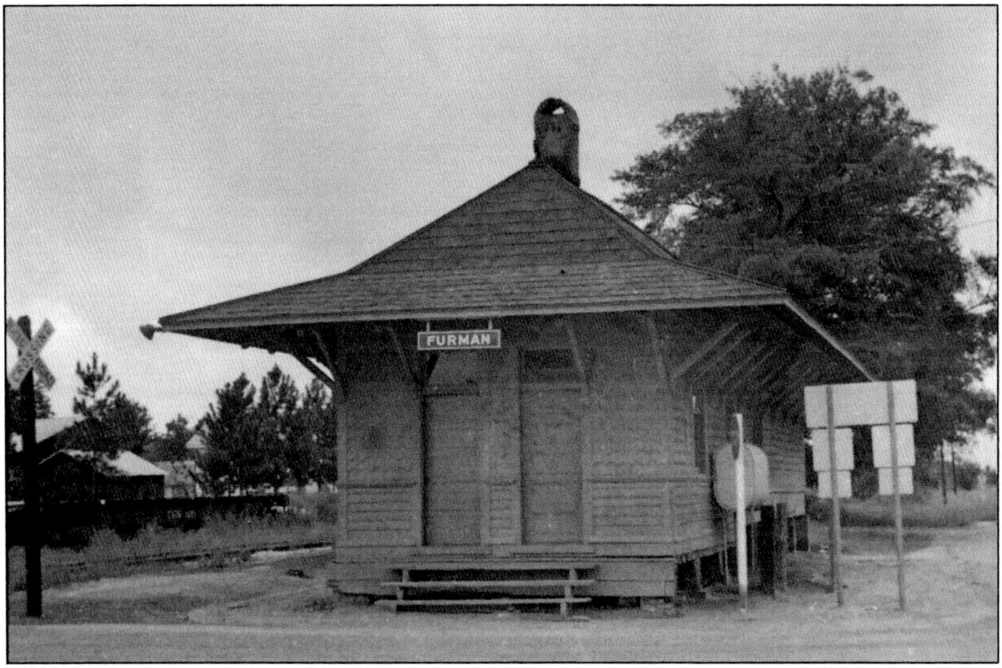


Pictured here on August 18, 1969, is the Furman Depot. One can judge by the size of the depot that it was not a major transportation hub for passengers, but Furman was a busy agricultural supply and shipping point in southern Hampton County. Farming and the agricultural supply business are still major livelihoods there for many families. (Courtesy of DM.)

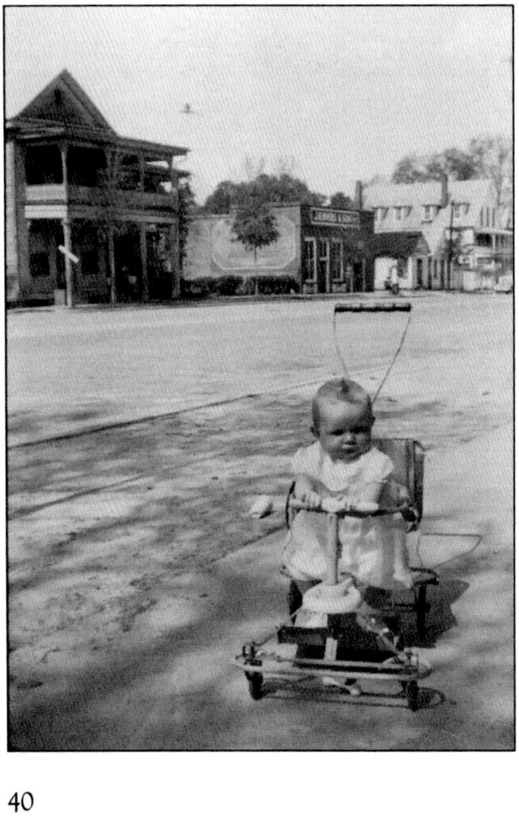

In this late 1930s photograph, an unidentified baby strolls down Lee Avenue in Hampton. Of the buildings in the background, only J.H. Rivers & Sons still stands today. Where the nearest two-story wooden home is located is now the general location of the present Frock Shop building, which was erected in the 1940s. (Courtesy of Becky Young and the Peeples family.)

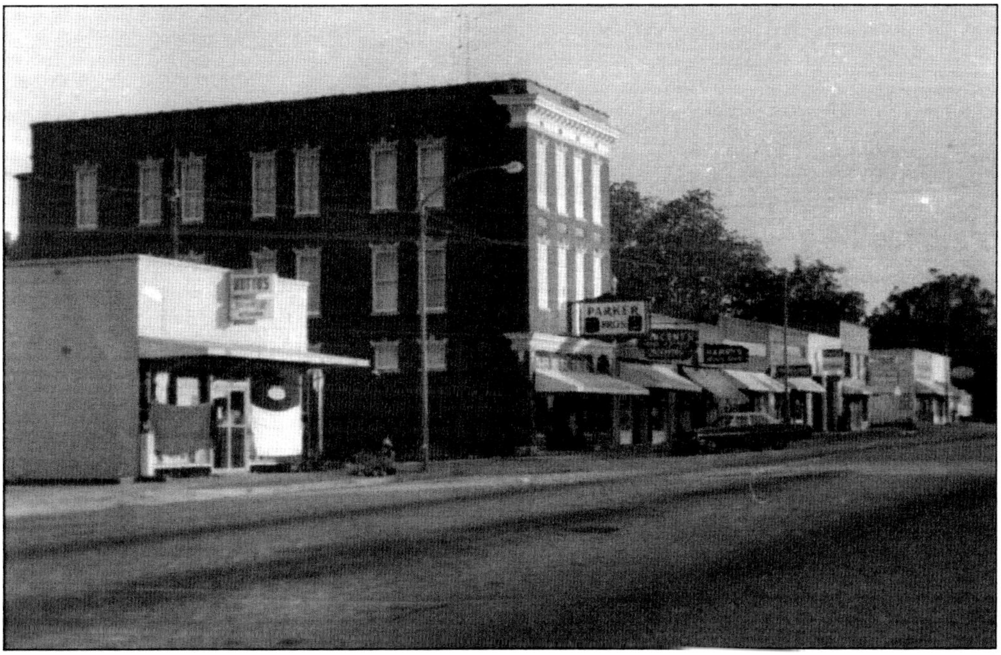


Pictured here is downtown Hampton's Lee Avenue as it looked in April 1969. Some of the local stores that were landmarks of the day included Hutto's, the three-story Parker Bros. department and shoe store, Vincent Drugs, and Harry's Men Shop. Of all of these, only Vincent Drugs is still going strong today. (Courtesy of DM.)

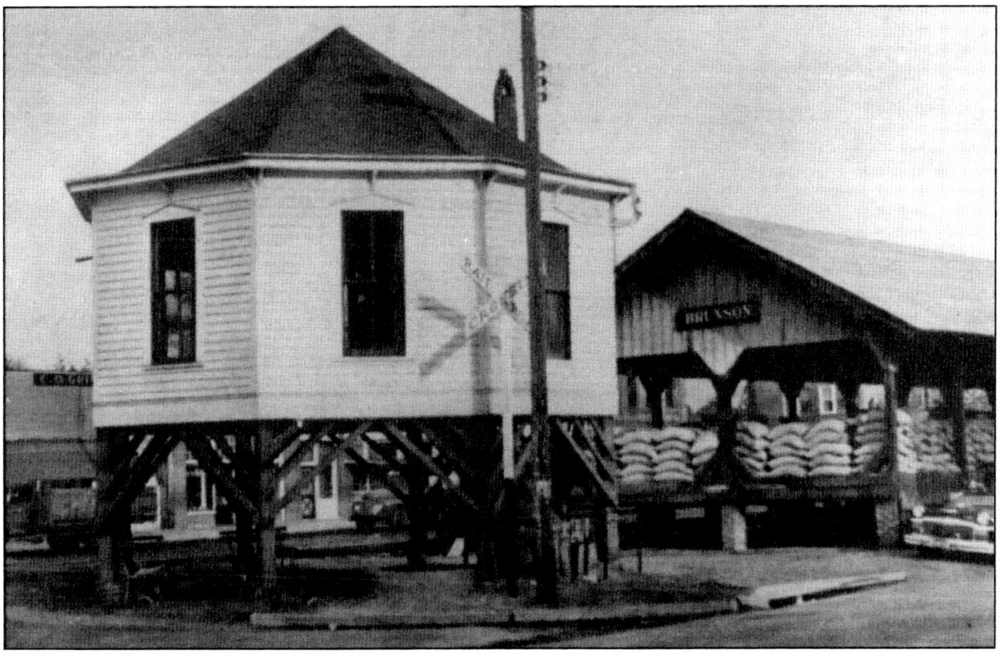


The original Brunson Town Hall, built in 1906, was cited in *Ripley's Believe It or Not* as the only octagonal town hall in the world built on stilts. It hosted town meetings and shaded the town's artesian well. In 1959, the stilts were removed, and it was relocated to its current location where it is now the home of the Brunson Museum and Visitors' Center. (Courtesy of BMVC.)

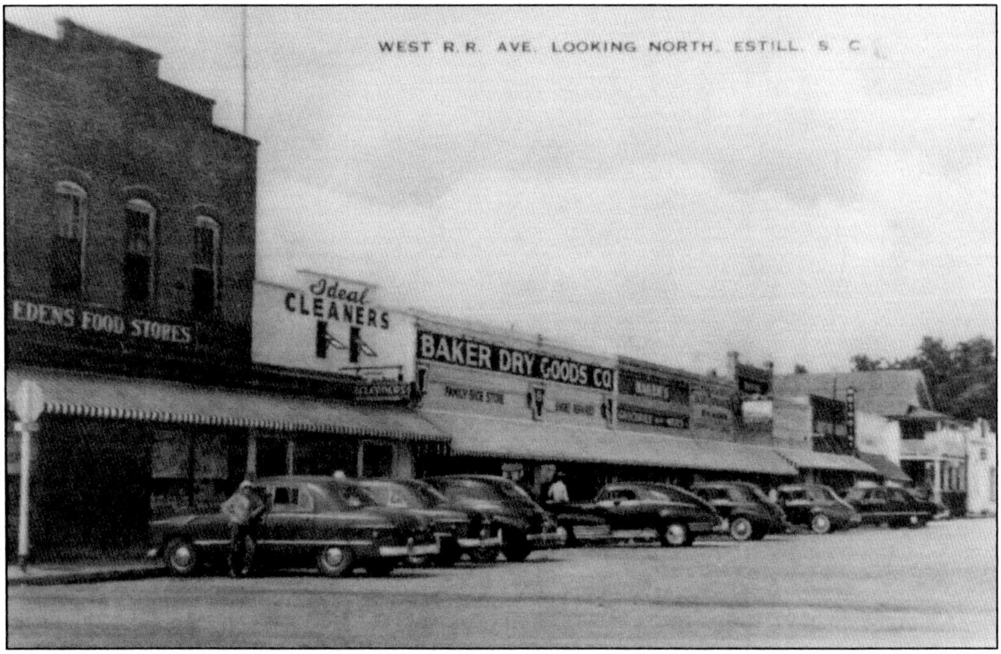


This is downtown Estill as it looked in 1948, a bustling time for commerce in Estill's history as evidenced by the many storefronts. This view is facing north on West Railroad Avenue. In particular, the Baker family ran a brisk enterprise, which included a dry goods and shoe store, grocery store, and furniture store (not pictured). (Courtesy of DM.)

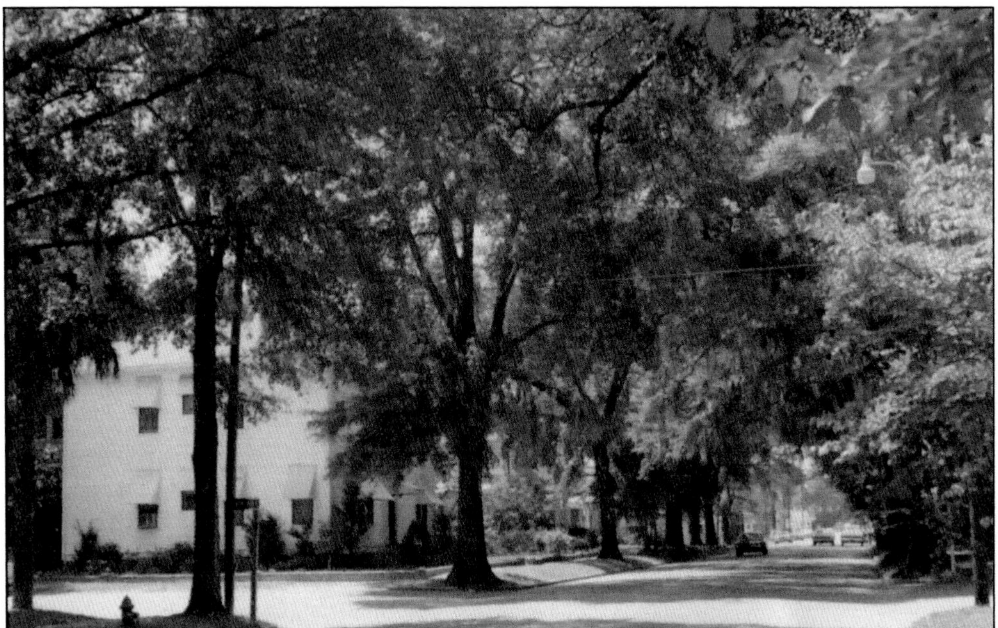

One of the most scenic views entering Estill is Highway 3 heading south. The shady tunnel of oak trees and Spanish moss escorts visitors past some of the finest homes in the county, including the Laffitte home, as well as the town library. This is how the avenue looked in 1973, and it has not changed much since. (Courtesy of DM.)

Pictured here is the Estill Pharmacy as it appeared on October 12, 1961. The corner drugstore located at the main intersection of Highway 321 and Highway 3 did a thriving business for years, but it is now an auto parts store. Today, Hanna's Discount Pharmacy, located just a block away, still proudly serves Estill-area customers. (Courtesy of DM.)

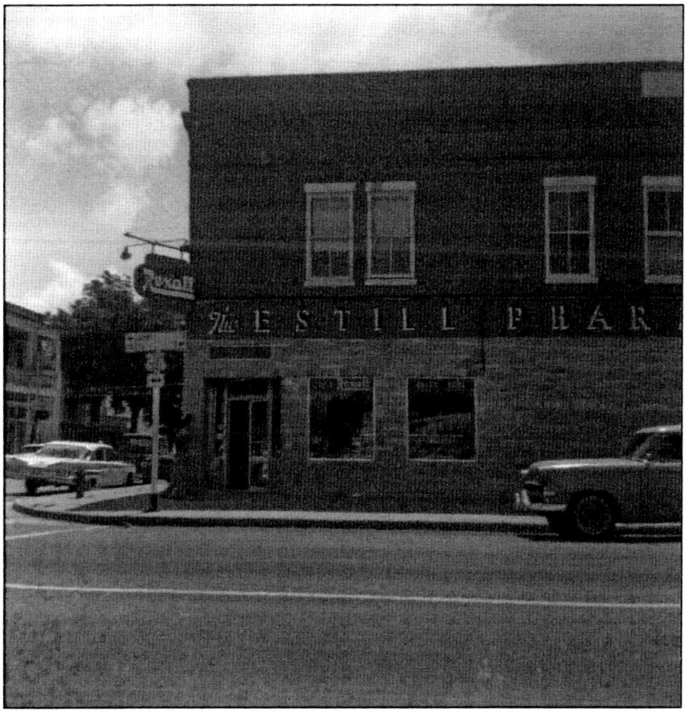


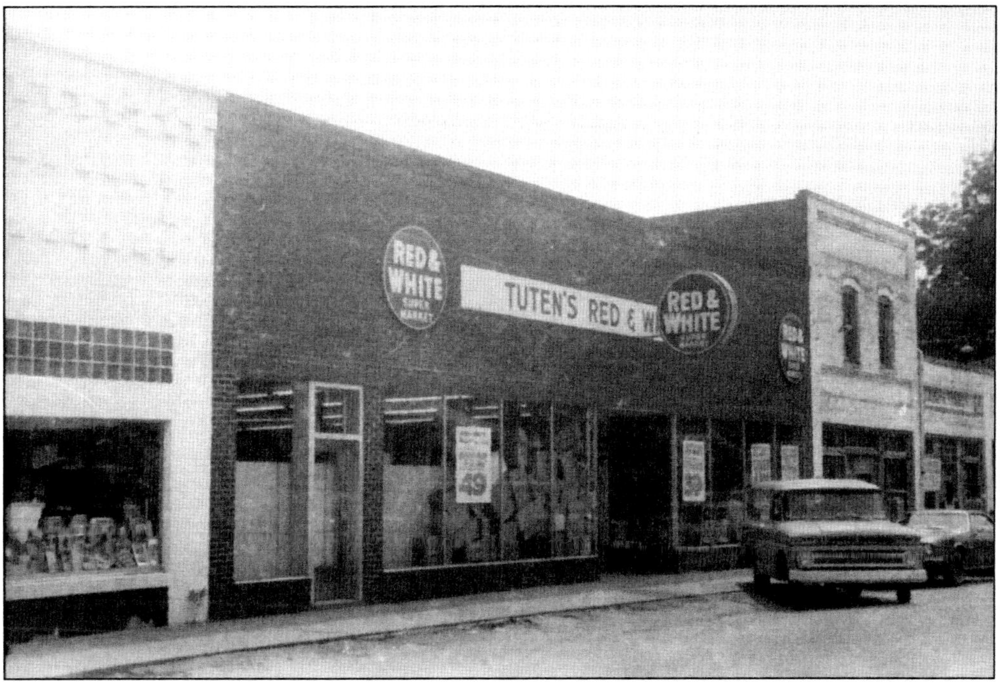


The Tuten's Red & White grocery store, pictured here on May 30, 1969, is still going strong in Estill. The family-owned store, well known for its meats and customer service, now operates as an IGA and has remained the largest grocery in Estill. Many Estill-area men fondly recall getting their first job at Tuten's and learning the art of sacking groceries properly for a nice 25¢ tip. (Courtesy of DM.)

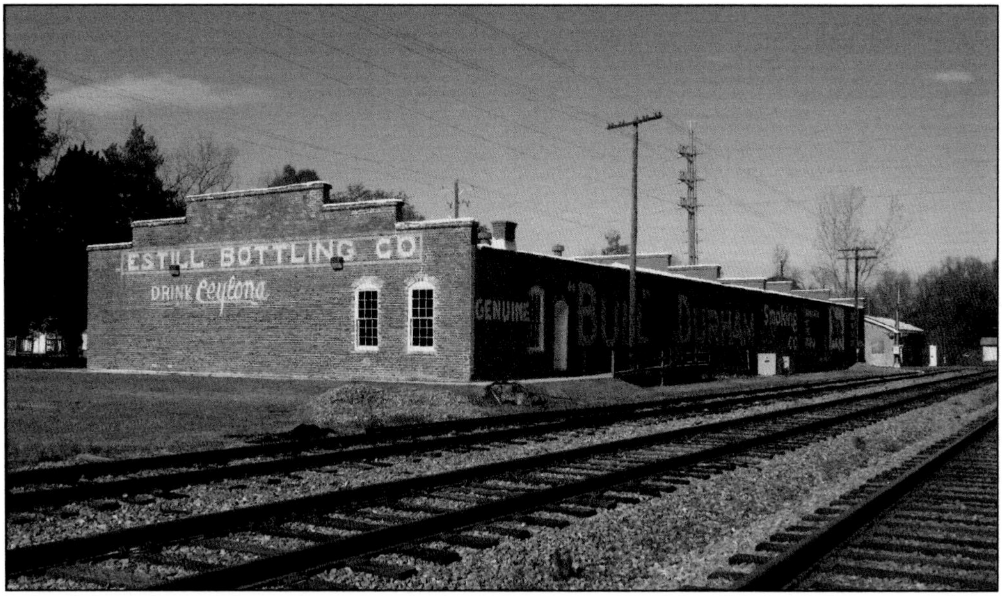


The Bull Durham Center, located at 380 Railroad Avenue, was constructed around 1910 as a cotton warehouse beside the busy railroad. In 1994, the Town of Estill acquired the building from Andrew Harper, and it was officially rededicated it as the Bull Durham Center, for use as a community center and reception hall, in August 2009. (Courtesy of HCG.)

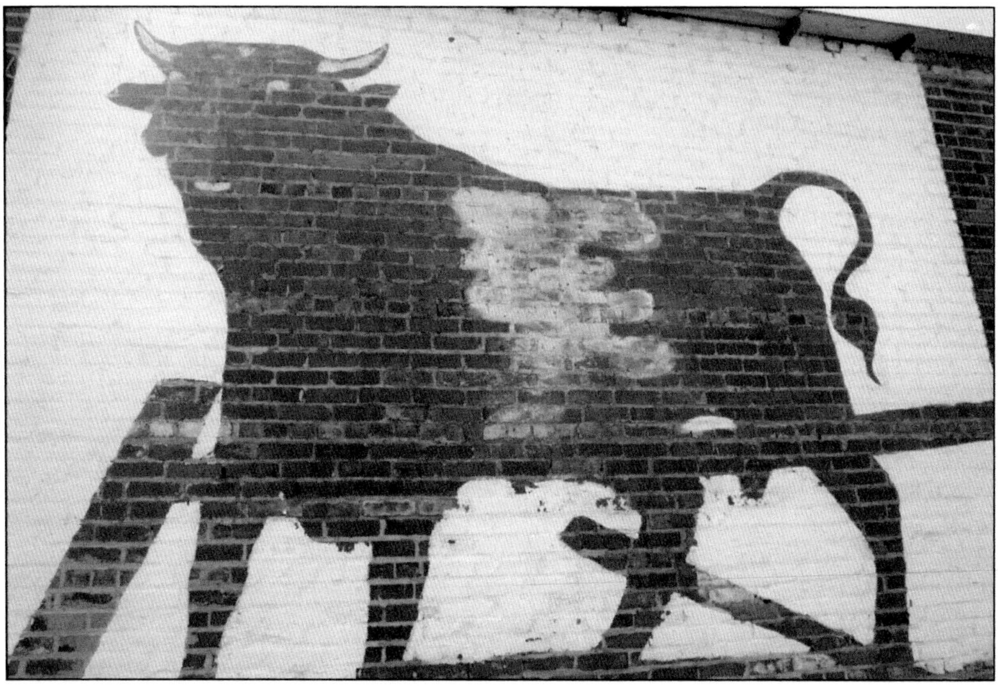

Originally a cotton warehouse, the Bull Durham Center became better known for the iconic Bull Durham tobacco advertisement painted on its brick exterior, a well-known advertisement all around the South. Local historians claim, however, the original depiction of the bull's anatomy was offensive to female passersby so a fence rail was painted in later for modesty's sake. (Courtesy of HCG.)

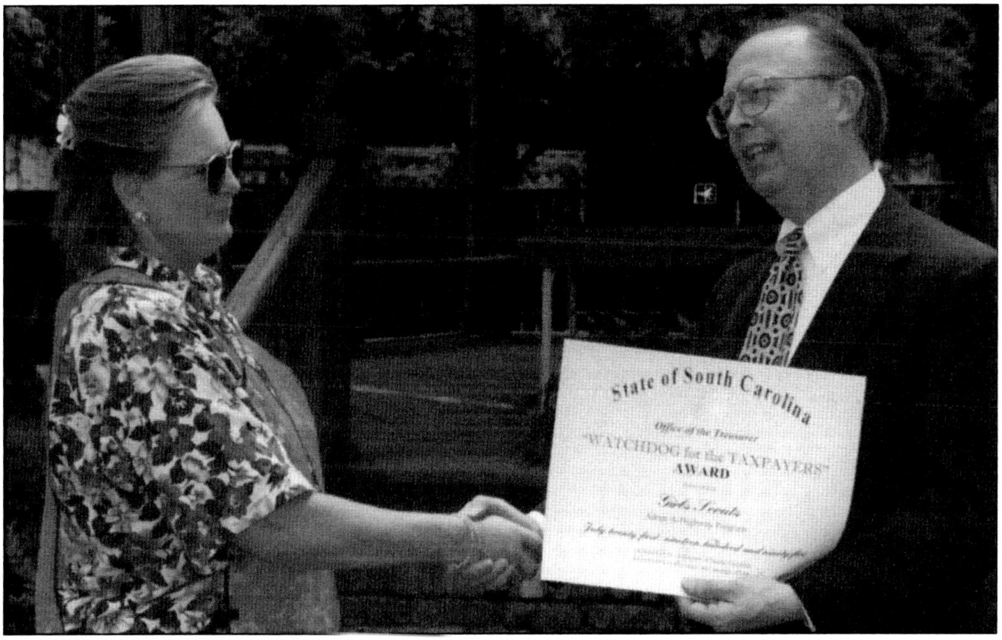


Around the early 1980s, Dr. Harrison Peeples presents a Watchdog for the Taxpayers award to Ann Long, a local Girl Scout leader. Dr. Peeples himself was highly regarded, having received the South Carolina Physicians' Award for Community Service. In November 1980, he was featured in *Good Housekeeping* magazine for being named one of the Top 10 Outstanding Physicians in the Nation by the Academy of Family Physicians. (Courtesy of HCG.)

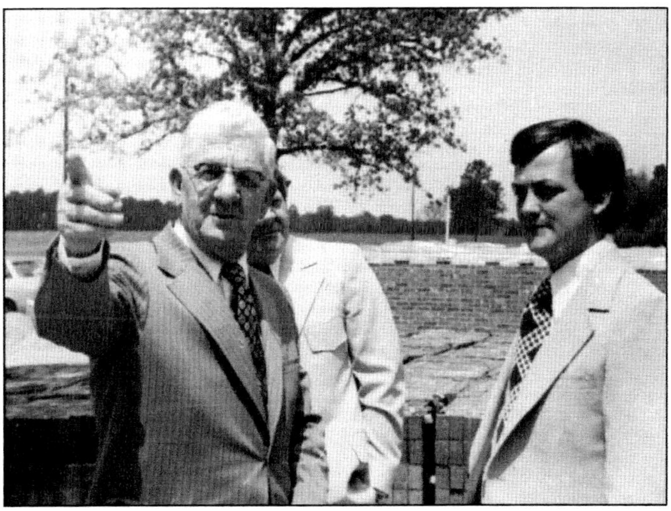

Lee Bowers (right) is pictured with Delacey Long at the Nix reunion on April 22, 1973. Bowers, an Estill native, founded his own Estill law practice, worked with the Estill Historical Preservation Society, was a longtime Hampton County magistrate, and served on the Hampton County Council from January 5, 1987, until January 6, 2003. In 2007, he was named council member emeritus. (Courtesy of HCG.)

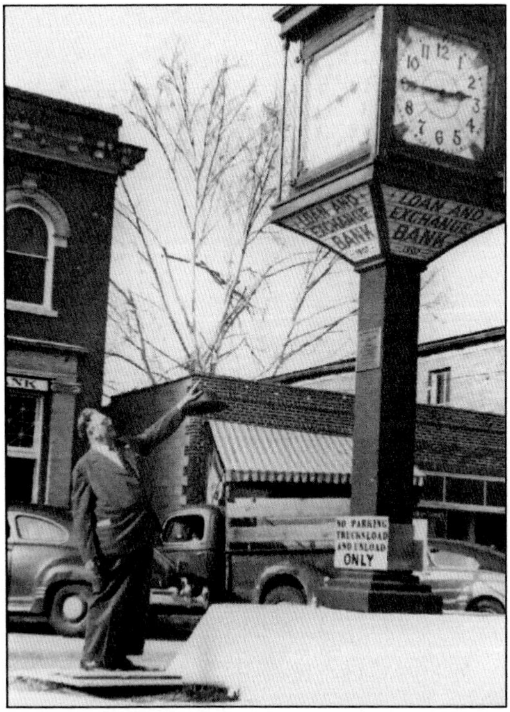


In 1910, the Loan and Exchange Bank of Hampton, once owned by banker R.O. Bowden (pictured), erected a grand clock on Lee Avenue. While the bank was demolished in 2014 to construct the Exchange Park of Hampton, the clock remains a downtown Hampton landmark. Some have joked that local historians would chain themselves to the clock in protest before they would see it torn down. (Courtesy of HCG.)

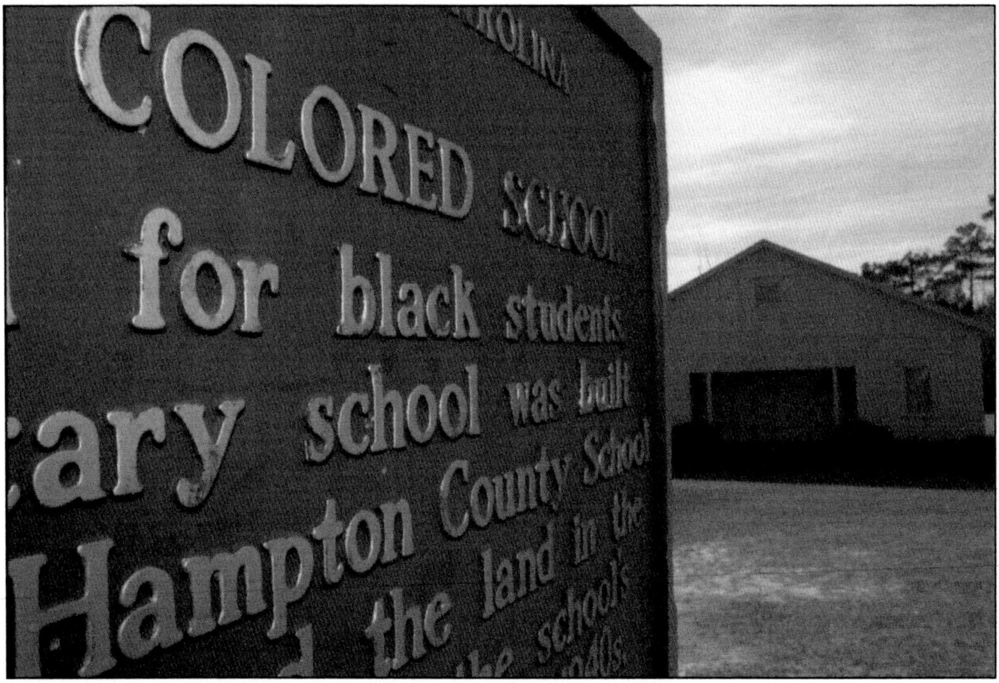


The Hampton Colored School, built around 1929, was one of several all-black schools scattered around Hampton County before integration came to South Carolina. An effort to restore and preserve these vacant school buildings began in the late 1990s, and James "Pete" Hagood, Hampton mayor pro tem, spearheaded an effort to transform the school into the Hampton Old Colored School Museum, which was dedicated on May 22, 1999. (Courtesy of HCG.)

This historic building stands strong at the corner of Lee Avenue in Hampton. Serving as the Bank of Hampton from 1892 to 1926, the two-story structure is now the home of the Hampton Museum and Visitors' Center and listed in the National Register of Historic Places. Longtime curator Marie Ellis, now retired, did an excellent job of keeping history vibrantly alive. (Courtesy of HMVC.)

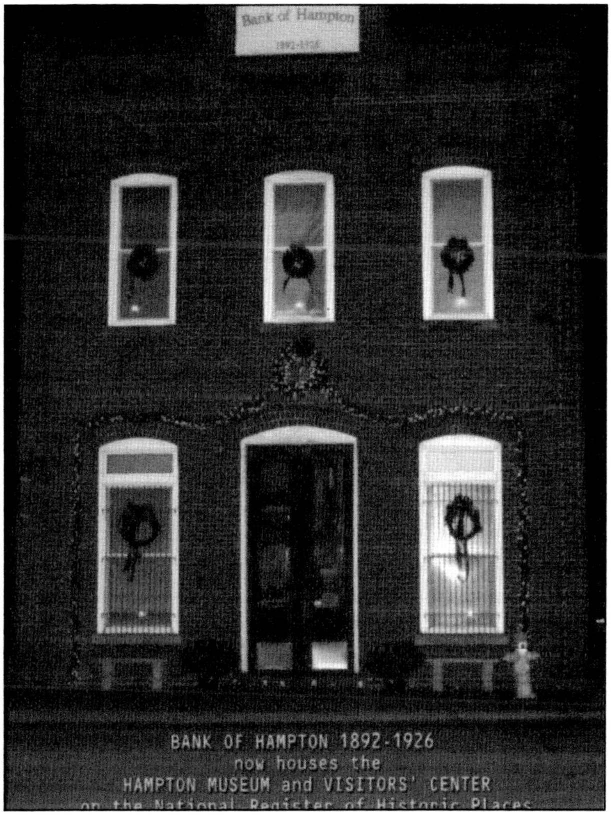


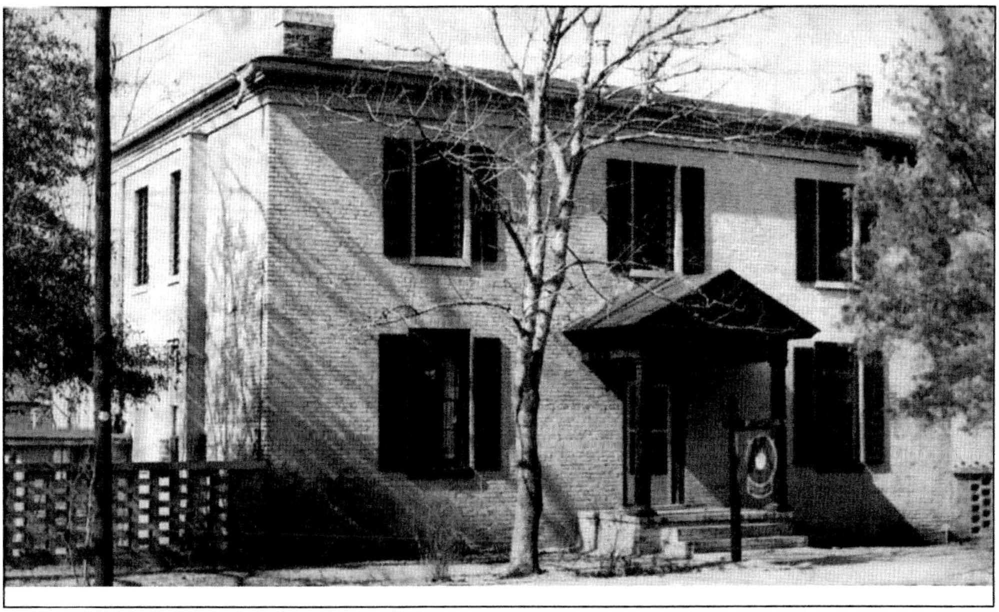

The former Hampton County Jail has been preserved by the Hampton County Historical Society and now serves as the Hampton County Museum. At the time of this writing, work is ongoing to restore the woodwork supporting its historic iron-bar cells in the second story, and the fortified and preserved structure is now a registered historical site. (Courtesy of HCG.)

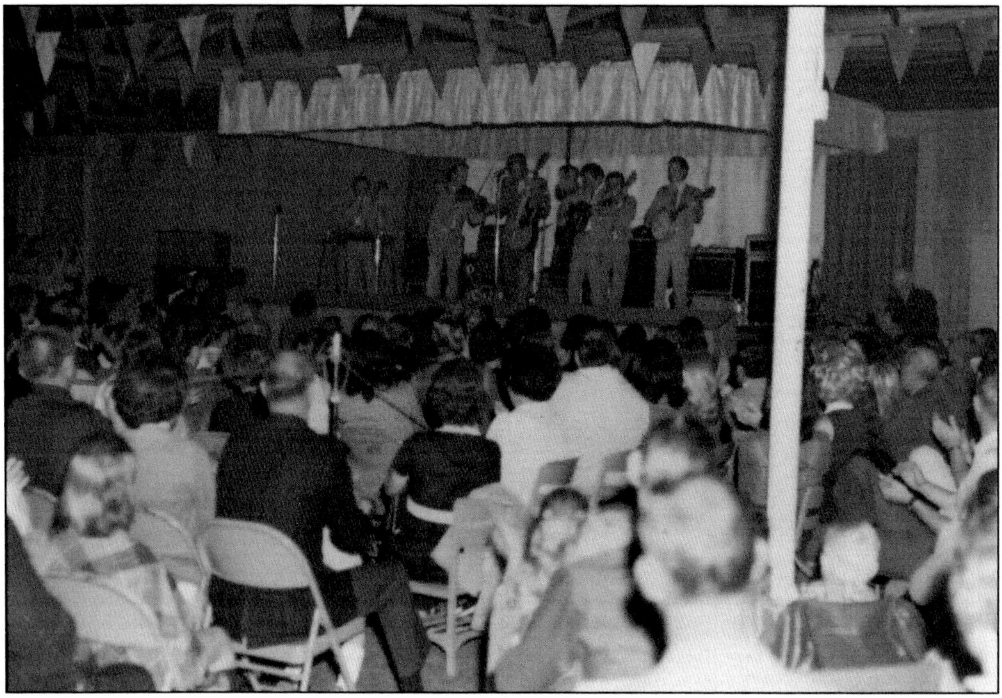

Cranel B. Herndon, a self-made businessman who built an international trucking business based in Hampton, kicked off another successful business venture in Varnville's United Door Company building in January 1968— the Low Country Arena. From that time through the 1970s and 1980s, Low Country Arena offered huge crowds a variety of country and gospel music, dances, Wild West shows, wrestling matches, and even auctions. Herndon also hosted church and community events, such as the June 1972 event in which Beaufort, South Carolina, native Joe Frazier (below), the heavyweight boxing champion who defeated Muhammad Ali in 1968, gave an inspirational speech and warned young people about the dangers of drugs. (Both, courtesy of Libby Smith.)

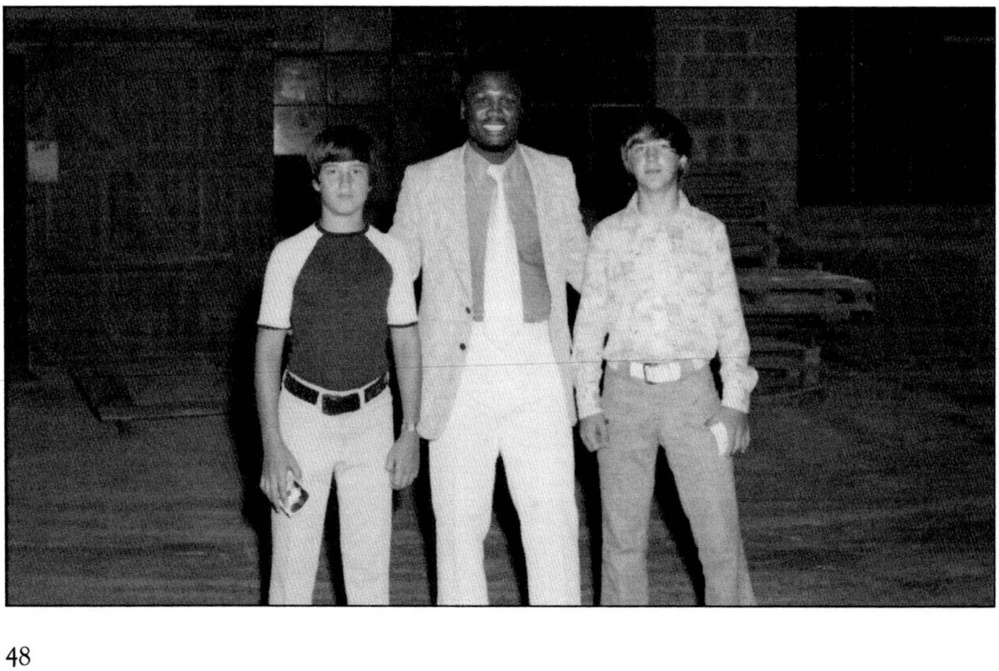

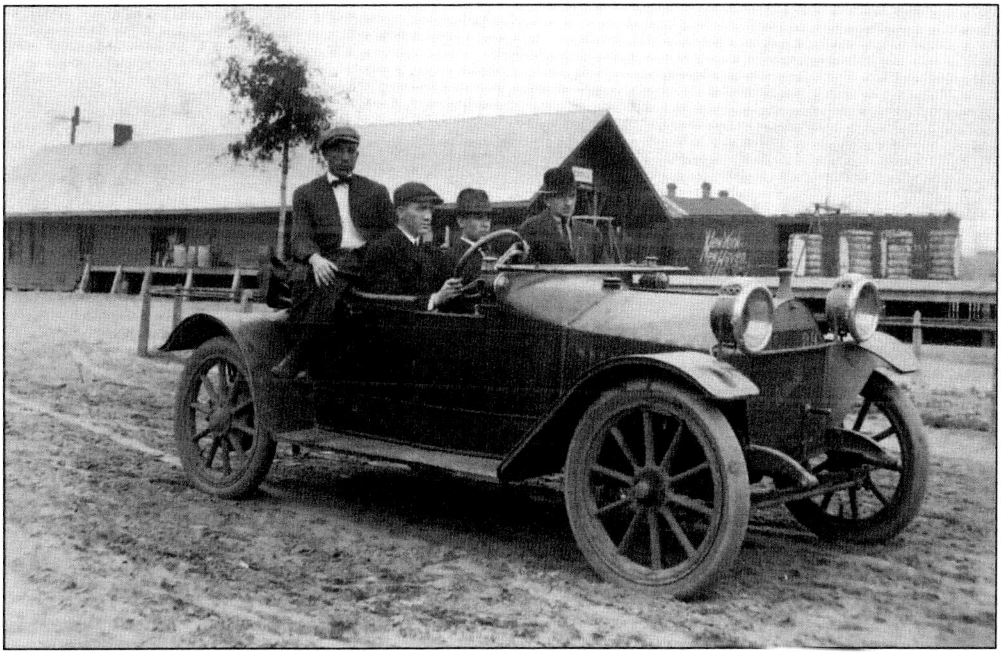

Pictured here is an unidentified group of men out for a ride in front of the Estill Depot in the early 1920s. During the early decades of the 20th century, the Estill Depot was a local landmark as well as a busy hub of commerce, a railroad link between southern Hampton County farmers and the big buyers in Savannah, Georgia, and Columbia, South Carolina. (Courtesy of HCG.)

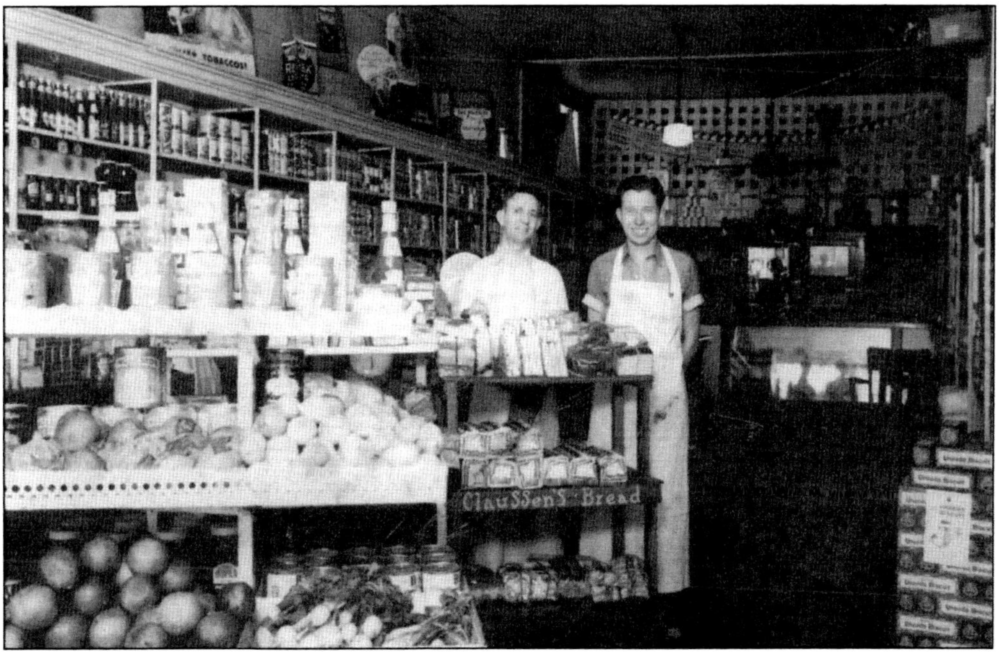


In this mid-1940s photograph, grocers Bissell Parker and Cliff Jemont pose amid well-stocked dry goods shelves and abundant locally grown produce. Parker's Grocery was one of several mercantile stores located in Hampton that folks patronized from miles around, along with Rivers' Five & Dime Store and Rivers' Dry Goods. (Courtesy of HMVC.)

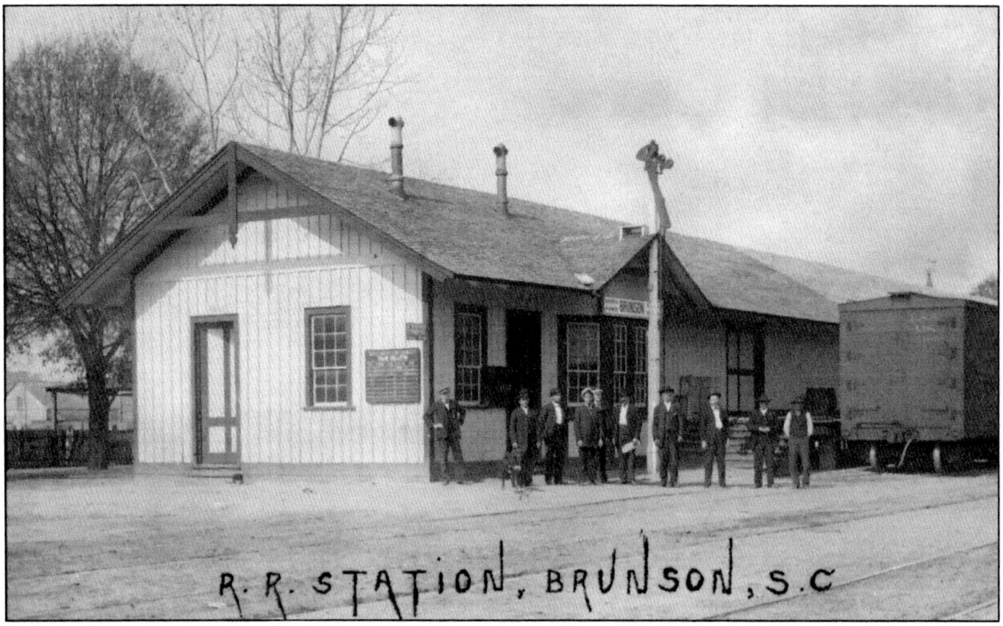


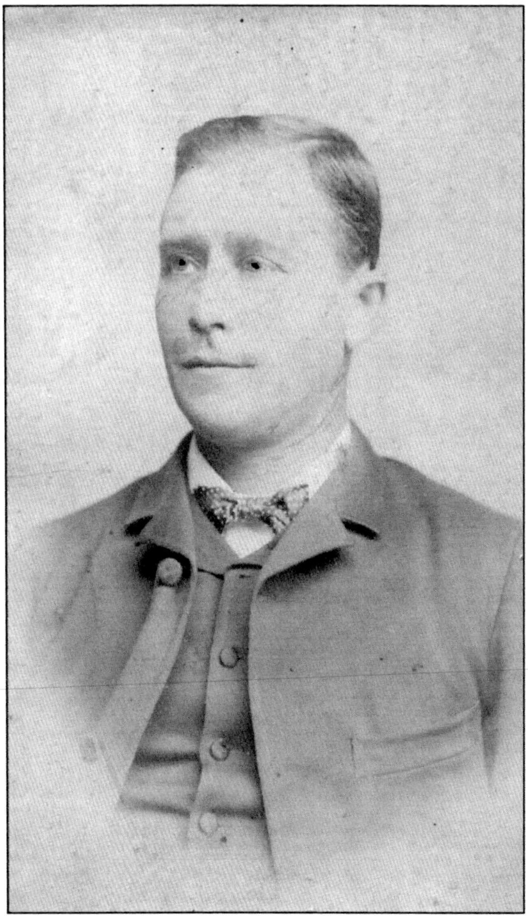

In this undated photograph, the Brunson Railroad Station is captured in its heyday. The depot was built in 1887, and the octagonal Brunson Town Hall on stilts (not pictured) was later built nearby in 1906. Eventually crowded out by the bustling railroad, which was an economic lifeline for many local farmers, timber dealers, and travelers, the town hall was moved to its present location in 1952. (Courtesy of BMVC.)

Thomas Wesley Williams (November 28, 1847–September 29, 1905) served in the Confederate army and was one of the early mayors of Brunson (1897–1899). He married Legatsy Caroline Brunson, daughter of the town's founder, William Edgar Brunson Sr. Their home still stands in Brunson, just behind the town hall on Main Street North. (Courtesy of BMVC.)

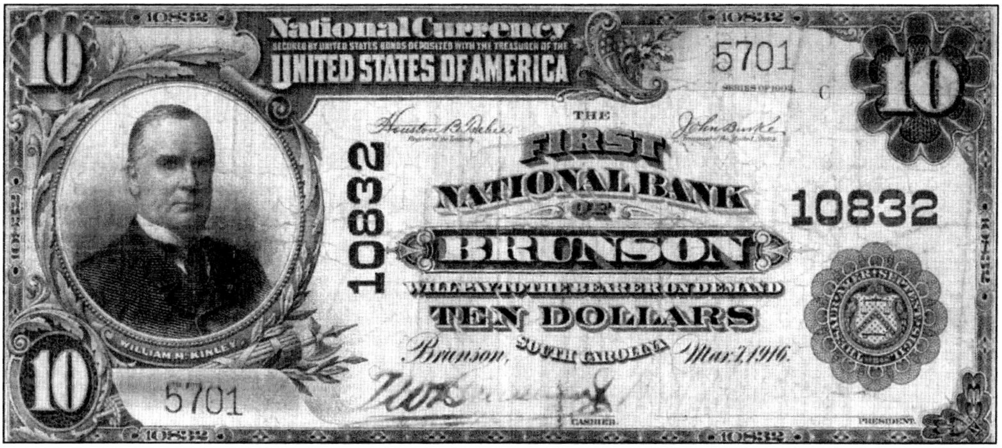


This $10 bill, series 1902, was printed at the First National Bank in Brunson in 1916. Not only did this federal bank print its own notes, but it was the only national bank in Hampton County. Brunson historians believe that it served the area from the early 1900s until the Great Depression era. (Courtesy of BMVC.)

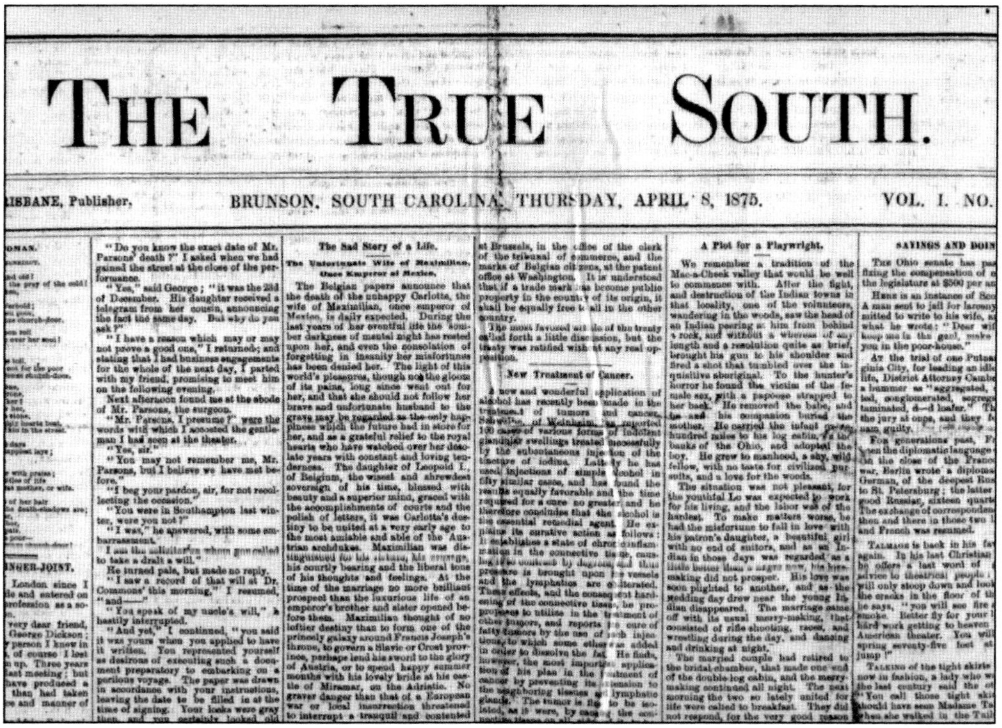

THE TRUE SOUTH.

...ISBANE, Publisher. BRUNSON, SOUTH CAROLINA, THURSDAY, APRIL 8, 1875. VOL. I. NO.

The Sad Story of a Life.

New Treatment of Cancer.

A Plot for a Playwright.

SAYINGS AND DOINGS.

The *True South* was a weekly newspaper established in Brunson in 1875 and discontinued the same year. During the late 1800s, there were three other newspapers printed in Brunson—the *Hampton County Elevator*, a black publication established in 1891; *Hampton County News Herald*, established in 1887; and *New Light*, a black publication founded in 1896. (Courtesy of BMVC.)

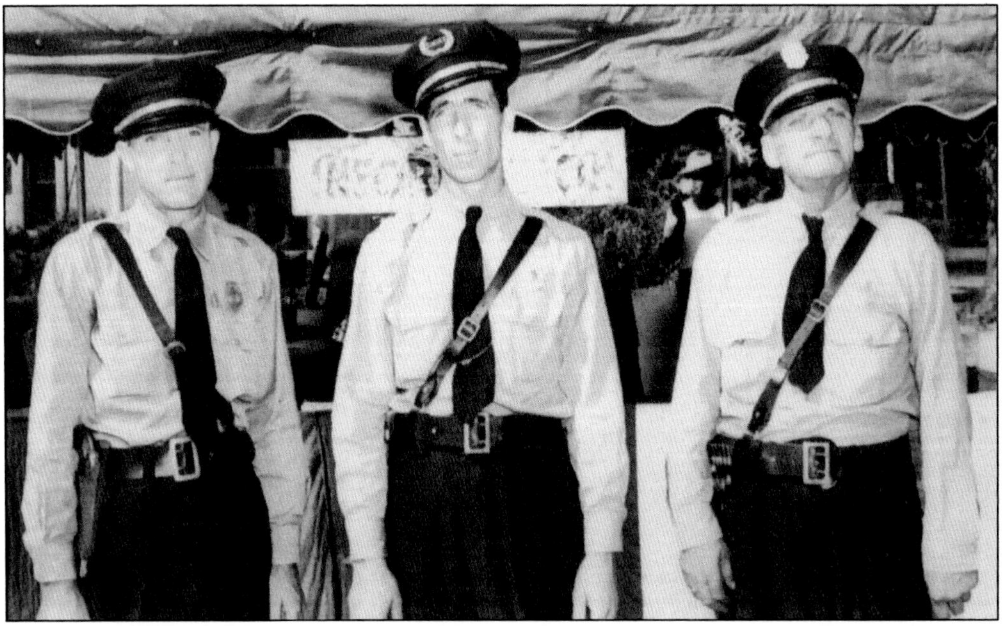

The town of Hampton's fire and police departments have long traditions of public service. In this 1940s-era photograph, believed to have been taken during the watermelon festival, are, from left to right, Wilfred Woods, Chief "Sassy" Lightsey, and John Dobson. Lest the Andy Griffith–style uniforms fool readers, they should know that the lawmen in those days had a reputation for not tolerating nonsense. (Courtesy of Anna Sue Rivers.)

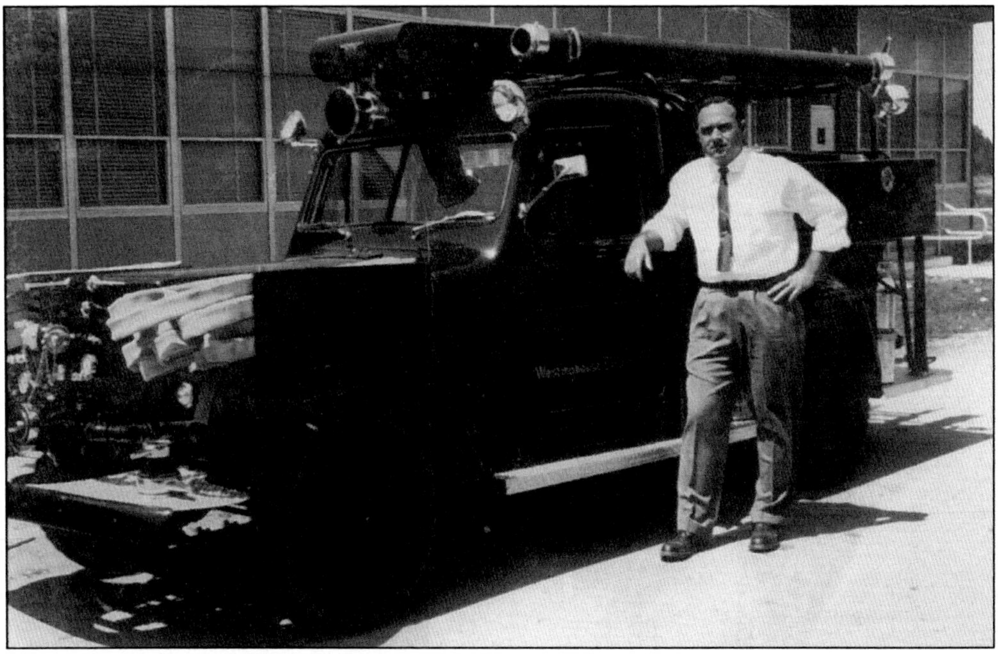

Jacob Rivers, husband of Anna Sue Rivers, poses in this 1950s-era photograph with his Westinghouse fire truck. This specialized fire truck was built with a narrow frame in order for it to be driven in the narrow aisles between the rows of manufacturing equipment. Rivers worked at Westinghouse and was in charge of fire safety. (Courtesy of Anna Sue Rivers.)

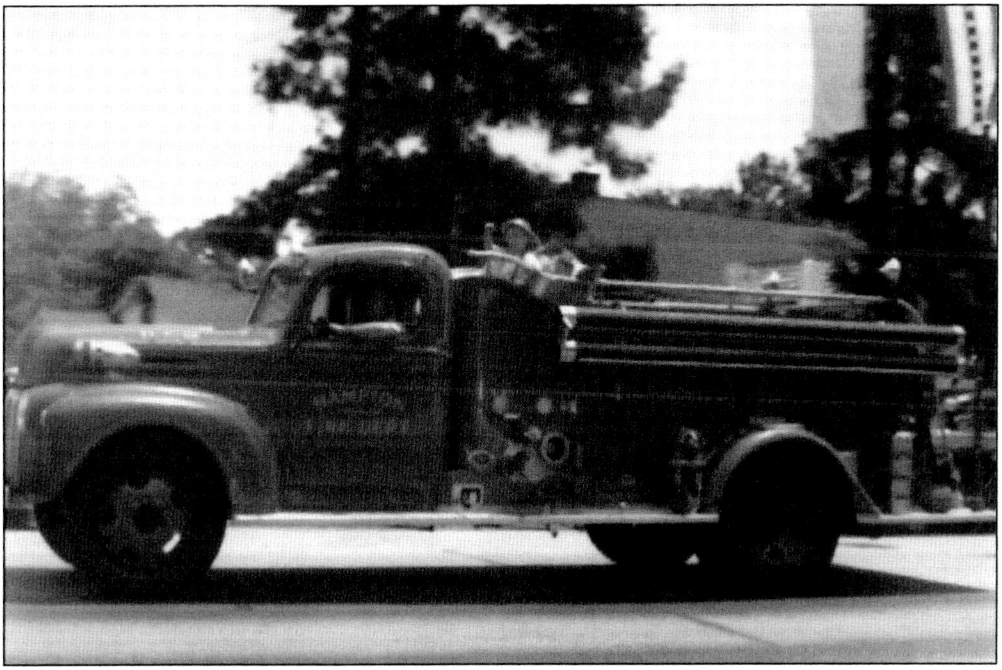

Pictured here is the Town of Hampton's 1946 Ford fire truck, the first real fire truck the town ever purchased. Driving the truck in the watermelon festival parade in the mid-1950s is W.E. "Billy" Ramsey, and his son Lewis E. Ramsey (current Hampton fire chief) is riding on the top of the truck bed. (Courtesy of Jerry Hatcher.)

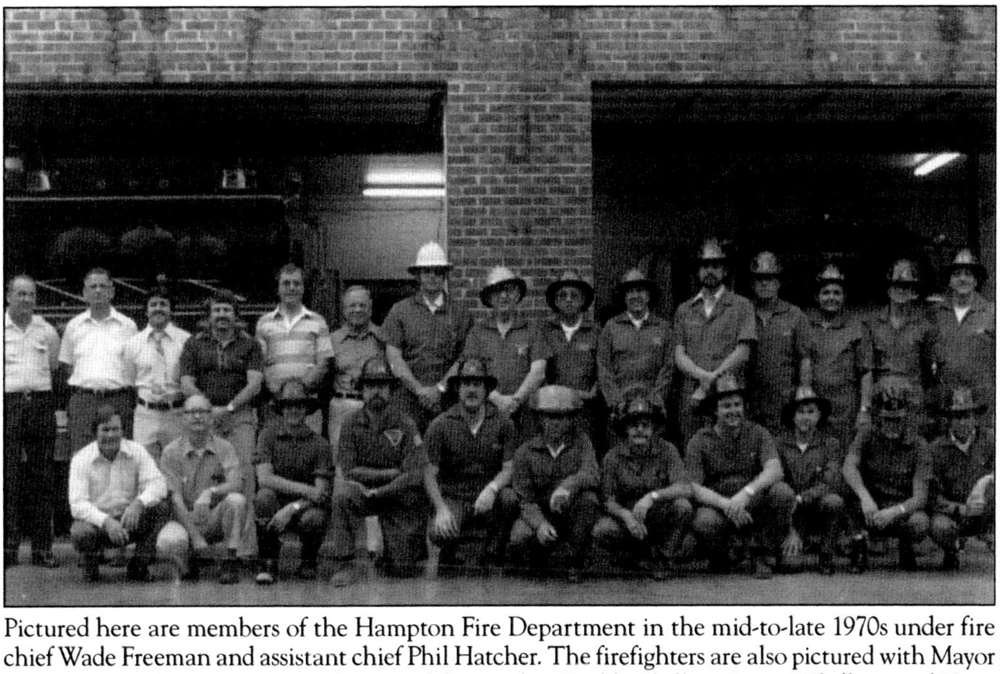

Pictured here are members of the Hampton Fire Department in the mid-to-late 1970s under fire chief Wade Freeman and assistant chief Phil Hatcher. The firefighters are also pictured with Mayor Harold McMillan; town councilmen Ralph Vaughn, Buddy Phillips, Jimmy Phillips, and Tony Gross; police chief Richard Pope; town administrator Richard Hutto; and town attorney Billy Anderson. The department offered volunteers much camaraderie. (Courtesy of Jerry Hatcher.)

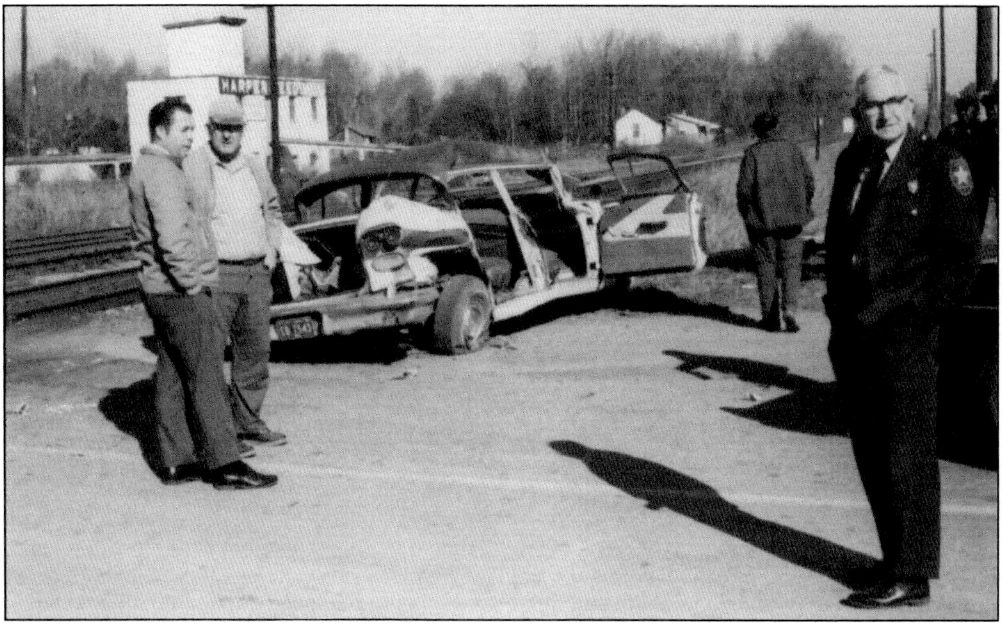

A tragic train-automobile wreck that occurred in southern Hampton County on January 21, 1971, was photographed by Dwight Moore, who captured the events of his day. It was said by those that knew him that Moore was a man of few words—when he spoke it was usually about photography, hunting, or fishing—but he loved having his photographs in the local paper, the *Hampton County Guardian*. (Courtesy of DM.)

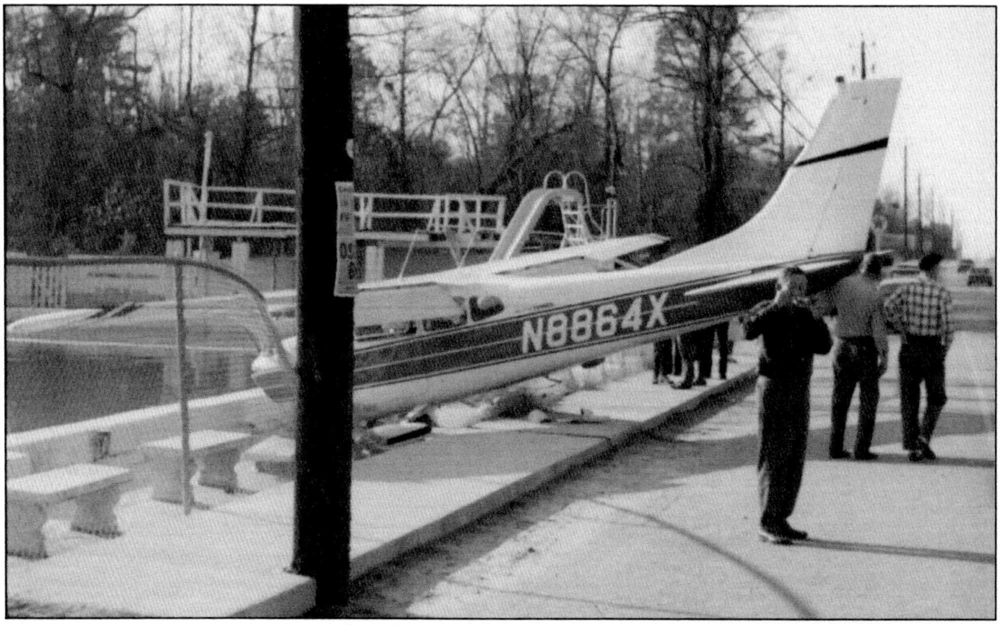


In 1970, a curious event occurred at the Varnville Swimming Pool: A Cessna 182D aircraft fell from the sky and crashed into the pool fencing, which stopped it from taking a dip into the water. Luckily, it was February 18 and there were no swimmers. Low on fuel en route to Savannah, Georgia, the pilot reportedly mistook the driveway for a runway in bad weather. (Courtesy of Marcia Wood.)

# *Three*

# The Watermelon Festival

By the 1930s, farming was both a way of life and big business for many in Hampton County. For most farmers, sweet, homegrown watermelon was the king of all crops. In 1939, a group of volunteers banded together with civic pride and decided to hold a watermelon festival. But this would prove to become more than just a small-town harvest festival.

It would grow to become the annual highlight event for the entire county, a community event that offers something for people of all ages: parades, mud racing, dancing, watermelon-eating contests, and more. But it would also become one of the biggest tourist draws in the Lowcountry. The Hampton County Watermelon Festival is now touted as the oldest continuously held festival in the state, and volunteers claim that it has the longest parade in the state, a route that covers two towns, for a whopping 2.4 miles, from Varnville to Hampton.

This festival, held continuously since 1939, attracts folks from around the country and packs thousands of people into two small towns that are normally sleepy and serene. The festival has drawn South Carolina governors and other state officials; Sen. Strom Thurmond was a regular here. Astronauts have mingled with beauty queens and other heavenly bodies at this event, and families share some of their fondest memories at the Hampton County Watermelon Festival. And the most amazing thing of all is this event is organized entirely by hardworking volunteers.

One will find a lot of Dwight Moore's photographs in this chapter. The watermelon festival was one of his favorite events, and he rarely missed it if he was in good health. In the final summer before Moore's death, one of his good friends, radio station owner Tony Gross, picked him up from the rest home where he was living to enjoy one final watermelon festival. Moore brought his camera.

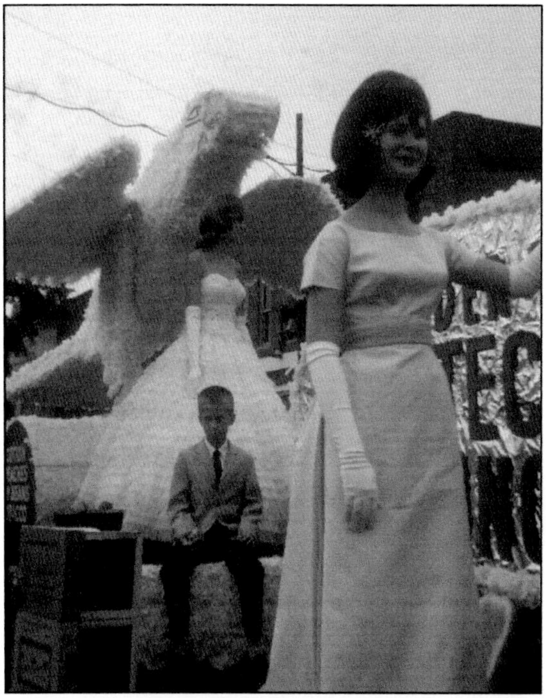

A waving beauty queen and a candy-slinging youngster ride on a decorated float during the 1965 watermelon festival parade. During recent decades, the watermelon festival parade, locally touted as having the longest route of any South Carolina parade, used to alternate between Hampton and Estill. It is now held each year in Varnville and Hampton. (Courtesy of DM.)

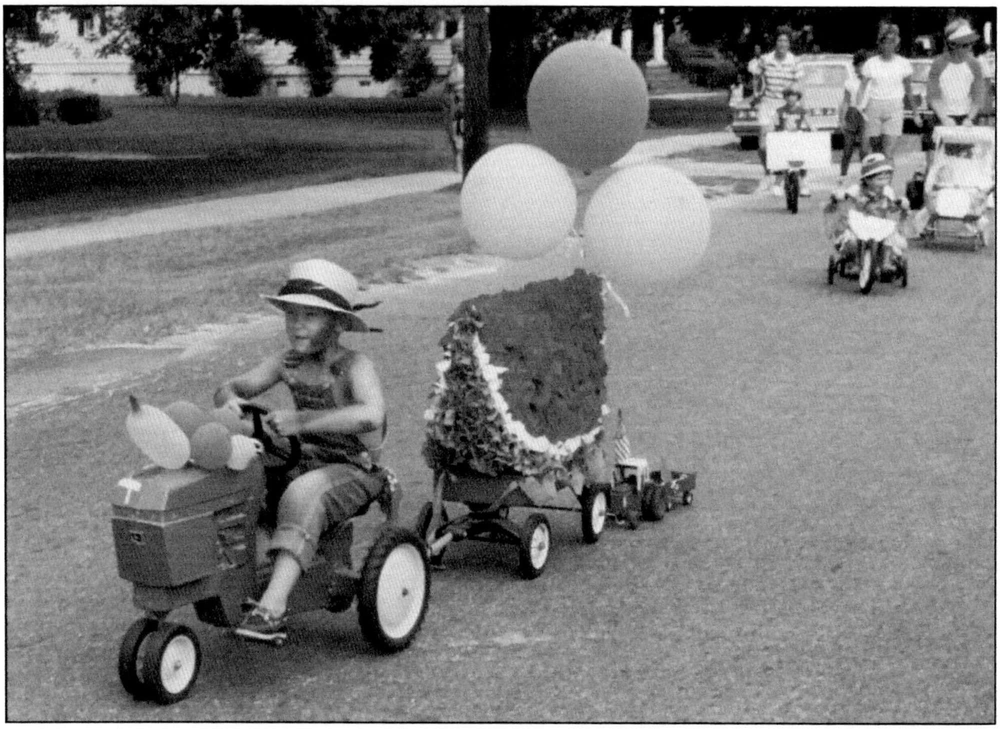

The festival spirit and Hampton County's agricultural legacy are clearly portrayed in this photograph of the 1985 watermelon festival youth parade. While the youth parade is much smaller than the annual flagship parade that has drawn people from across the Southeast for more than 70 years, it makes up for its small scale with a huge amount of cuteness. (Courtesy of DM.)

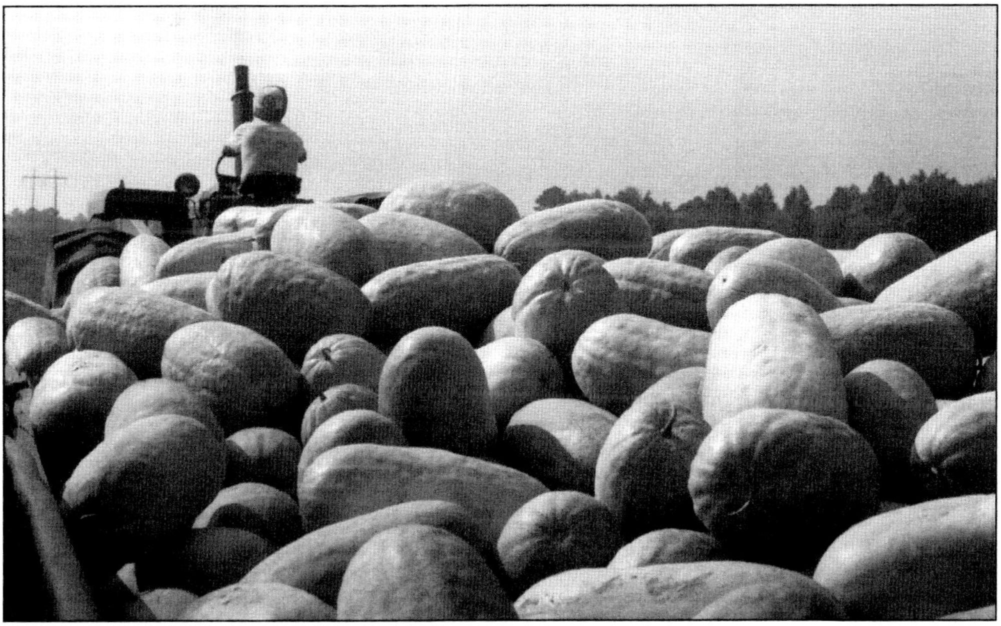

Hampton County watermelons go to market—what a beautiful sight! Picked by strong hands, hired help, family, and helpful neighbors, Hampton County watermelons were shipped around the nation and put the county on the map via the watermelon festival. Although the sweet and sinfully juicy watermelon is no longer the king crop in terms of acreage, it will always reign supreme in Hampton County hearts. (Courtesy of HMVC.)

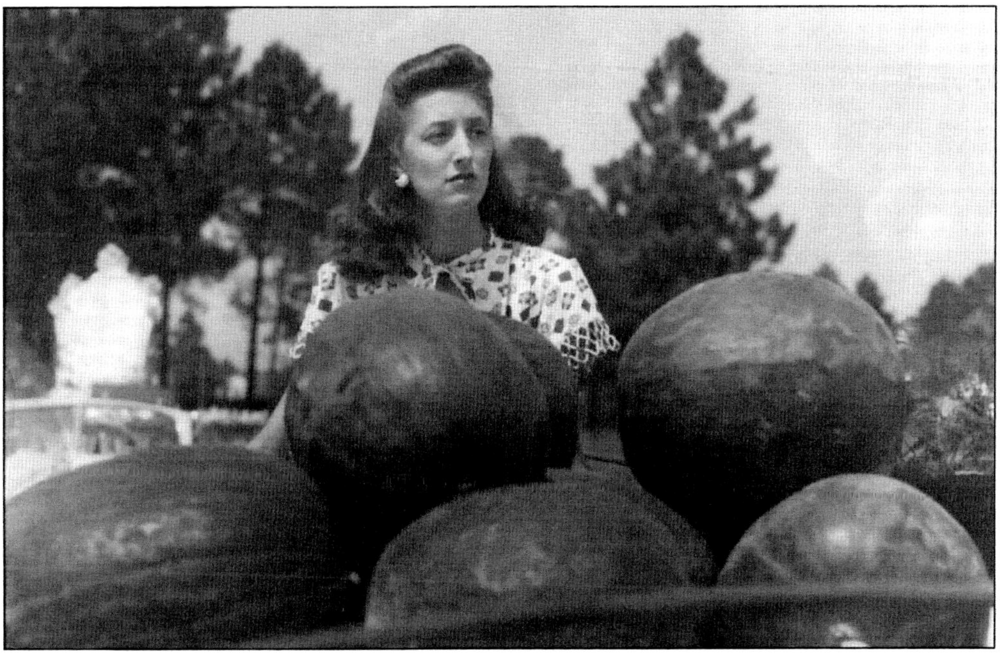

An unidentified young beauty queen rides in sweet company, a truck full of cannonball watermelons, during the 1946 Hampton County Watermelon Festival. Hampton County produced a good variety of beauty queens every year for the festival and an even wider variety of melons, including cannonballs, Congo, Charleston Gray, and Jubilee varieties. (Courtesy of HCG.)

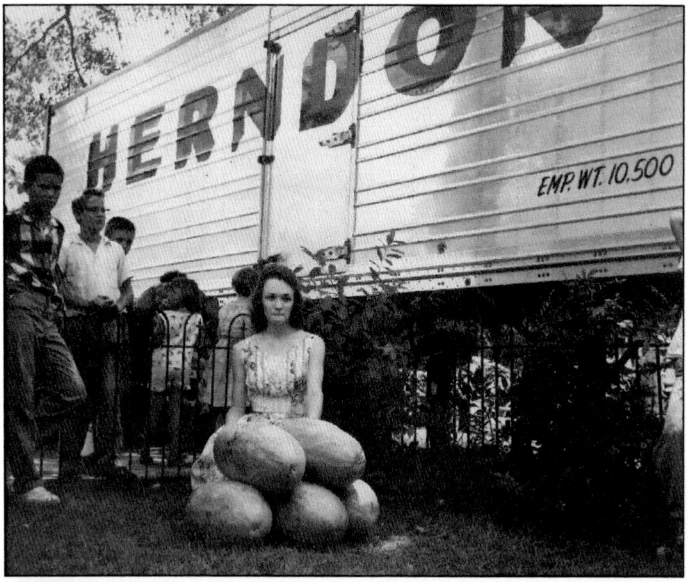


In this 1960s-era photograph, elementary school teacher Ellen Phillips poses for photographs during the watermelon festival with the stars of the show, a pile of juicy, sweet Hampton County watermelons, as curious youngsters look on. The C.B. Herndon trucking company of Hampton was a proud sponsor of the festival, and their trucks were a common sight in the parade during those days. (Courtesy of Libby Smith.)

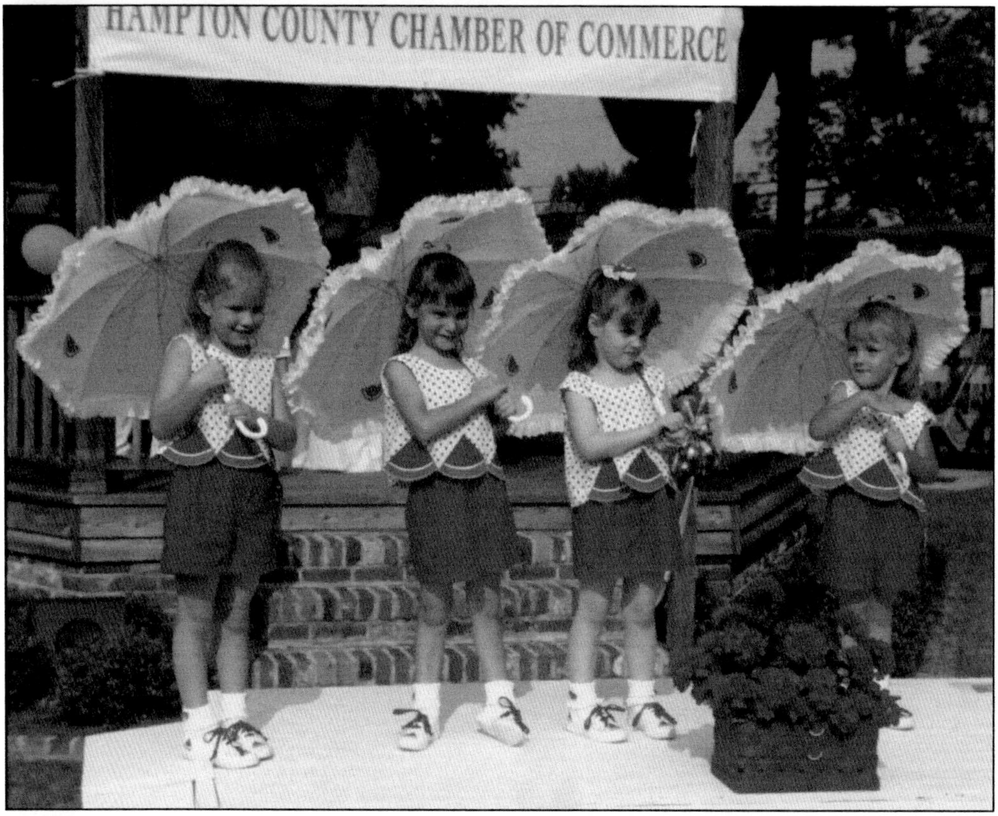


These young ladies enjoyed the 1991 edition of the watermelon festival with smiles, melon-themed outfits, and matching umbrellas on the steps of the Hampton Gazebo. As the overhead banner denotes, local organizations like the Hampton County Chamber of Commerce, the Rotary Club, and area Shriners endorsed and enjoyed the festival just as much as the youngsters. (Courtesy of DM.)

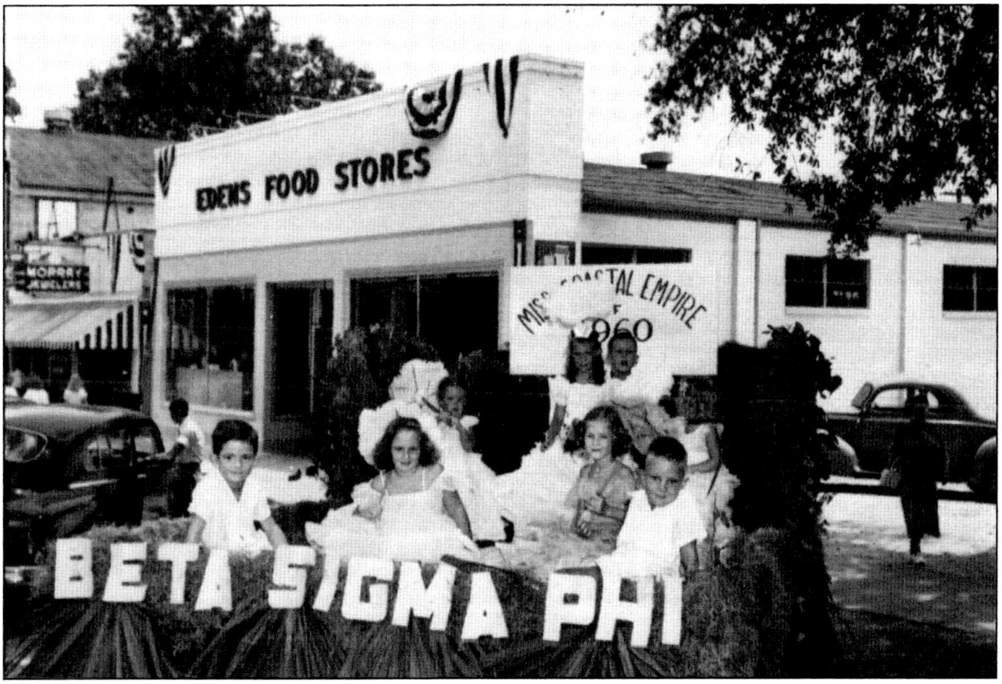


The Beta Sigma Phi sorority sponsored this Miss Coastal Empire float full of smiling youngsters during the 1960 watermelon festival parade, back when the parade still traveled down Main Street in Hampton. Morray Jewelers and Eden's Food Store, pictured in the background, have long since retired to the annals of history. (Courtesy of HMVC.)

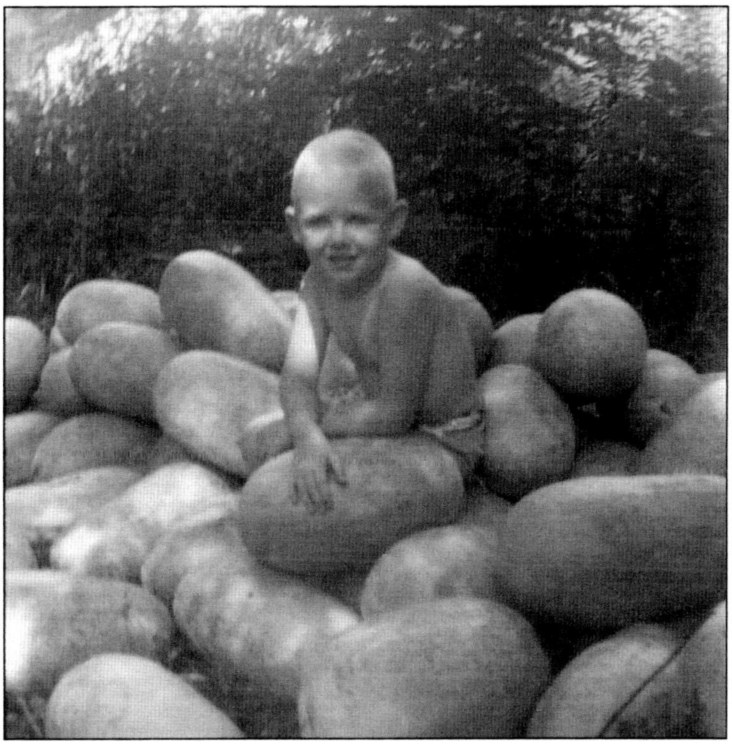

Five-year-old Carl Anderson is enjoying the annual watermelon harvesttime in this photograph from August 1959. The summer months of June and July hold vivid memories for many local residents: working in the hot sun all day to pick and load the sweet watermelons while looking forward to watermelon festival activities later that week. (Courtesy of HMVC.)

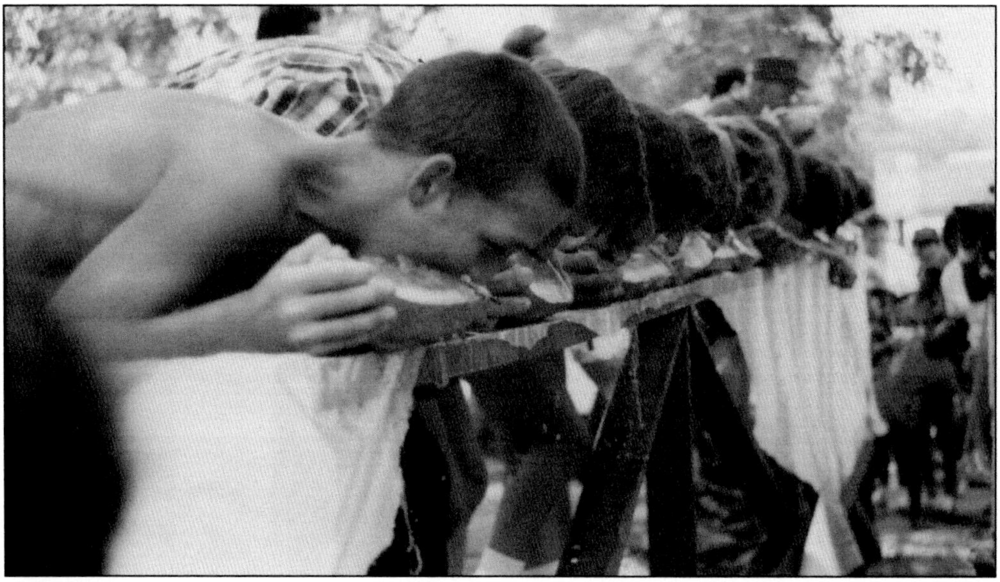

Shirts off, chins down, elbows flying, and juice dripping—that pretty much describes the action during the watermelon festival's watermelon-eating contest. The contest has been an annual tradition for decades and is usually held under the shady oaks of the courthouse square or at the Hampton Gazebo. Modern winners take home a T-shirt as a prize; they certainly need clean shirts afterward. (Courtesy of HMVC.)

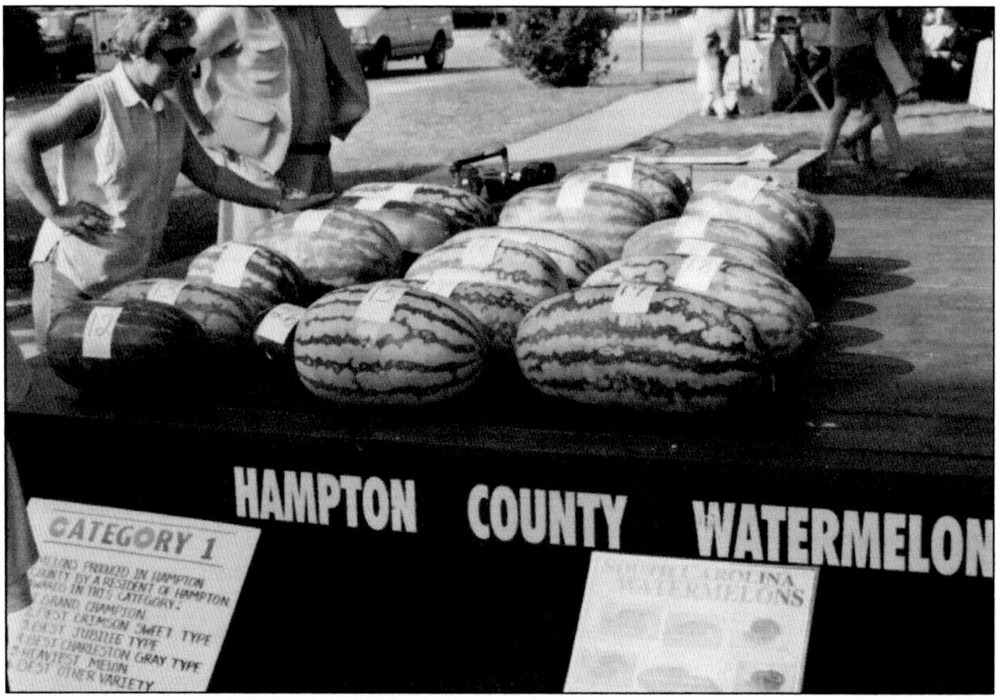


The watermelon festival melon-judging contest has also been an integral part of the festival in recent decades. Categories titles include Grand Champion Melon, Best Crimson Sweet, Best Jubilee, Best Charleston Gray, and Heaviest Watermelon. Regardless of what type of melon is entered, it must be grown in the fertile soils of Hampton County to qualify. (Courtesy of HMVC.)

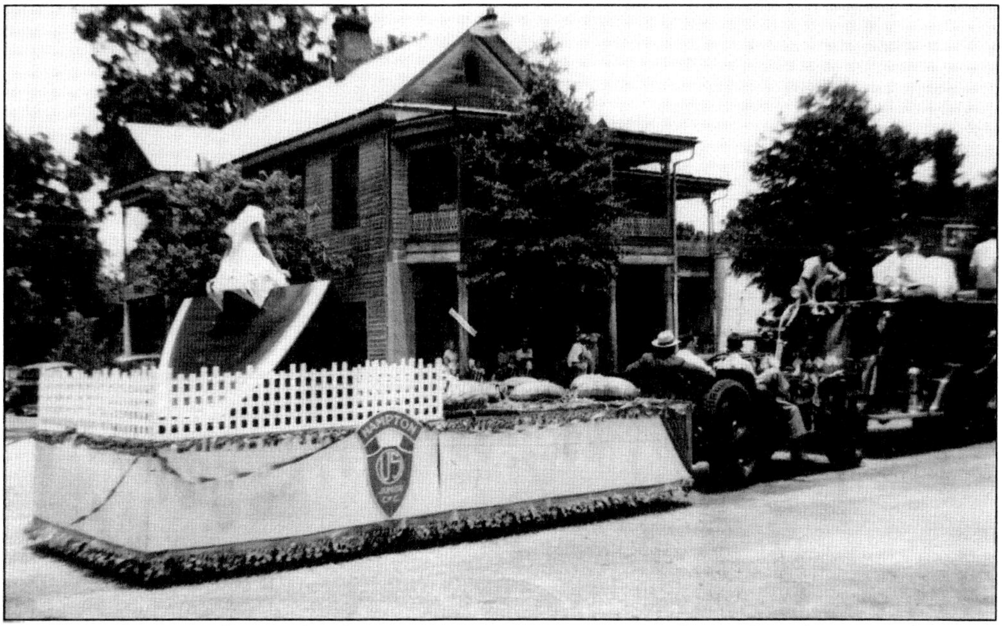

A Hampton Jaycees float glides down Hampton's main street and past the John Rivers home in this early 1940s–era photograph. The home, now demolished, is on the future site of the Frock Shop, a local business that has been a Lee Avenue landmark since 1946. (Courtesy of Dorothy Vincent Moore.)

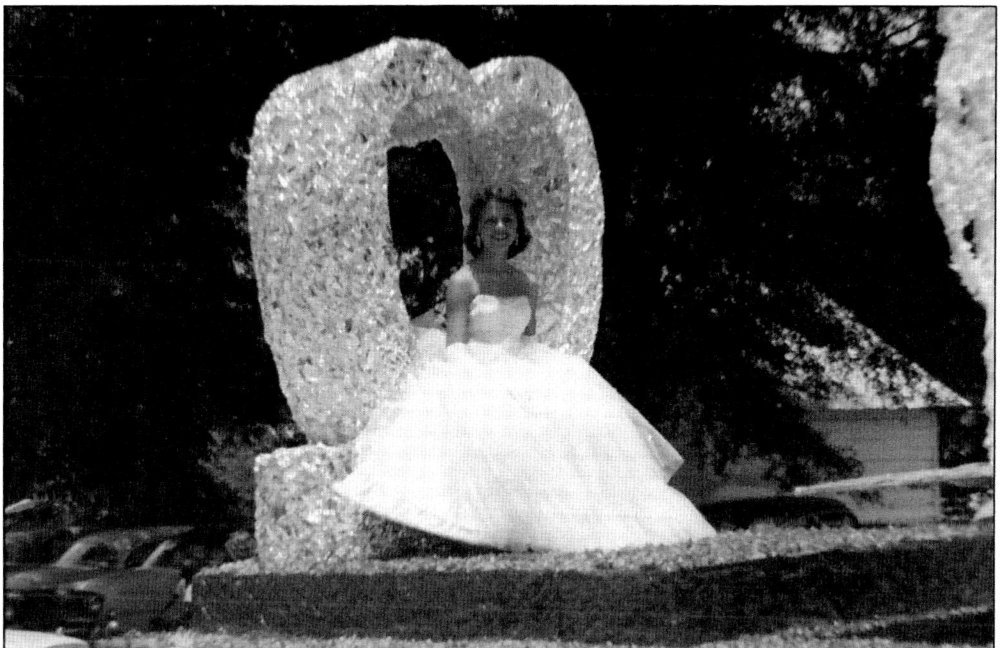

Beauty queen Rita Kittles gracefully adorns the Estill float during the 1959 watermelon festival. The honorary guest speaker of that year's festival was R.C. Edwards, and the Miss Coastal Empire queen that year was Ann Stevens of Conway, South Carolina. The festival chairman that year was E.R. Bullard. (Courtesy of DM.)

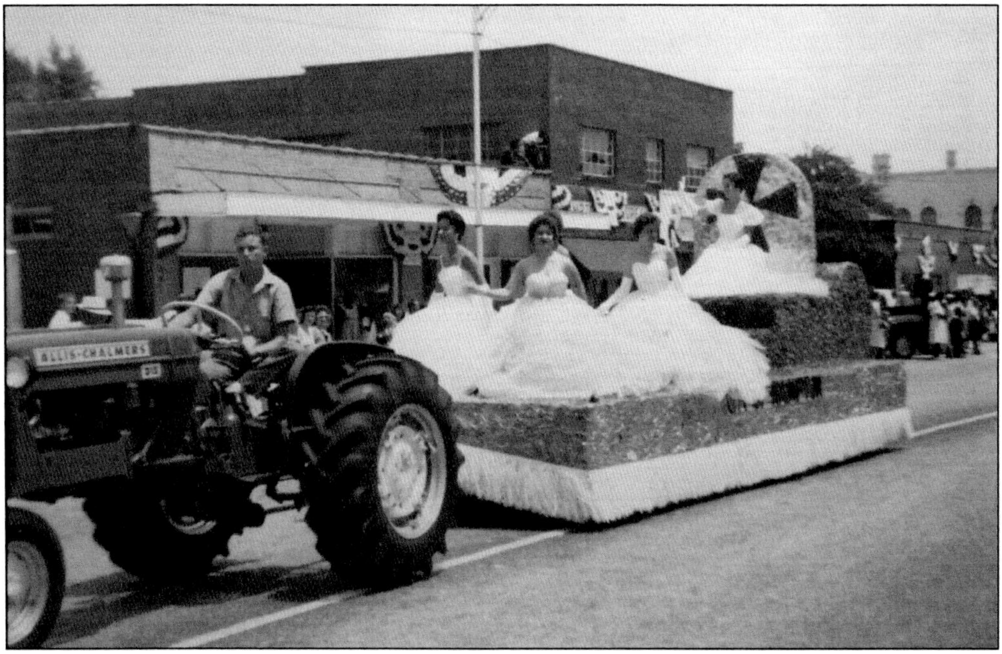

A laid-back lad on a handy tractor pulls the Town of Hampton float full of beauty queens down Lee Avenue during the parade on June 9, 1961. The one-story building behind the float is the current home of the *Hampton County Guardian*. Note the adventurous spectators observing from the rooftop. (Courtesy of DM.)

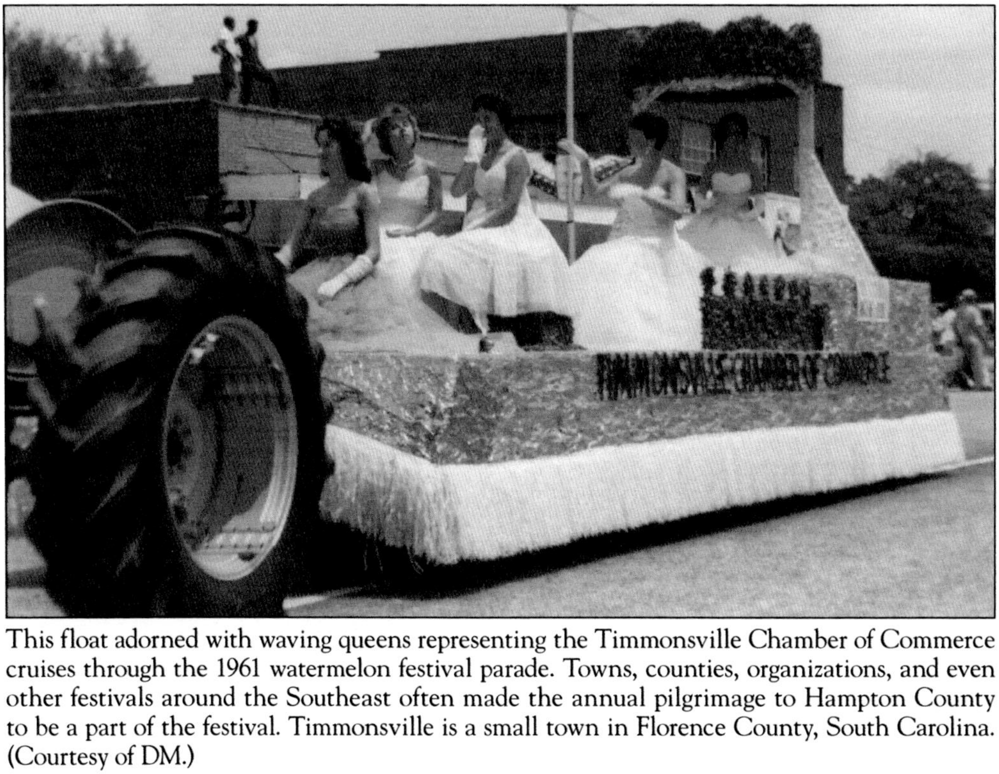

This float adorned with waving queens representing the Timmonsville Chamber of Commerce cruises through the 1961 watermelon festival parade. Towns, counties, organizations, and even other festivals around the Southeast often made the annual pilgrimage to Hampton County to be a part of the festival. Timmonsville is a small town in Florence County, South Carolina. (Courtesy of DM.)

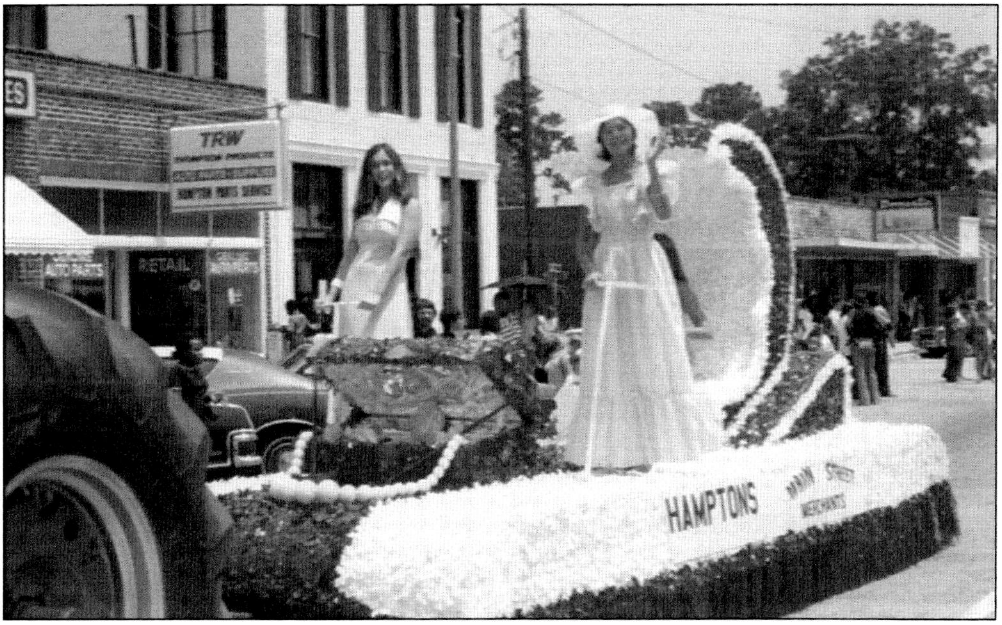

A big-wheeled tractor pulls the Hampton Main Street Merchants float during the 1974 Hampton County Watermelon Festival parade as it makes the loop down Lee Avenue. These days, the local merchants' group is known as the Hampton Downtown Business Association, and all of the businesses seen in the background have long since been replaced with new ones. (Courtesy of DM.)

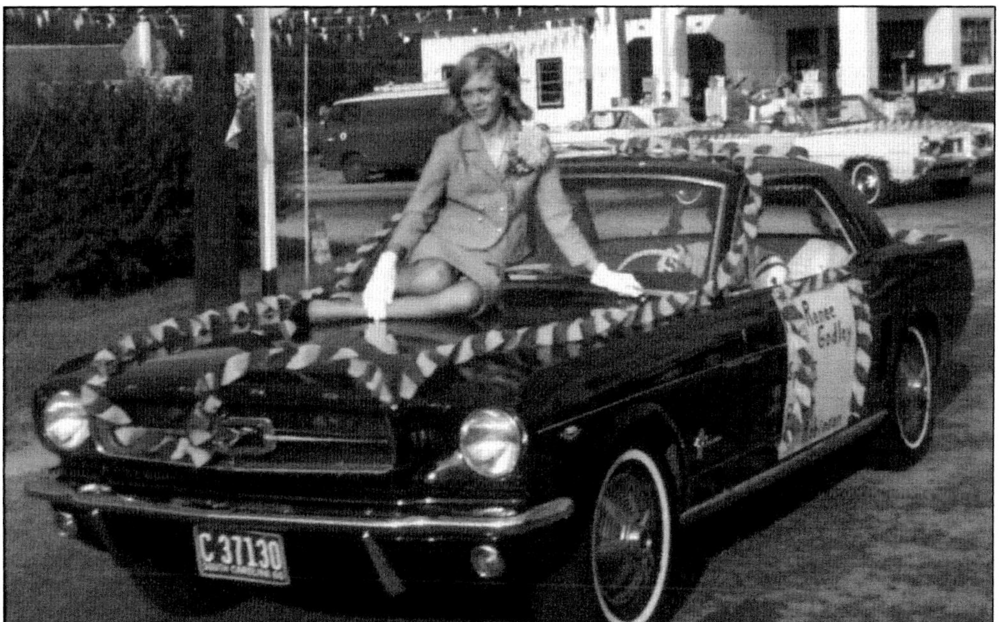

Local beauty queen Renee Godley cruises through Varnville's Main Street during the 1966 watermelon festival parade. For most of its history, the festival parade has begun in Varnville and ended in Hampton, except for a brief time when it rotated years with Estill. The American gas station in the background has long since been torn down. (Courtesy of DM.)

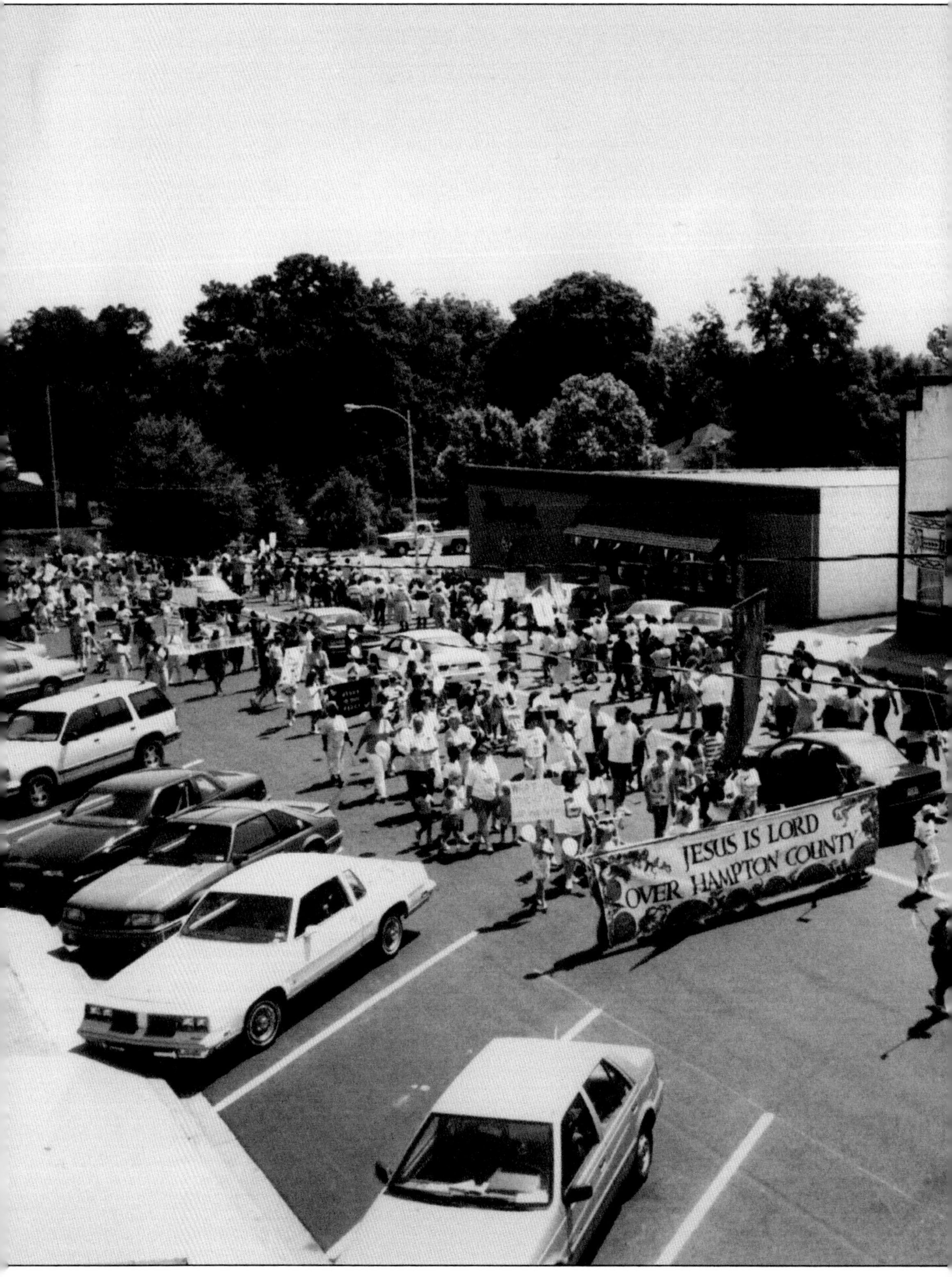
JESUS IS LORD
OVER HAMPTON COUNTY

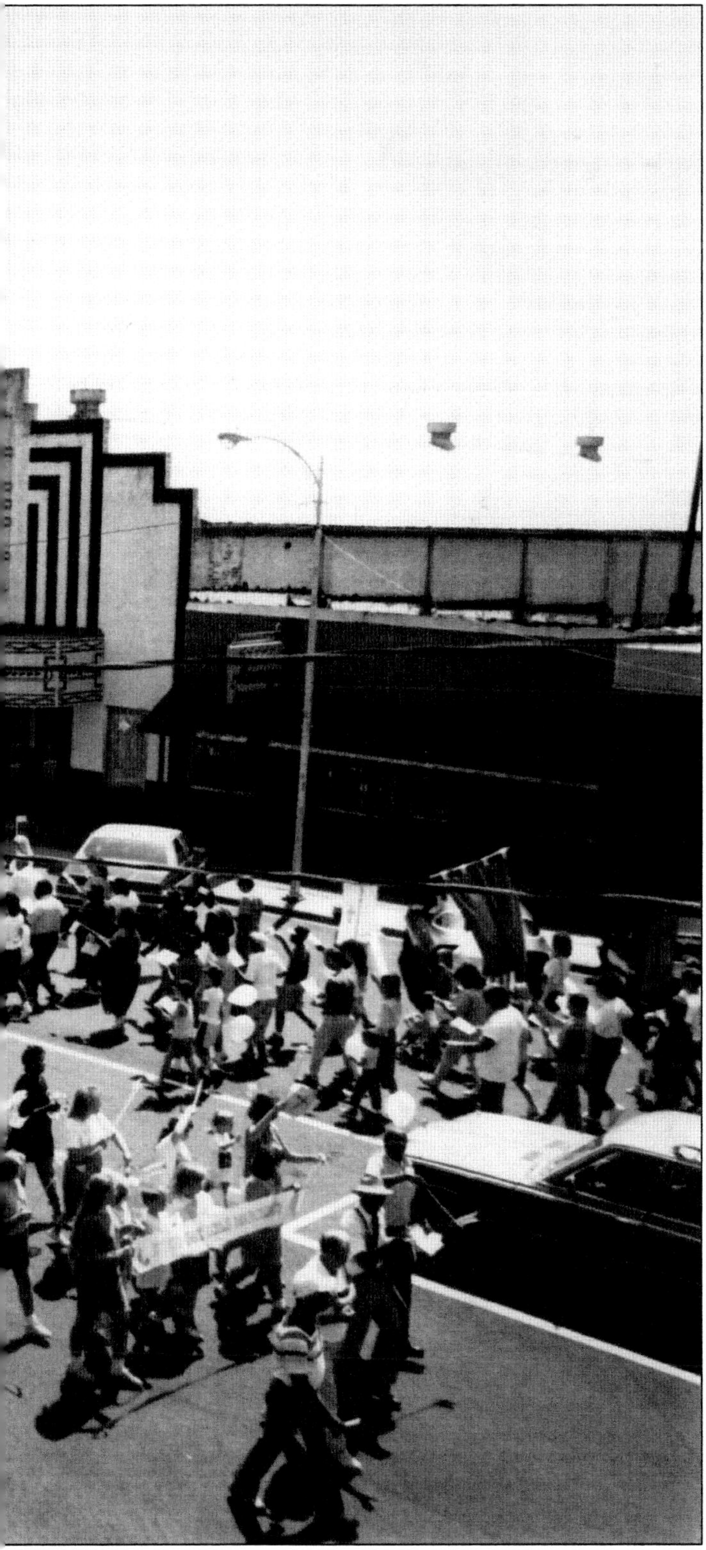

Local bands, youth, and church groups bearing signs proclaiming that "Jesus Is Lord Over Hampton County" and "What a Mighty God We Serve" lead the watermelon festival parade down one side of Lee Avenue, Hampton, and march back up the other. Although this photograph is undated, it was likely taken during the 30th annual watermelon festival in 1972. The theme was "Dedicated to our Churches of all Faiths." There was no grand marshal that year, but the official guest speaker was the Honorable Robert E. McNair, the 108th governor of South Carolina, who served from 1965 to 1971. The festival chairman that year was Perry Padgett. Note the historic Palmetto Theater in the background. B.C. Moore's building to the left of the theater is now the T.G. and Allie Cultural Arts Center, an annex of the Palmetto. (Courtesy of HMVC.)

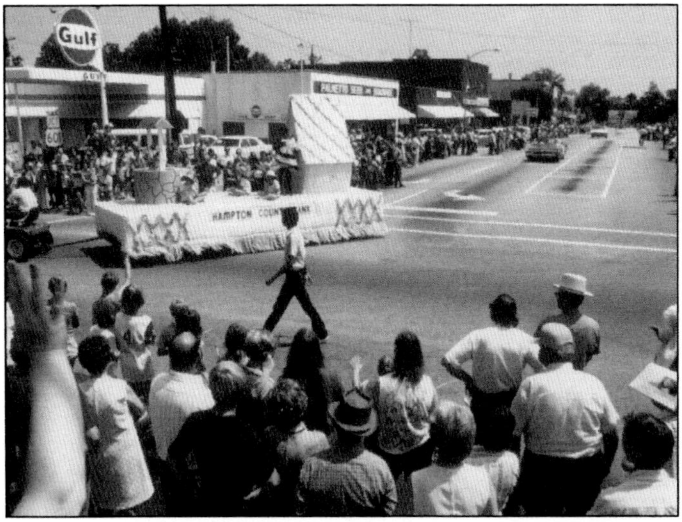


In this undated photograph, the Hampton County Bank float, pulled by a sturdy garden tractor, and several following units in the watermelon festival parade clear Lee Avenue and make the turn west back onto US Highway 278, along the traditional parade route, as throngs of spectators look on and wave. The Gulf station and the Palmetto Seed and Hardware businesses in the background no longer exist. (Courtesy of HMVC.)

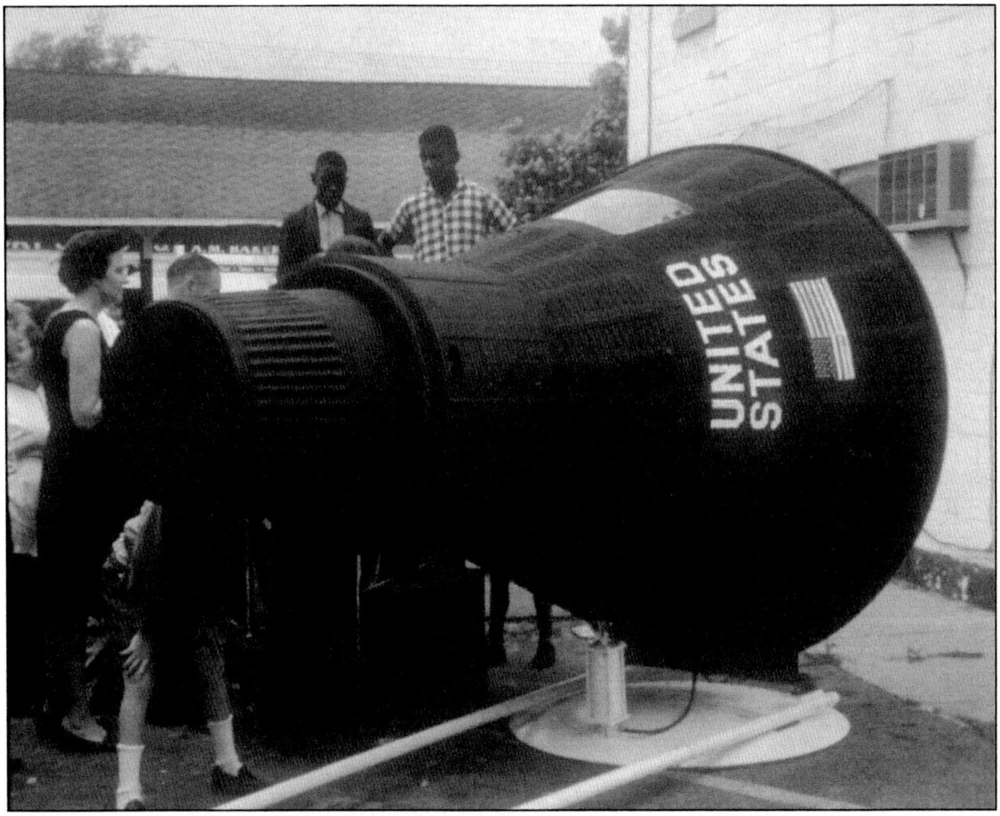


In this photograph of the 1965 watermelon festival, adults and children gaze with curiosity at a NASA rocket cone on display. The honorary guest speaker that year was Air Force astronaut Lt. Col. Virgil "Gus" Grissom, the second American to fly in space. That year's parade also featured several other famous astronauts. (Courtesy of DM.)

A Brunson queen cruises down Lee Avenue during the 1966 watermelon festival. The J.H. Rivers & Son Inc. and Rivers Grocery stores in the background were founded in the early 1900s and still operating during the late 1960s, selling everything from feed and seed to everyday grocery items. The historic buildings remain a part of the Lee Avenue landscape. (Courtesy of DM.)

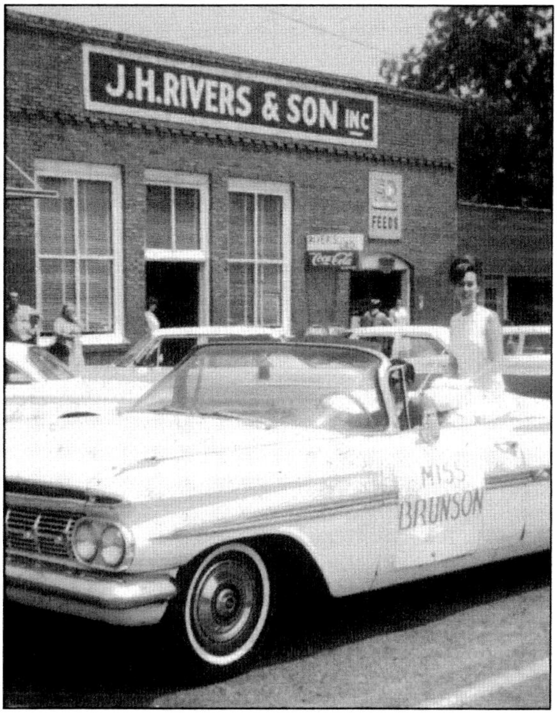


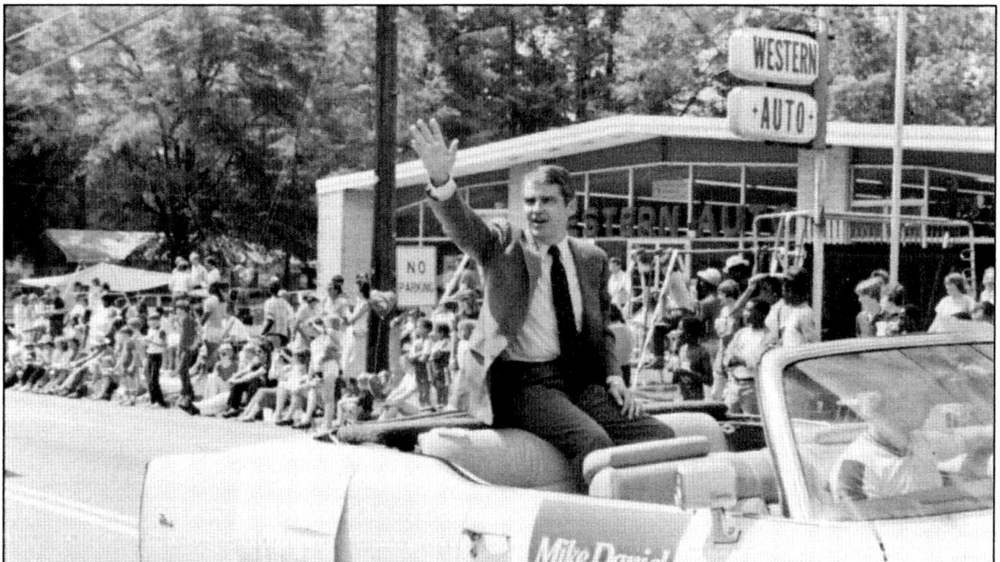


The watermelon festival draws more than fun-loving families; politicians from around the state flock to its keynote Saturday parade in droves during election years. Here, Mike Daniel, Democratic candidate for lieutenant governor, waves to the crowds in Hampton during the 1982 festival. The Western Auto hardware store, pictured in the background, is still in operation. (Courtesy of DM.)

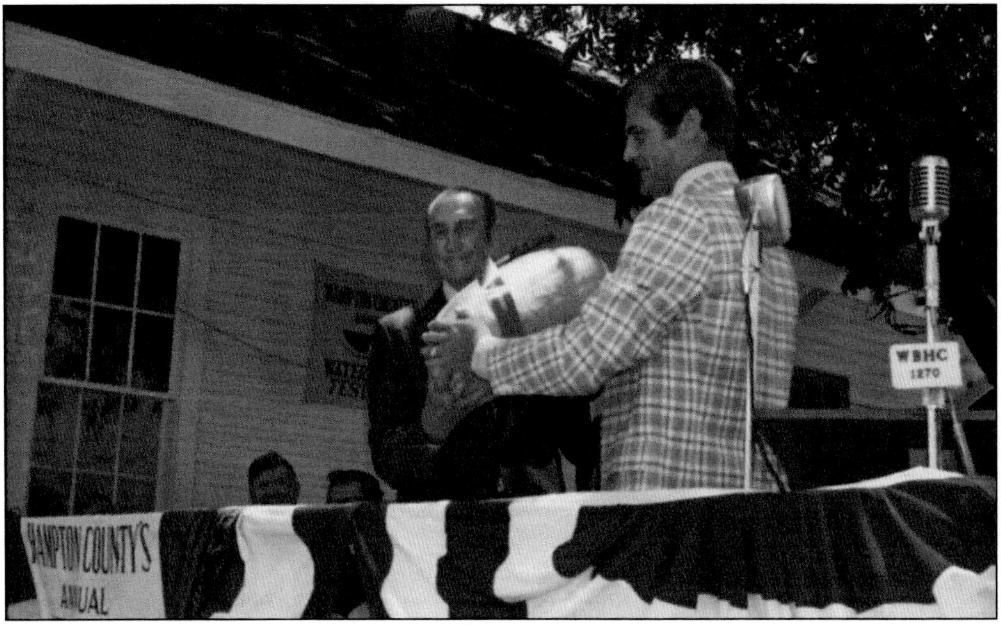


Sen. Strom Thurmond (left) and Estill's Karl Bowers present prizewinning watermelons during the 1973 watermelon festival. Bowers (1941–2012) was the youngest magistrate elected in South Carolina, served as chairman of the South Carolina Highway Commission from 1974 to 1977, when he was named chairman emeritus, and was appointed a federal highway administrator by Pres. Jimmy Carter, where he served from 1977 to 1980. (Courtesy of DM.)

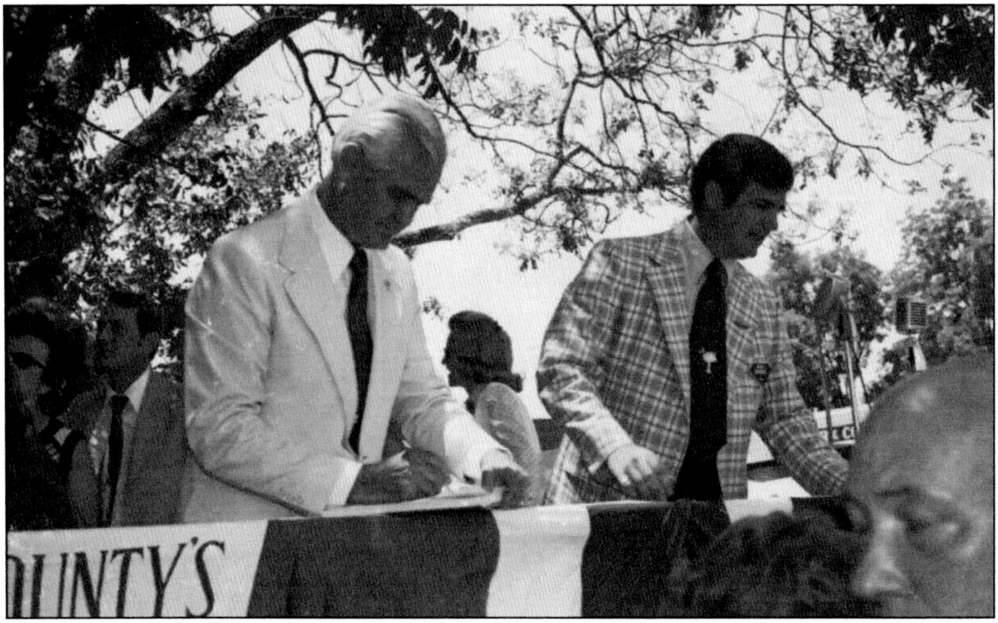

Army general William C. Westmoreland (left) and Karl Bowers are pictured here during the 1973 watermelon festival official ceremonies. A four-star general, Westmoreland (1914–2005) was a South Carolina native who served in the US Army from 1936 to 1972. During the peak of his career, he was in command of all US military operations during the Vietnam War from 1964 to 1968. (Courtesy of DM.)

Pictured here is an unidentified Miss Coastal Empire contestant during the 1971 watermelon festival. Miss Costal Empire that year was Susan Moore Stallworth of Aiken, and the official guest speaker was Sen. Strom Thurmond. The Miss Coastal Empire Pageant was a Hampton County Watermelon Festival tradition that began when the festival started in 1939, and it was just recently discontinued, in 2012. (Courtesy of DM.)

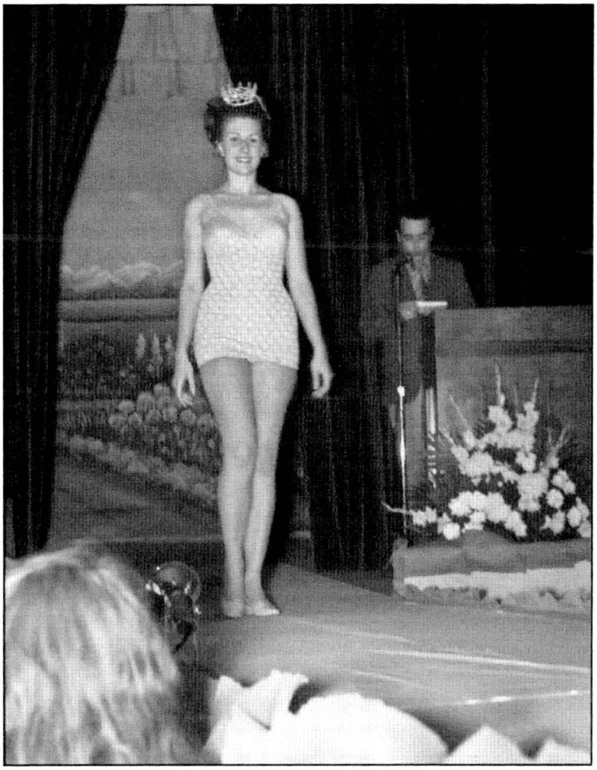

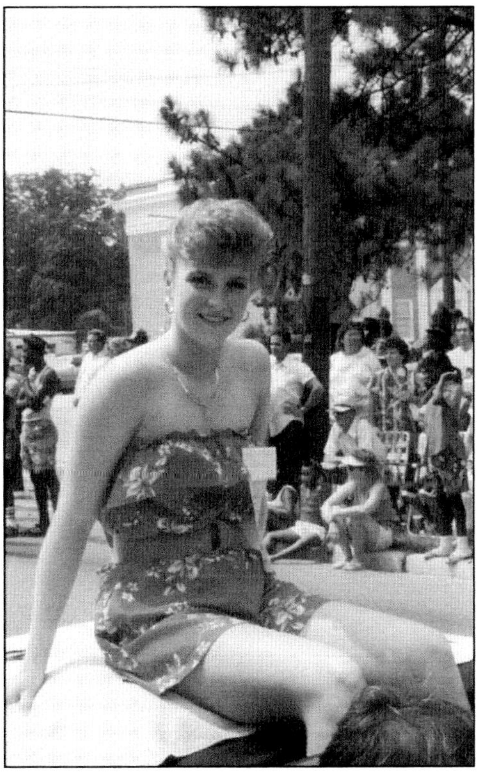

Pictured here is lovely local queen Eleanor Wiggins riding through the town of Hampton during the 1987 watermelon festival parade. The Wiggins family was a prominent family in Hampton and Estill and owned several businesses, including Wiggins and Son Hardware in Estill and Wiggins Concrete, which are still going strong today. (Courtesy of DM.)

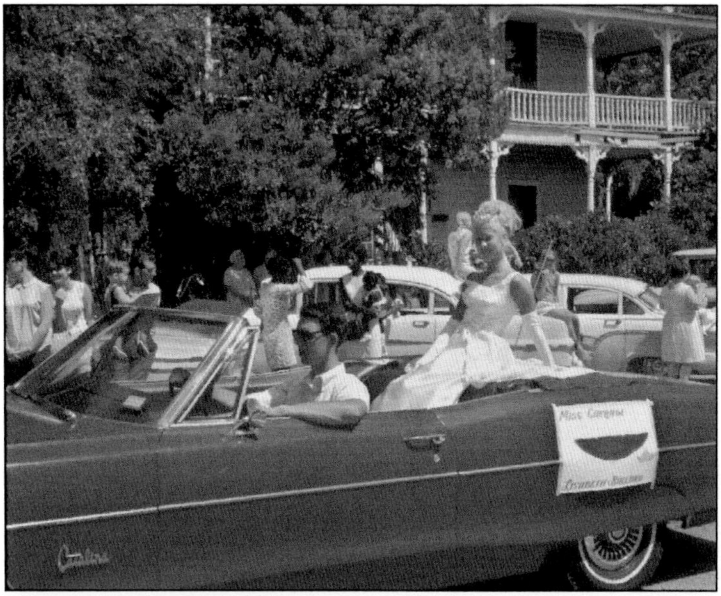

The elegant Miss Cheraw cruises down Elm Street in Hampton in a classic Catalina during the 1970 watermelon festival parade. Since its founding as a mere countywide harvest festival in 1939, the watermelon festival grew to become one of the biggest traditions in South Carolina— drawing politicians, queens, and dignitaries from all over the Palmetto State. (Courtesy of DM.)

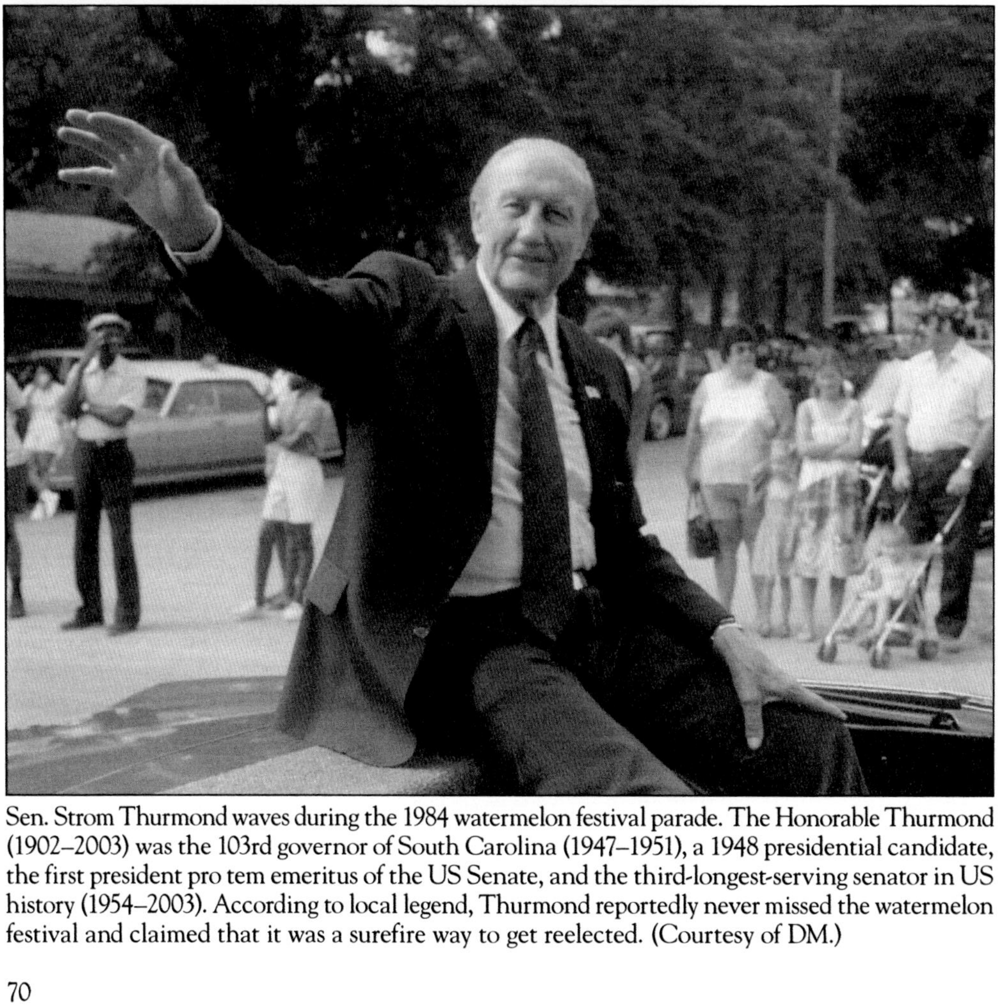

Sen. Strom Thurmond waves during the 1984 watermelon festival parade. The Honorable Thurmond (1902–2003) was the 103rd governor of South Carolina (1947–1951), a 1948 presidential candidate, the first president pro tem emeritus of the US Senate, and the third-longest-serving senator in US history (1954–2003). According to local legend, Thurmond reportedly never missed the watermelon festival and claimed that it was a surefire way to get reelected. (Courtesy of DM.)

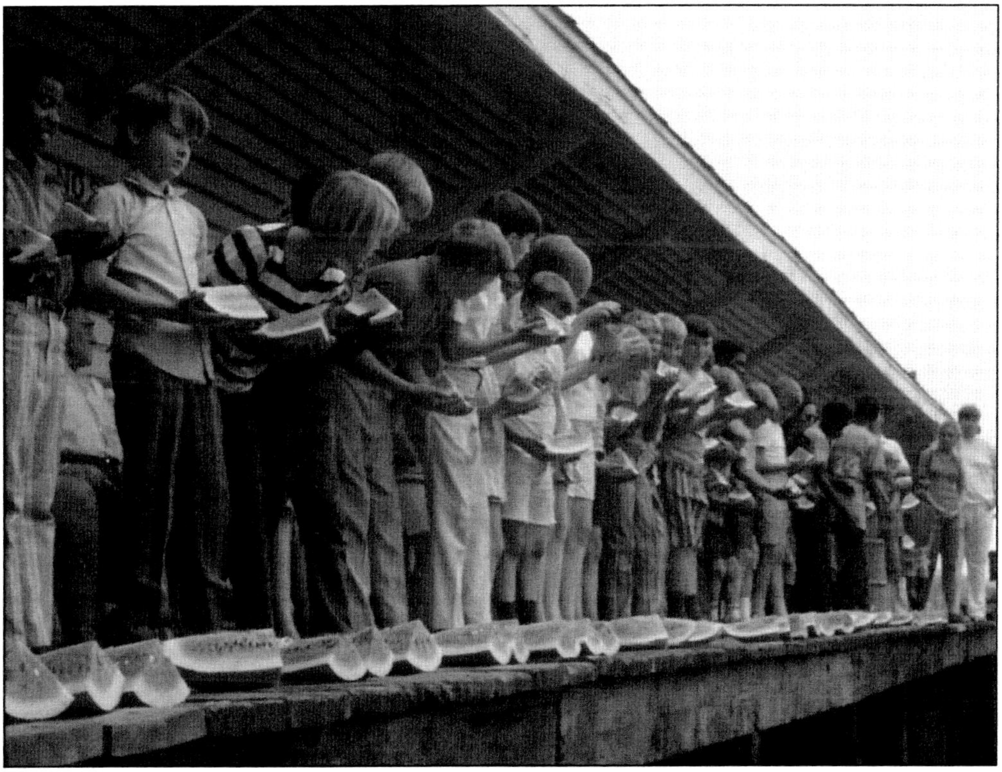

Youngsters of all ages and races line up on a platform and eagerly await the start of the annual watermelon-eating contest during the 1971 watermelon festival. For youngsters far and wide, this contest is one of the most enjoyable traditions of the festival. And may the biggest sweet tooth win! (Courtesy of DM.)

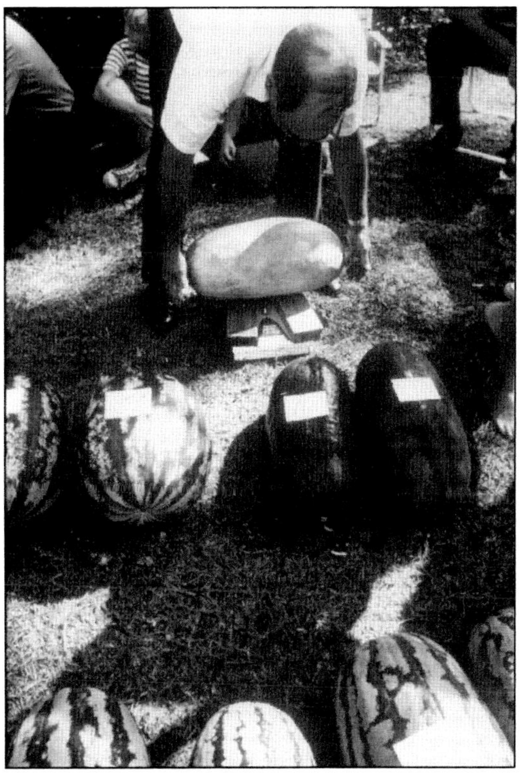

In this 1970s photograph, an official watermelon judge weighs and measures several melons as part of the annual watermelon-judging contest. Watermelons of all varieties, sizes, and colors are grown in Hampton County, but most locals will argue that all of them taste just a little sweeter during the festival. (Courtesy of HMVC.)

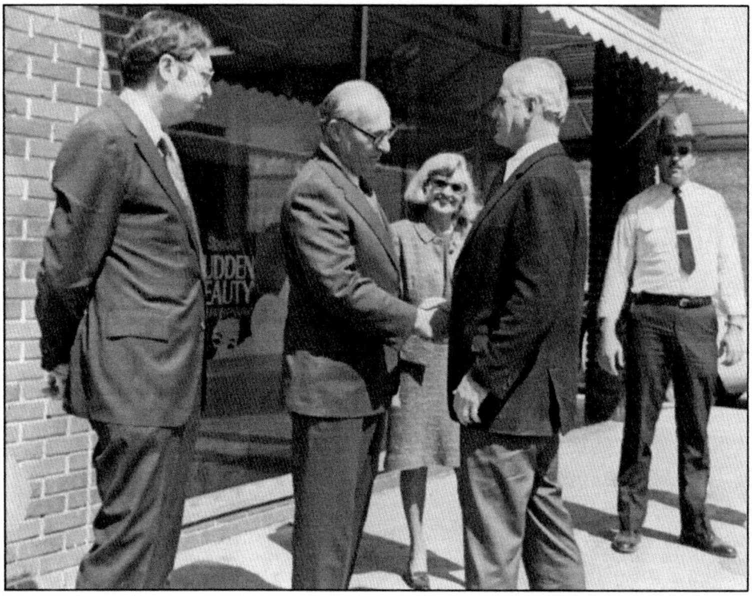

Gen. William Westmoreland (second from right) visits with county and town officials, surrounded by the watchful eyes of local law enforcement, during the 1973 watermelon festival. The four-star general was the festival's official guest speaker during the 31st annual festival, which was dedicated to Sen. Strom Thurmond. (Courtesy of HCG.)

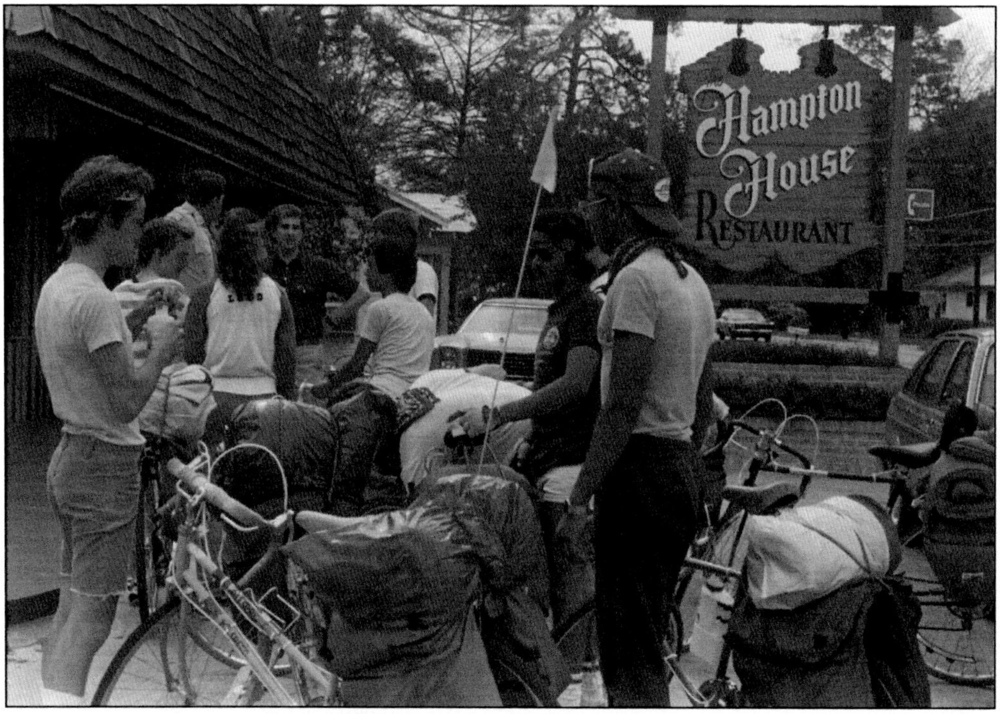


Captured in this 1979 photograph is an out-of-town bicycle club visiting with locals at the Hampton House Restaurant during the watermelon festival. The annual festival parade attracts bicycling enthusiasts, motorcycle clubs, car clubs, equestrians, and more. The parade can give participants a nice workout; it is 2.4 miles from its starting point in Varnville to its finish in Hampton. (Courtesy of DM.)

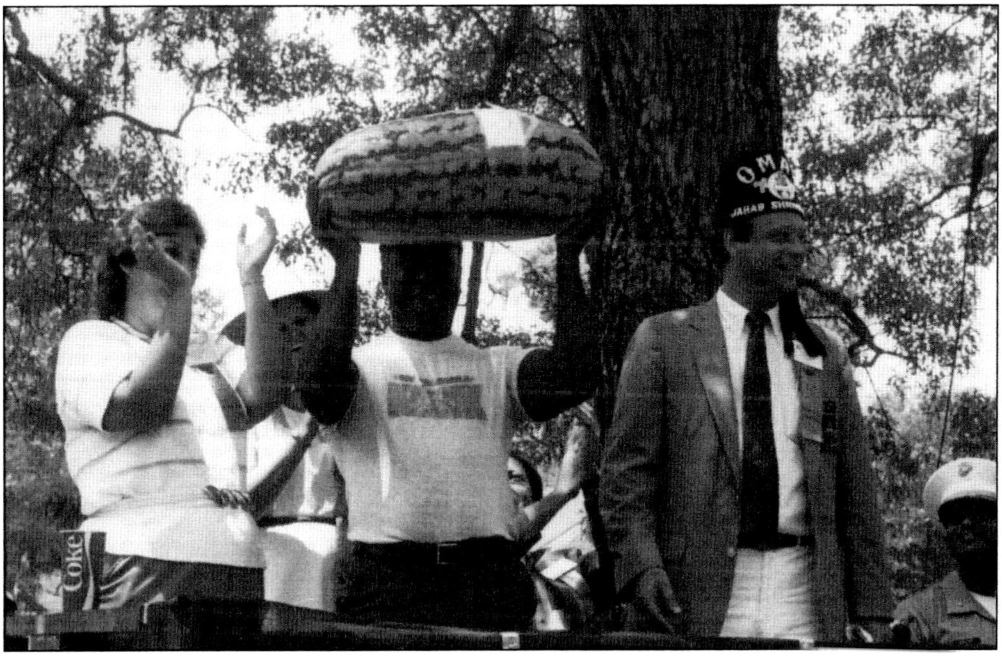


In this 1980s photograph, an unidentified watermelon grower has won a prize for his Hampton County melon and hoists it proudly. For many local families, the festival is a once-a-year opportunity to showcase their gardening skills and perhaps even take home a blue ribbon. Many farmers also rely on the festival for income. One can often see trucks full of melons for sale along roadsides during the festival. (Courtesy of HMVC.)

First place and grand champion watermelons are lined up for display during the 1975 watermelon-judging contest. This is what the festival is all about: sweet Hampton County–grown watermelons. Although today the watermelon is no longer the king crop in the county in terms of acreage due to advances in technology that have made other crops more profitable, the watermelon will always be king in Hampton County hearts. (Courtesy of DM.)

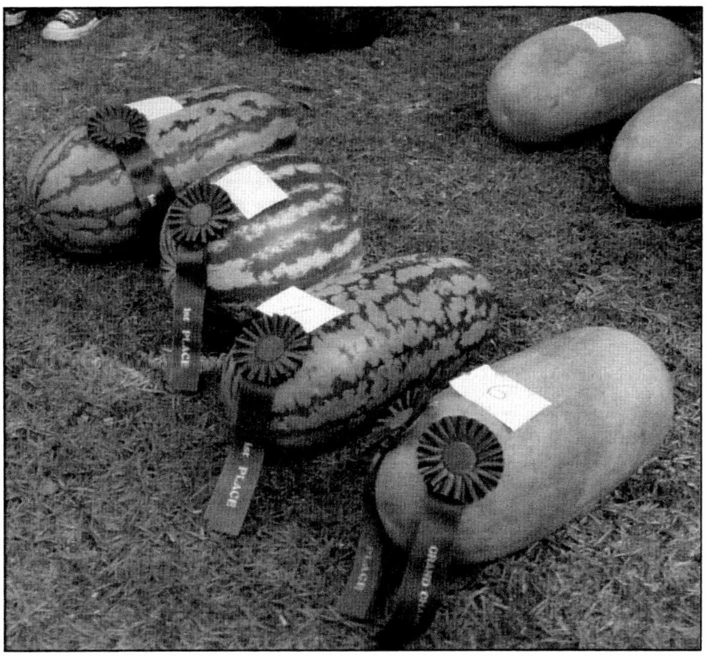

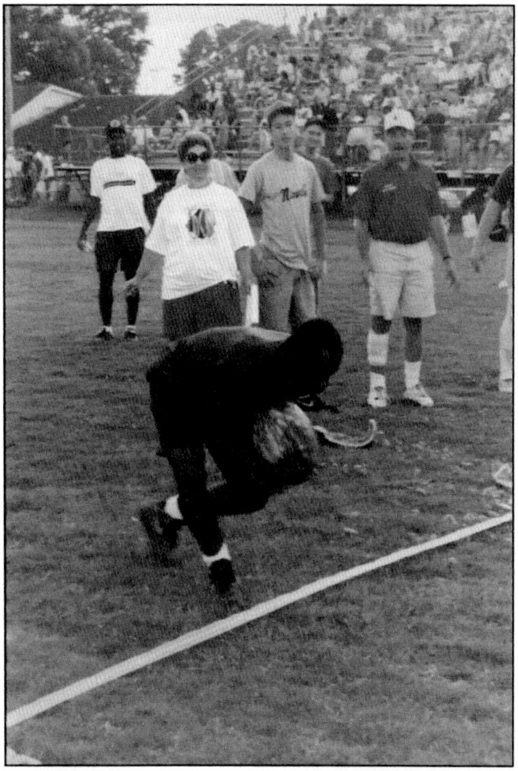

In this late 1980s photograph, Battle of the Towns contestant Jeffrey Johnson hustles across the starting line with a cumbersome melon as a festival volunteer judge looks on. The Battle of the Towns is one of the most popular annual events of the festival and features athletic youngsters (and a few not-so-youngsters) from almost every town in the county competing in various competitions involving watermelons. One of these events is a seed-spitting contest between the mayors of each town. (Courtesy of HMVC.)

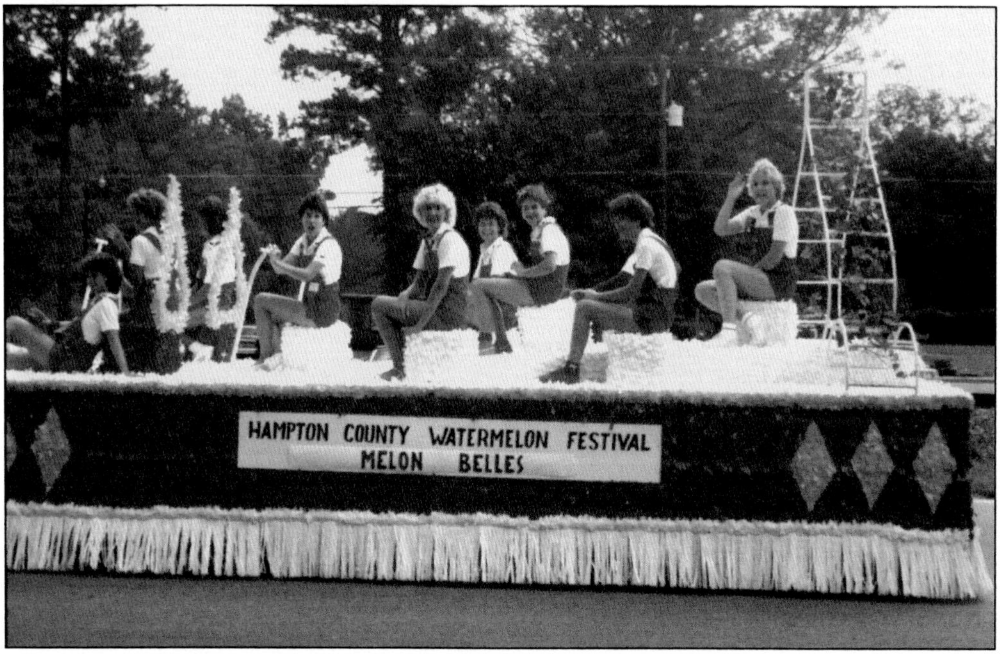


Pictured here in 1984 is the first crop of Melon Belles the watermelon festival ever produced. The Melon Belles, founded that year by Victoria Tuten, a Girl Scout leader and festival volunteer, are now a Hampton County tradition. Melon Belles lend a helping hand at almost every festival event, and it is considered an honor to be one. (Courtesy of JoAnne Lamprecht.)

# *Four*

# A Hunting and Fishing Paradise

It should come as no surprise that a rural area surrounded by pine forests, hardwood swamp bottoms, and blackwater rivers would be a hunting and fishing paradise. From centuries ago, when the region was inhabited by thriving Native American populations and later European settlers struggling to make a foothold in a strange new world, through its modern American history, Hampton County and surrounding environs have been a source of abundant natural resources, which means abundant wild game and sporting fun.

South Carolina writers such as Havilah Babcock and Archibald Rutledge penned glowing tributes to the sporting life in the Lowcountry, an area rich in fish, four-legged game, and game birds of various feathers. Babcock, a sportsman who traveled and hunted widely along the East Coast, wrote on more than one occasion that he would rather hunt quail in the South Carolina Lowcountry than anywhere else in the world.

History has been kind to the sporting life here. Antebellum plantations, once toiled by slaves to raise cash crops, have long since been converted into some of the finest hunting plantations one can find in this part of the country. Combine that with the fact that Hampton County has one of the longest deer-hunting seasons in the Palmetto State and has historically proven to be one of the top deer harvest producers in the state, and it should also be no surprise that hunting and fishing is now a multimillion-dollar industry in this part of the state. Visitors from Florida to New England and beyond return to Hampton County for a good shot and a better story.

In this chapter in particular, one can see the love of the outdoor life in the photography of Dwight Moore. He devoted countless pleasant days of his life to the outdoors, photographed many adventures during the 1950s and 1960s, and a number of his favorite photographs are here to report his success and record this enjoyment for future generations to come.

In 2015, the Hampton County Watermelon Festival proclaimed the theme of the festival "The Outdoor Life in Hampton County."

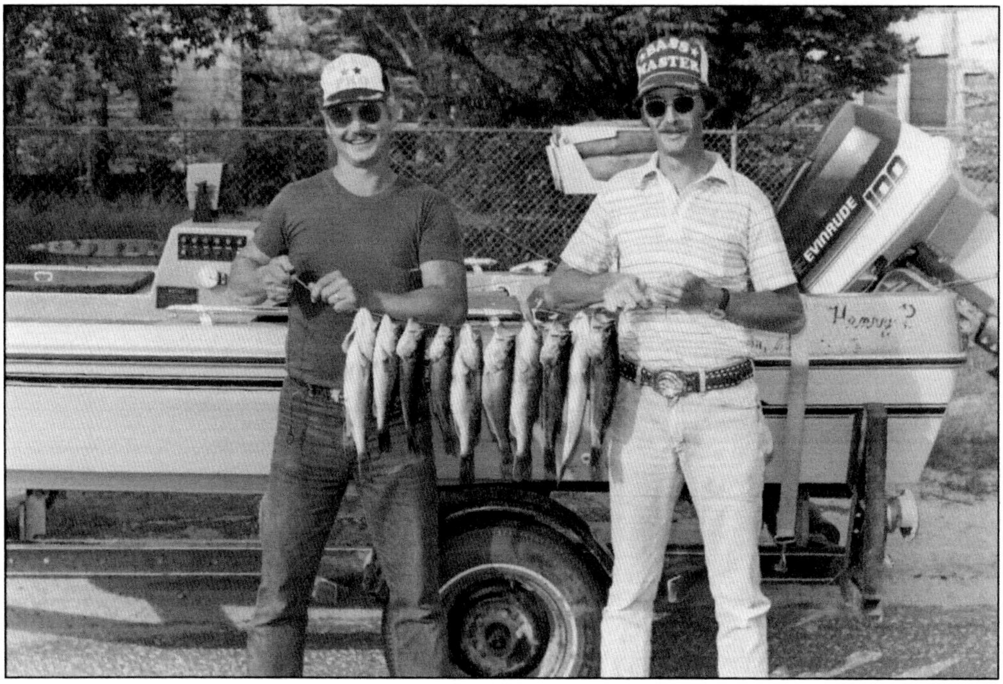


The watermelon festival fishing contest held at Lake Warren is an annual tradition that combines two of the county's greatest assets, the festival and the great outdoors, for lots of family fun. In this photograph taken by *Guardian* freelance photographer Jerry Thomas, Henry Peeples (left) and Carl Wilson display their prizewinning stringer caught aboard the *Henry P.* (Courtesy of HMVC.)

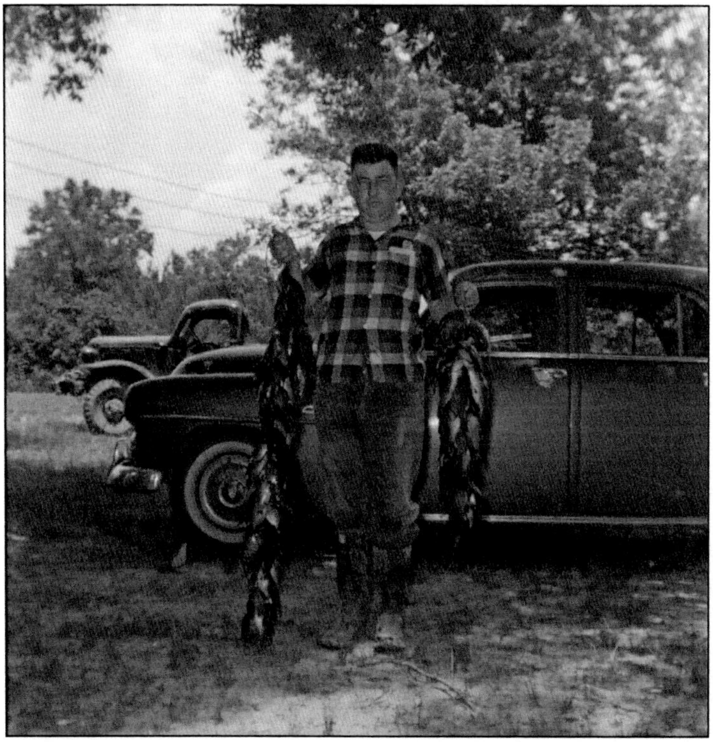

Garnett sportsman and photographer Dwight Moore was photographed by a friend on June 7, 1958, after helping catch a personal record of 300 fish in one day. According to friends and family members, Moore loved three things in life: fishing, hunting, and taking photographs. Many of the images in this volume are a product of Moore's eager, busy lens. (Courtesy of Jeff Hunt and the Moore family.)

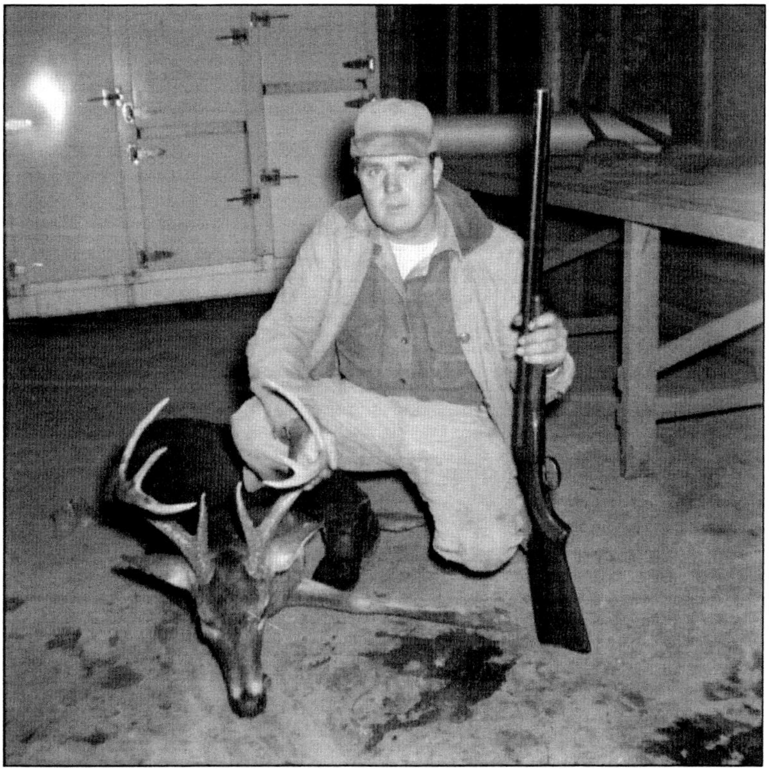

Hunter G.C. Miken is pictured with an eight-point buck he harvested on December 14, 1957, with a trusty double-barreled shotgun, an economical yet efficient weapon used by many Lowcountry hunters. Note the skinning shed in the background. Most farms, plantations, and hunting clubs were self-sufficient, and many hunters processed their own game. (Courtesy of DM.)

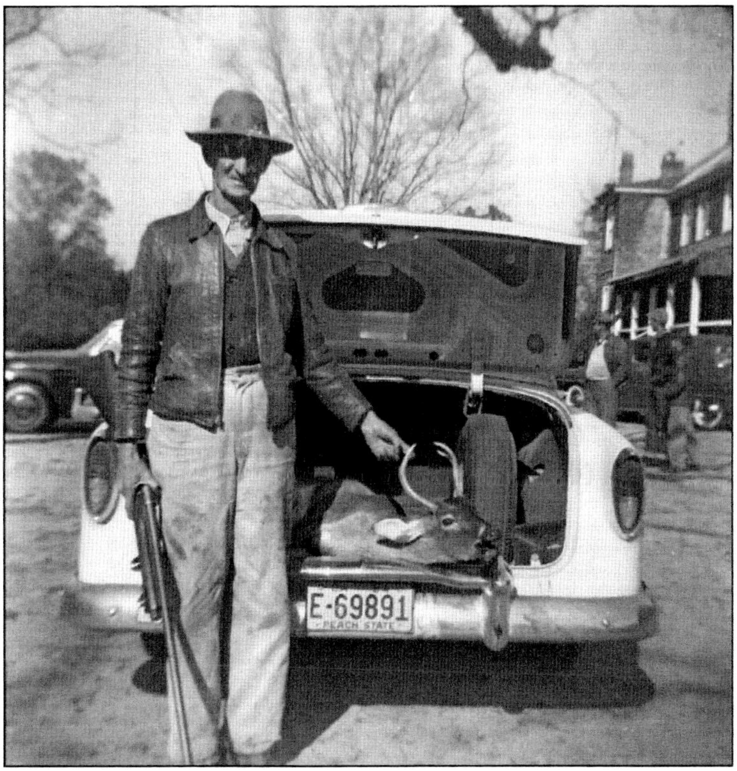


A lanky, grinning Peach State hunter, Flynt Moore shows off a modest five-point buck brought back to the Union Camp plantation in the trunk of a car on November 8, 1954. A successful hunter would think nothing of throwing his trophy in the trunk or even across the hood of the family station wagon, often making for some interesting and lively conversations once he arrived home. (Courtesy of DM.)

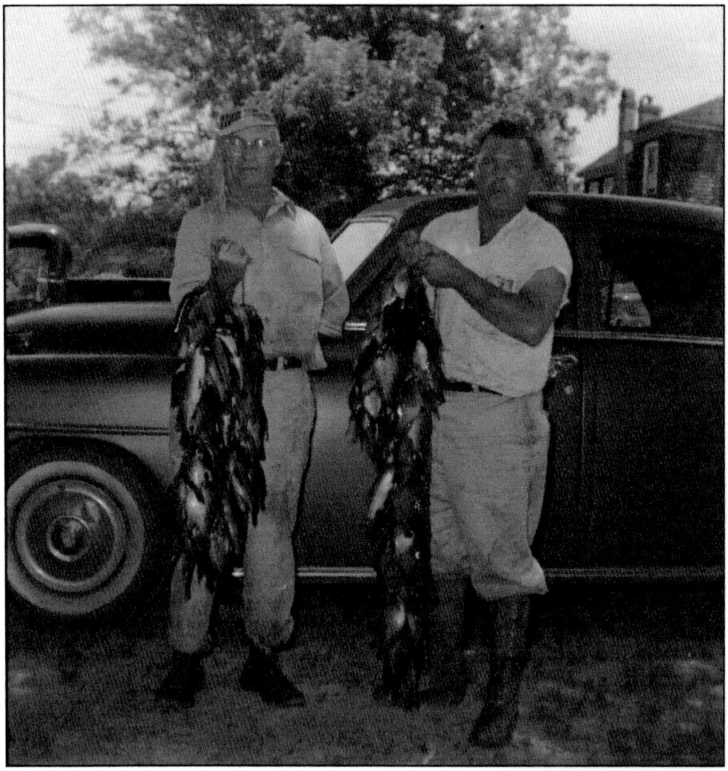

Clad in muddy trousers and snake boots, C.E. Lively (right) and C.S. Endenfield hoist the rewards of a June 5, 1958, fishing expedition: approximately 300 bream and red breast, a popular and sweet-tasting panfish common in the rivers, lakes, and streams of the Southeast. If hauling that heavy stringer of fish was not enough work, imagine the job of cleaning them for supper. (Courtesy of DM.)

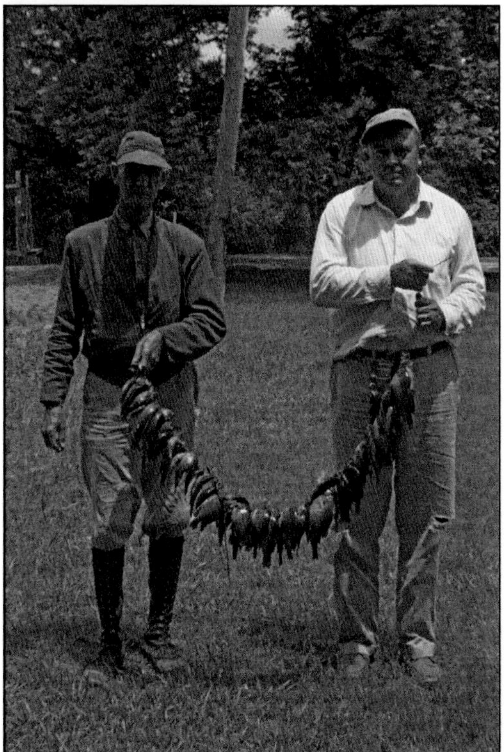

Anglers F. Moore (left) and G.E. Jackson show off a lengthy stringer of fish caught on June 5, 1958, in the Savannah River area near Garnett. The photographer noted that 125 fish were caught, and while no one has ever suggested that fishermen sometimes stretch the truth or tell tall fishing tales, one can only wonder at how quickly that number grew with every repetition of the day's events. (Courtesy of DM.)

On June 5, 1955, with just a hearty cane pole, M.J. Nelson snagged four catfish out of Fowl Craw Lake on Hamilton Ridge plantation. Hamilton Ridge, in southern Hampton County along the Savannah River, is now a South Carolina Department of Natural Resources–managed wildlife management area open to public fishing and hunting for locals and visitors alike. (Courtesy of DM.)

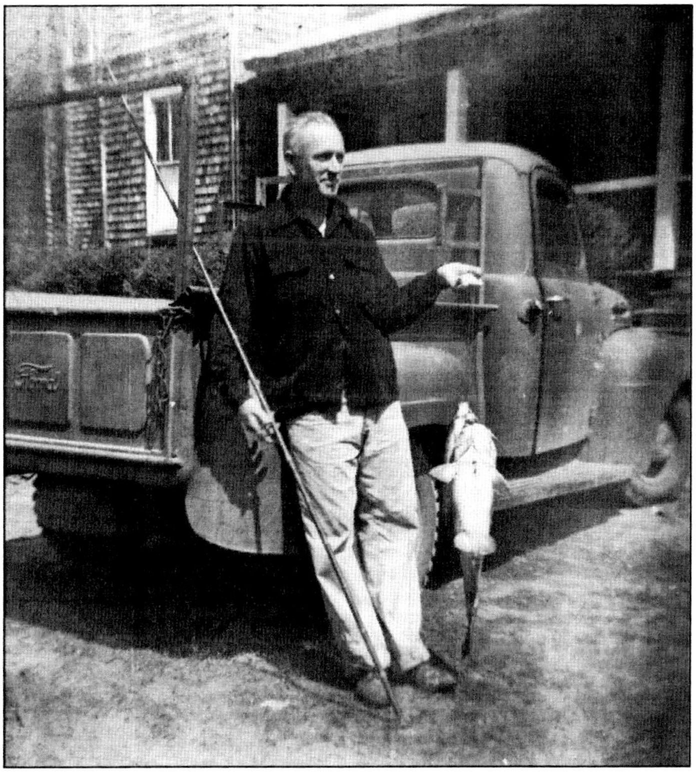

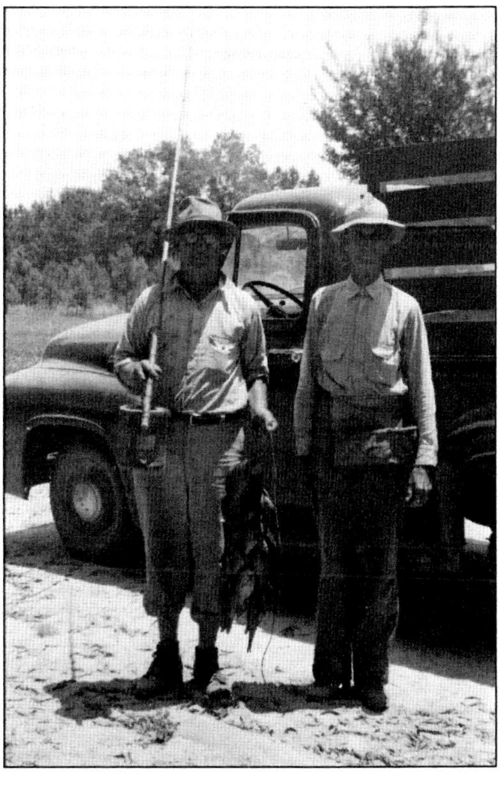

A sturdy old Ford, cane pole, cricket cage, and rolled-up pants are all that J.M. Daley (left) and Flynt Moore needed to catch this mess of fish from Fowl Craw Lake on June 5, 1955. One of these gentlemen has also apparently converted a carpenter's cloth nail apron into a fishing creel/ tackle box, a clever, handy technique for those times when the fish are biting and speed is important. (Courtesy of DM.)

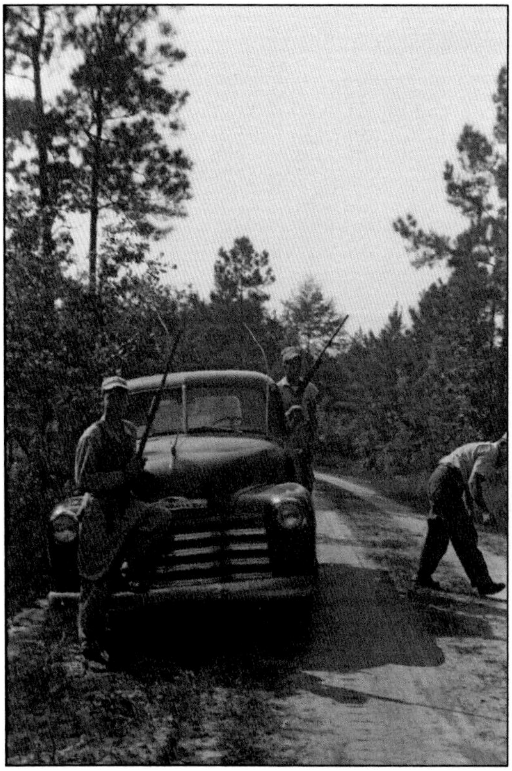

Several young hunters wait patiently along an opening on a dirt road during a Hampton County dog-drive deer hunt on December 8, 1954. Using dogs to drive and track deer used to be a very common practice in the Lowcountry but, because it requires so much acreage, now only a few families and hunting clubs still work with canines. (Courtesy of DM.)

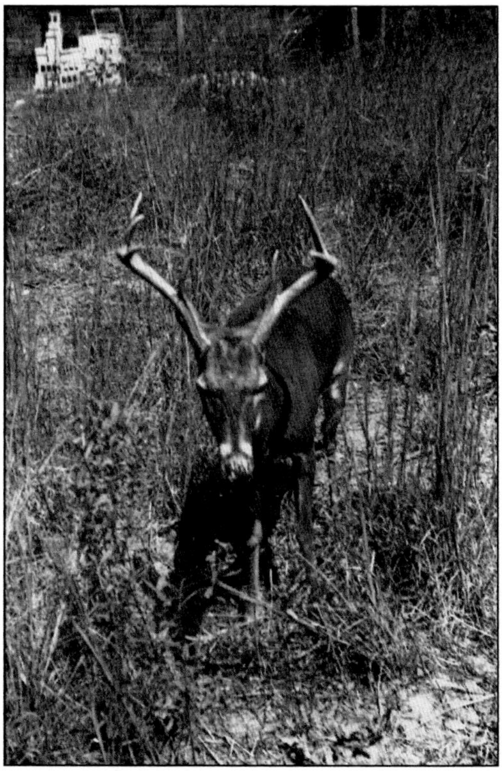

Pictured here on August 11, 1959, is a fenced-in captive deer labeled "Mason's Deer, 8 point bambi." Juvenile deer, or fawns, and even injured adult deer are sometimes separated from their population, and well-meaning country folks have been known to take them in and nurse them back to health. (Courtesy of DM.)

R.D. Nix pauses on the banks of a favorite fishing spot to display a healthy stringer of approximately 103 fish caught on June 10, 1958. A productive and lucky fishing hole, whether it is a farm pond, a bend in the swamp, or a spot on a local river, is often a closely guarded secret, and the photographer did not make note of this location. (Courtesy of DM.)

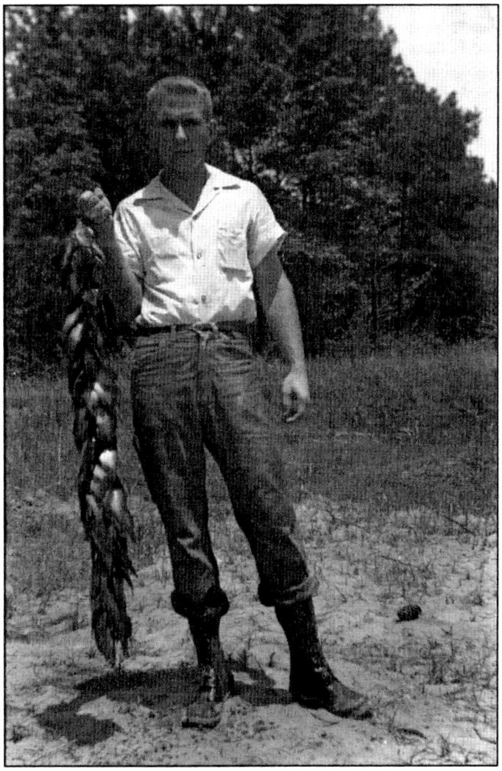

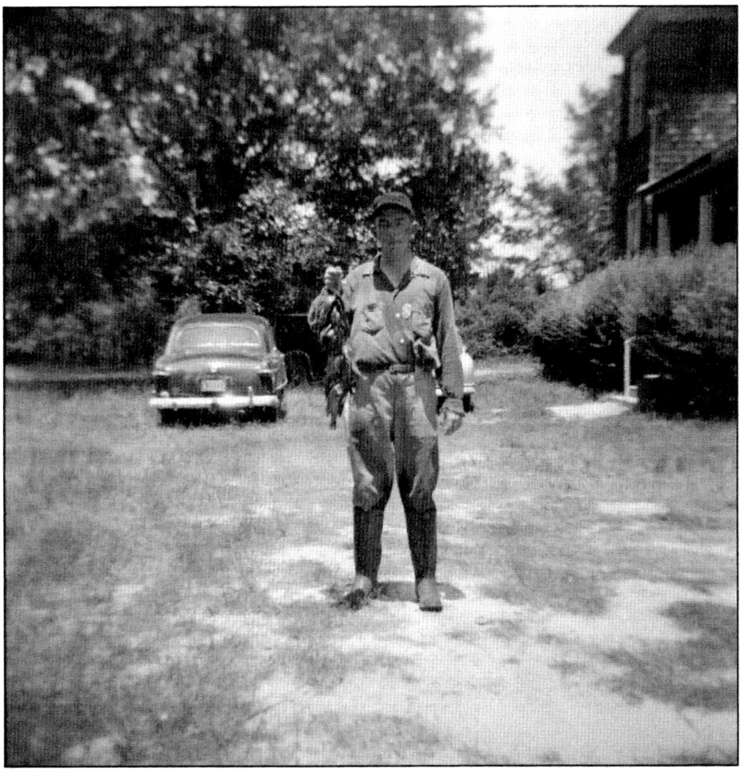

No doubt loaning his camera to a friend, Garnett photographer Dwight Moore is pictured here with this modest stringer of 26 keepers caught near his home on June 5, 1955. As most anglers will likely attest, an old saying claims that even a bad day of fishing beats a good day of working any time. (Courtesy of DM.)

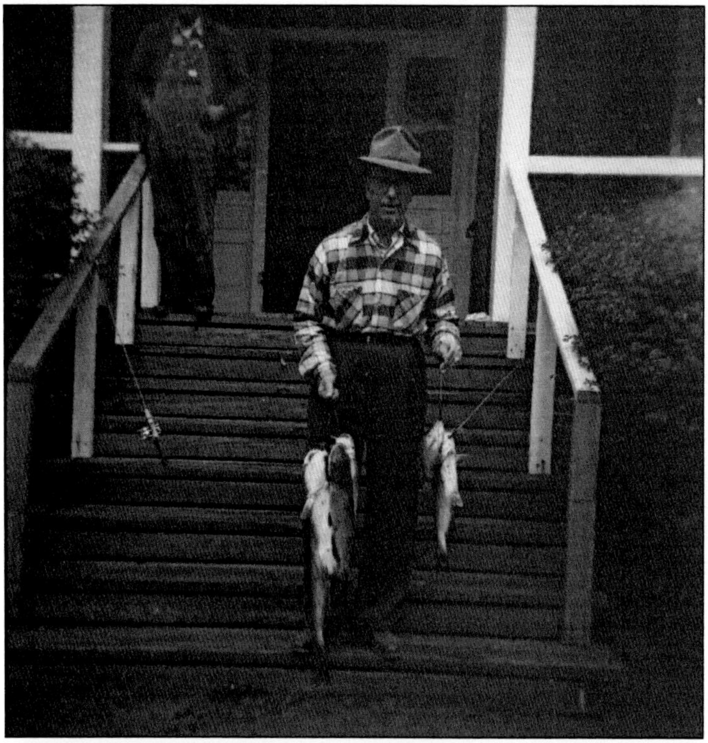

With his trusty spinning reel and fishing buddy in the background, Lowcountry angler J.P. Smith is photographed with a stringer of six hefty catfish caught on June 2, 1955. The fish would likely make for a good fish fry with family or friends or perhaps even a simmering pot of catfish stew, a popular Southern favorite. (Courtesy of DM.)

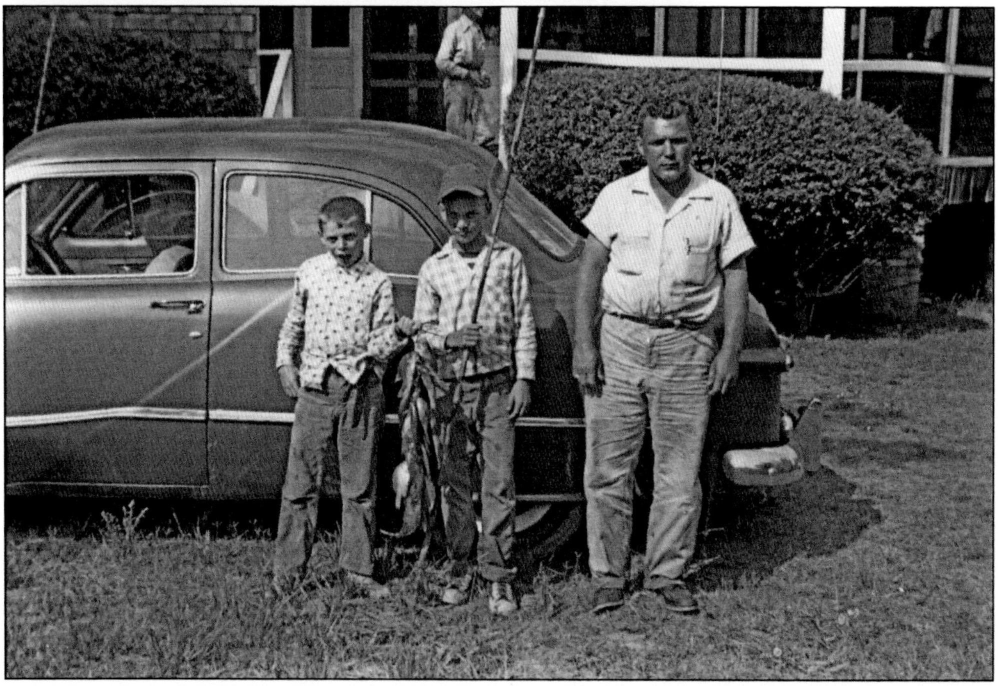

C.E., Danny, and Billy Lively are pictured here with a mess of 27 fish caught on June 3, 1956. Many a lad—and lots of young ladies, too—eagerly remember the magical days when one loaded into the family wagon with Dad and set out for angling adventure to return with supper, stories, and lifelong memories. (Courtesy of DM.)

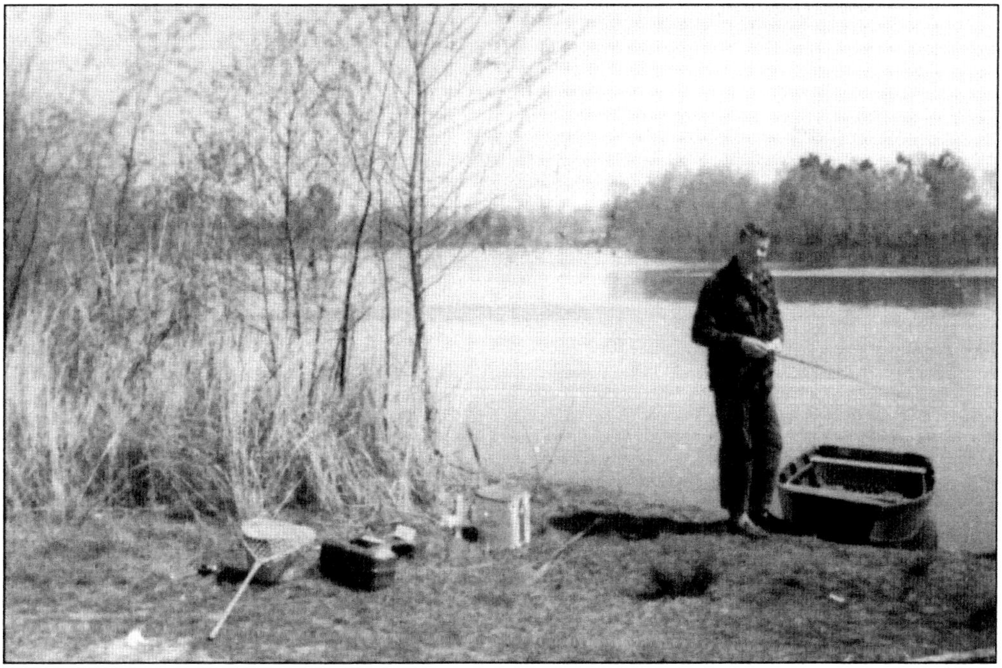

With his gear ready for action, Nick Hunt prepares for a productive outing at Ramsey's Pond on December 30, 1963. For true, diehard angling enthusiasts, fishing was a year-round hobby. An experienced fisherman knows that catfish and even some bass and panfish bite during the colder months. (Courtesy of DM.)

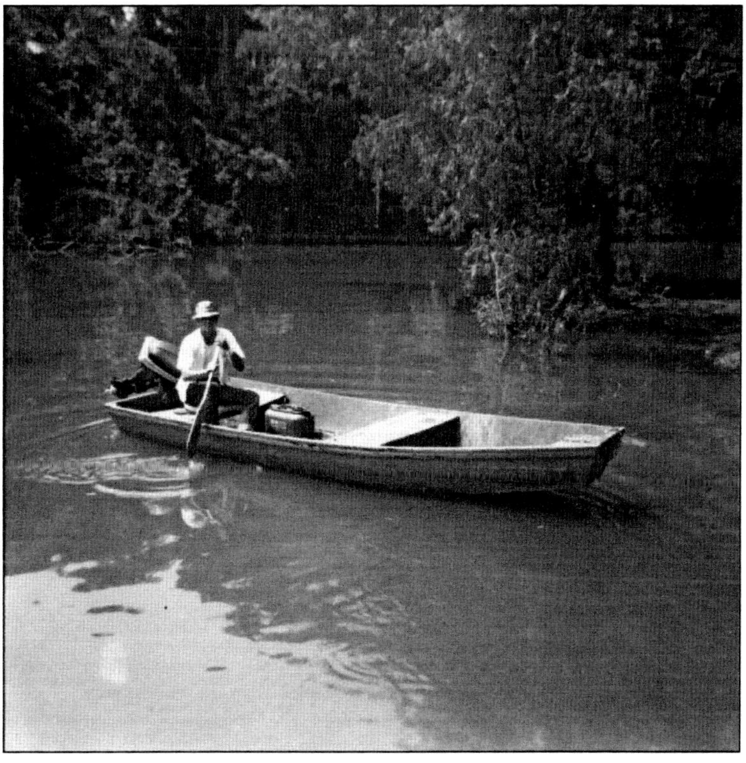

Hampton County's Lawton Maner paddles the last few feet toward the bank during this Savannah River–area boating expedition photographed on August 26, 1966. From a historic and prominent Estill family, Maner became well known around the state as a surveyor and real estate broker, a career that allowed him to spend a lot of time in the freedom of the outdoors. (Courtesy of DM.)

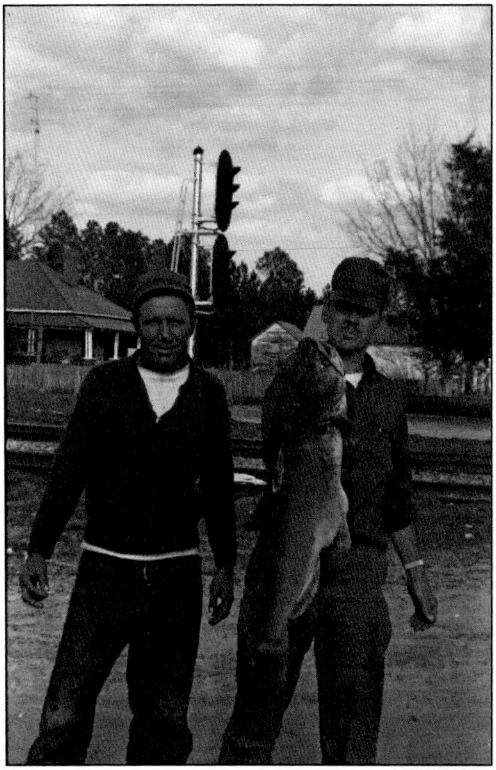

Fishing in Hampton County is a fun-filled adventure no matter the size or quantity of the catch. Pictured at left are Joe Mason and his friend Sonny near the railroad tracks in Garnett with a whopping 23-pound catfish taken on June 10, 1959. Photographed below is a young Nick Hunt proudly displaying a modest stringer with a trio of largemouth bass taken in 1966, his Volkswagon fishing wagon by his side. From the tiniest bream and perch to the mightiest of lunker bass, giant catfish, monstrous pike, or mudfish, Hampton County's lakes, rivers, and streams have produced fun, food, and fellowship for generations of outdoor enthusiasts. (Both, courtesy of DM.)

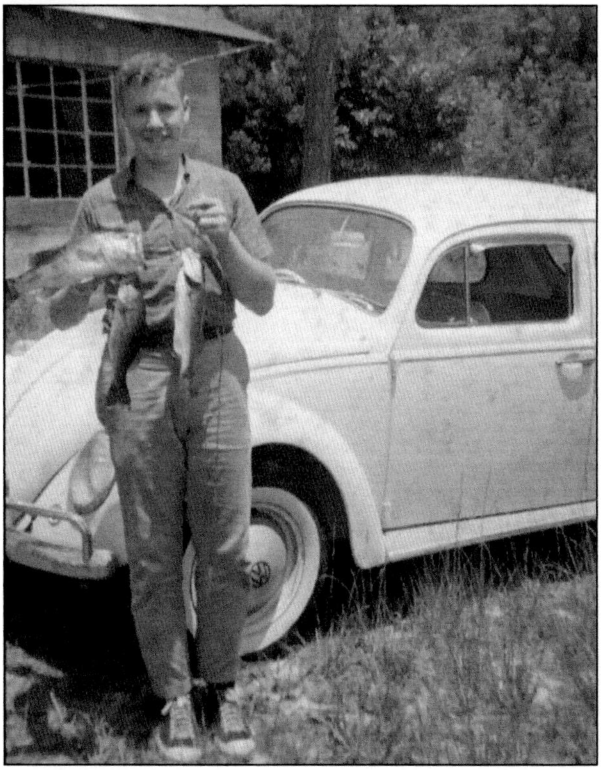

One of Moore's favorite outdoor subjects to photograph, Flynt Moore is pictured with a five-point buck in his truck bed that was taken on August 23, 1957. The deer-hunting season in Hampton County and the surrounding Lowcountry is one of the earliest and longest in the state, running from August 15 to January 1, making it very attractive to out-of-state sportsmen looking for trophies. (Courtesy of DM.)

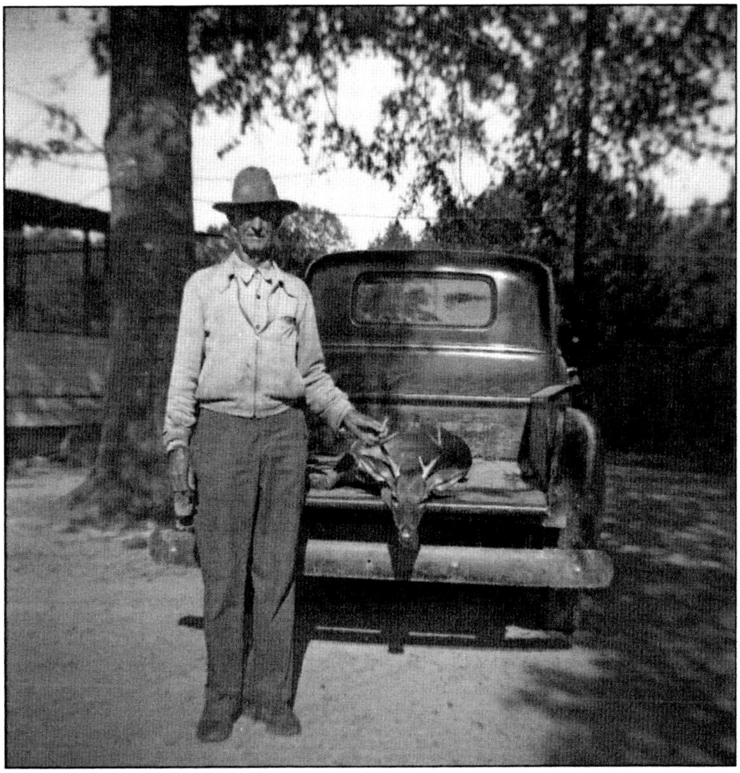

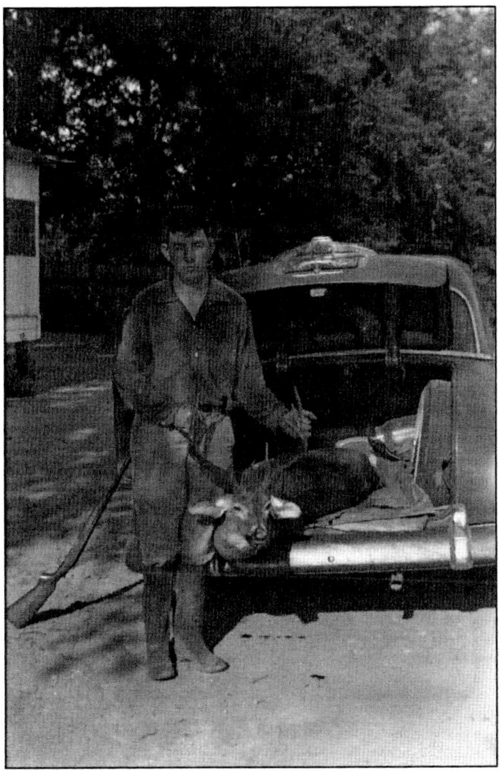

Both an outdoor photographer and enthusiast, Moore shows off this nine-point buck taken at the Union Camp Hunting Club on September 11, 1955. Much of the hunting acreage near his Garnett home, along the Savannah River basin, was owned by timber companies like Union Camp and later acquired by the state and placed in conservation easements as wildlife management areas (WMAs), including Webb and Hamilton Ridge WMAs. (Courtesy of DM.)

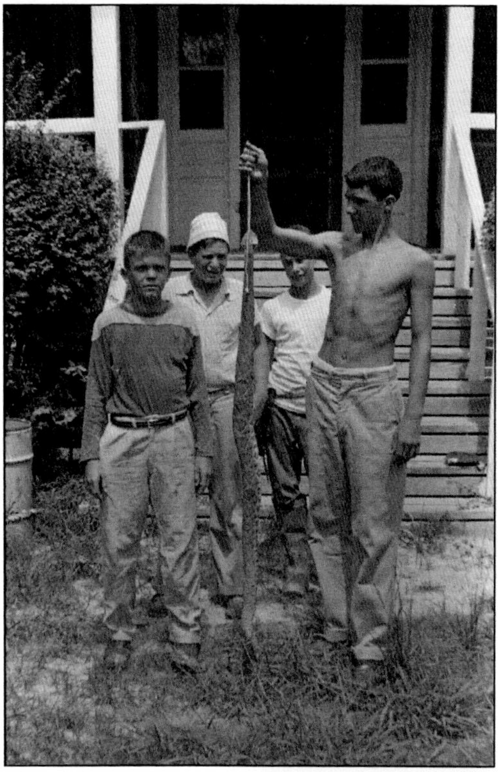

On the left, Jacky Jackson, Sonny Mobley, and two unidentified friends display with awe a five-foot-plus rattlesnake killed in the rural, heavily wooded Garnett area of Hampton County on June 10, 1957. But giant venomous vipers are not just found in backwoods habitats. Below, in this May 1965 photograph, Hampton businessman Richard Hutto holds up the carcass of a six-foot-plus rattlesnake killed near Lee Avenue in Hampton. Every outdoorsman and farmer knows to keep a watchful eye on the ground because venomous snakes can be underfoot from spring to fall, on land and in the swamps. (Above, courtesy of DM; below, courtesy of HMVC.)

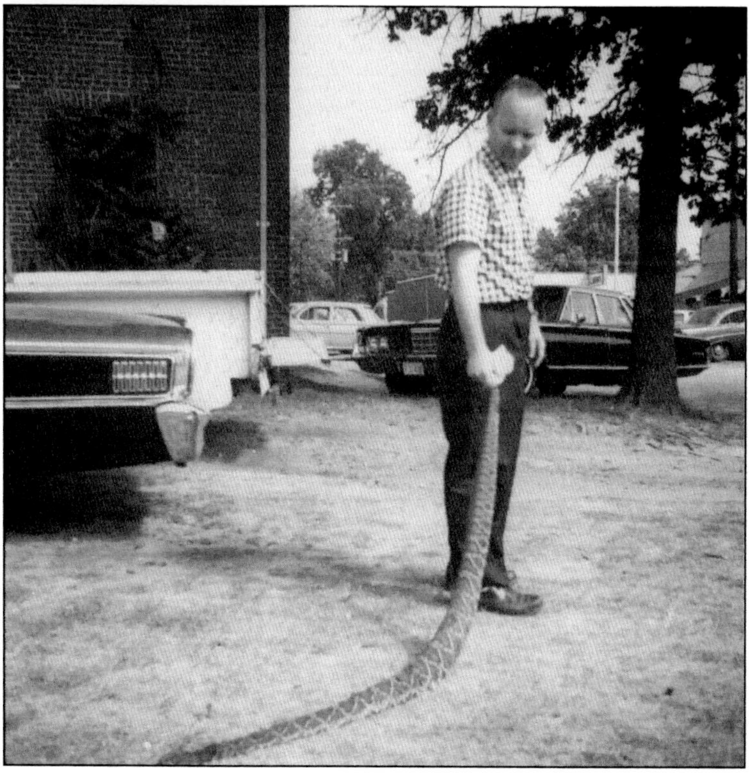

In this undated photograph, a man displays a dried and preserved rattlesnake skin from a reptile killed in Hampton. Sometimes even pests and reptiles were sought after by outdoorsmen and could be useful for making unique belts, wallets, or boots or even simply hung as trophies on the wall, all the while making the woods safer to tread. (Courtesy of HMVC.)

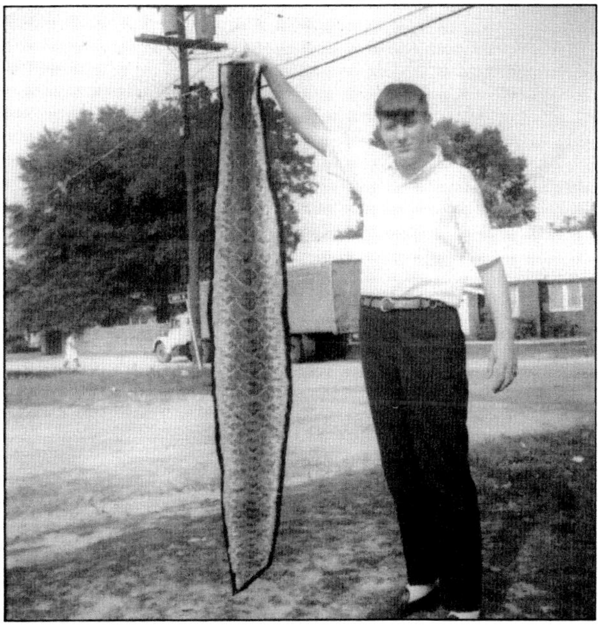

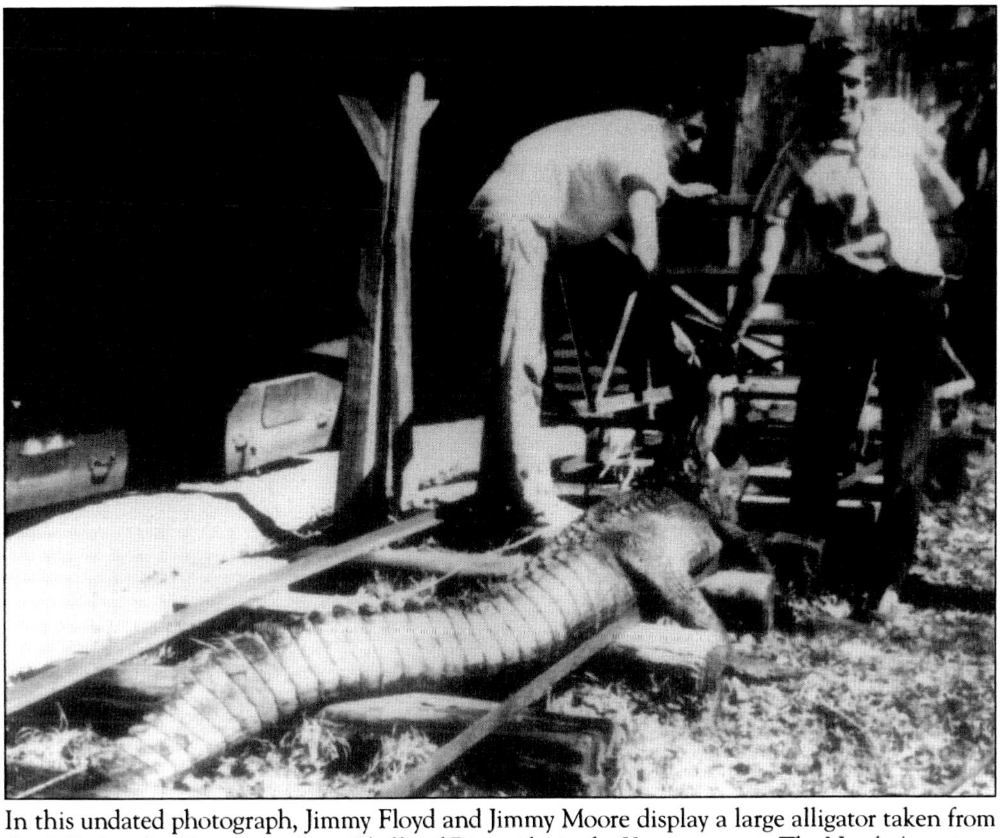

In this undated photograph, Jimmy Floyd and Jimmy Moore display a large alligator taken from the Salkehatchie River, near Rum Bluff and Riverside, in the Yemassee area. The North American alligator, once listed as a threatened species and protected from hunting, has since made a comeback and limited gator-hunting is once again allowed in South Carolina. (Courtesy of HMVC.)

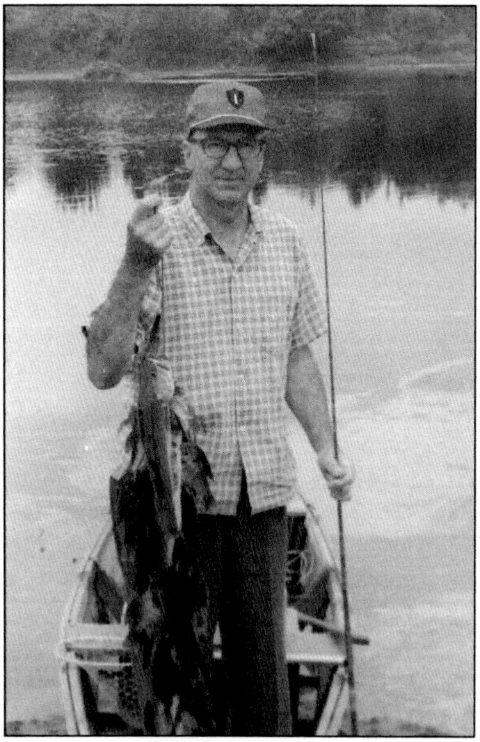

A fish a day keeps the doctor away. Well, maybe not, but it is true that even a physician can relieve stress and find health benefits from outdoor activities. Here, Dr. J.A. Richardson displays a stringer of 48 bass and bream caught in the Savannah River area of Hampton County in May 1968. (Courtesy of DM.)

Avid hunter Dwight Moore poses atop a pickup truck's dog box with his 1978 state-record buck. In December, he harvested the animal while hunting as a member of the Jones 601 Hunt Club based out of the old Brighton Oaks Grocery in Brighton (Garnett). (Courtesy of Jeff Hunt and the Moore family.)

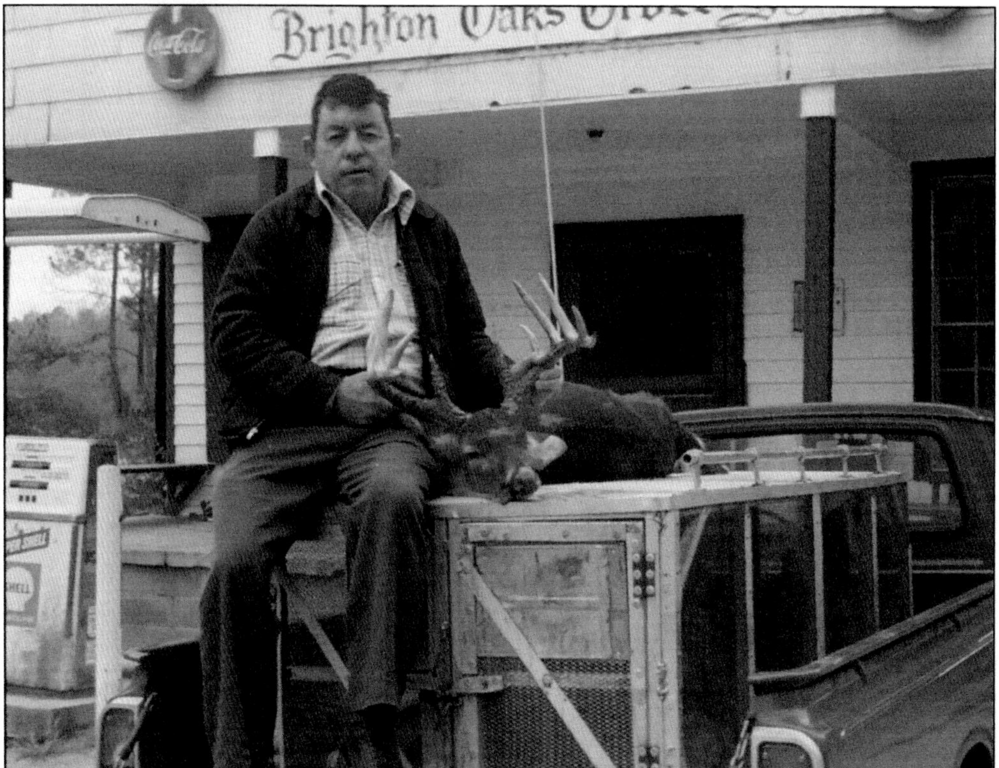

Photographer Moore labeled this September 7, 1958, photograph simply as "Mason's Hunt," which captures the productive climax of a Hampton County hunt where four older men skin and butcher a massive buck hanging from the stout limbs of a hearty oak tree. The oak is a fittingly meaningful element in this composition, the ancient tree's longevity is symbolic of Lowcountry hunting traditions almost as old as nature itself. (Courtesy of DM.)

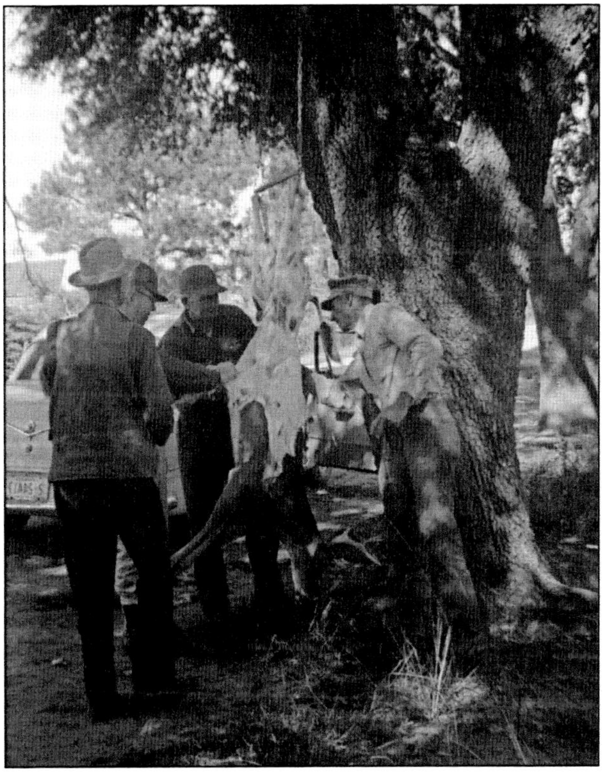

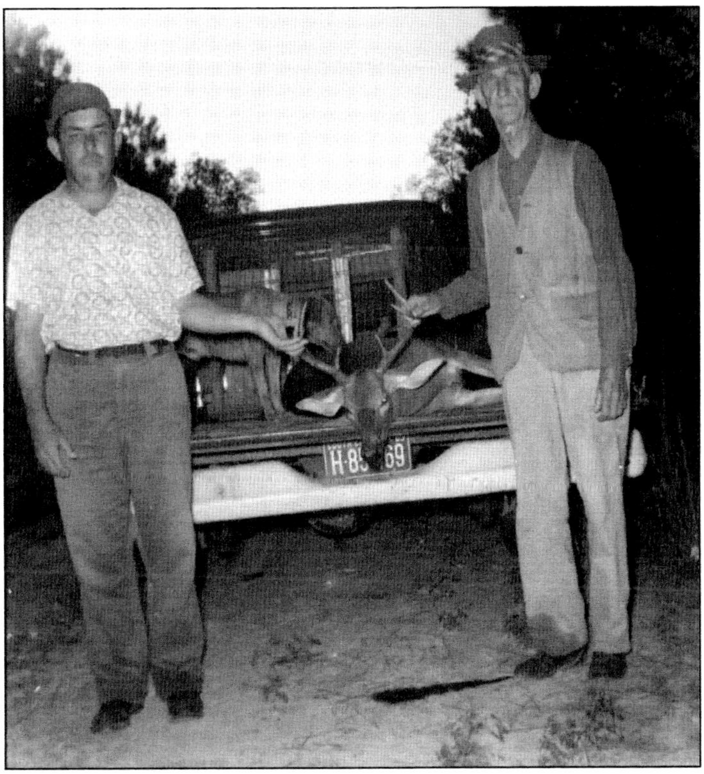

Flynt Moore (right) and Dwight Moore show off an eight-point buck killed during a family hunt on September 24, 1972, as a faithful deerhound stands watchful guard in the pickup bed. For most, hunting in South Carolina was not just about outdoor adventure and fresh game on the table, but a way to spend time with family and friends, continue lasting traditions, and create lifelong memories. (Courtesy of Jeff Hunt and the Moore family.)

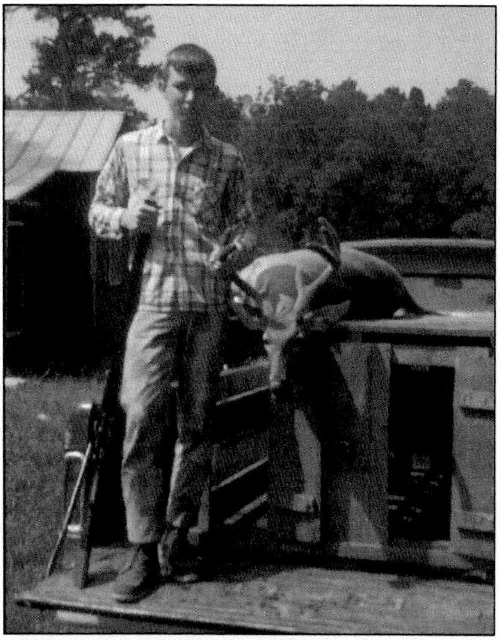

In this 1965 photograph, a proud young Marty Jones poses with a trophy buck, velvet still on its antlers. Dwight Moore also photographed Jones with a big buck during the 1966 hunting season. Once the love of whitetail deer hunting gets into a youngster's blood, it becomes an annual obsession, and he or she is likely hooked for life. (Courtesy of DM.)

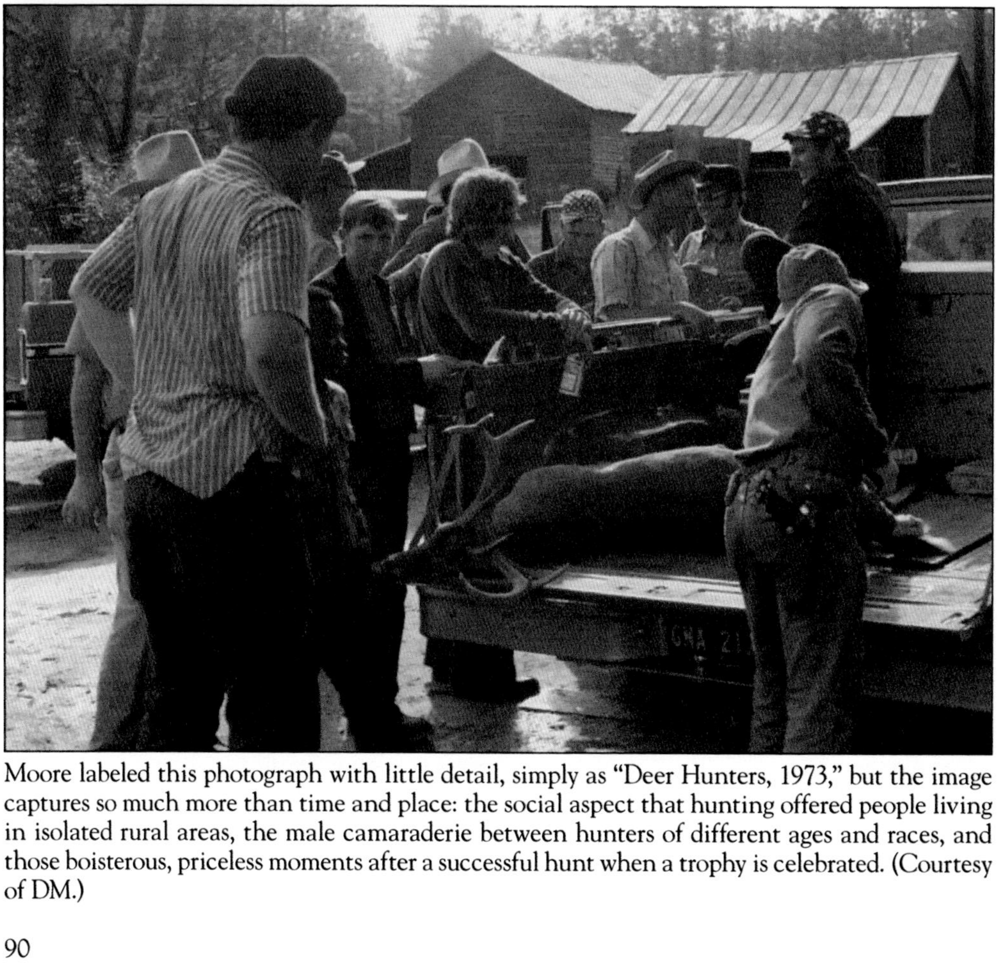

Moore labeled this photograph with little detail, simply as "Deer Hunters, 1973," but the image captures so much more than time and place: the social aspect that hunting offered people living in isolated rural areas, the male camaraderie between hunters of different ages and races, and those boisterous, priceless moments after a successful hunt when a trophy is celebrated. (Courtesy of DM.)

# *Five*

# A Heart for the Arts

Nestled deep in the lower part of South Carolina, an hour and a half from the culture of the nearest cities, lies a jewel in the rough that is quickly becoming a center for the arts in the Lowcountry.

Folks from Hilton Head, Aiken, and points beyond make day trips to the little town of Hampton to sample its artistic offerings, but it was not always so. Hampton's heart for the arts truly began in 1989 when the Hampton County Arts Council was formed, and volunteers began working to purchase and preserve the crumbling, dormant Palmetto Theater. Today, the 1946 theater has been transformed into a cultural arts center where visitors and residents alike can enjoy musicals such as *The Sound of Music*, *The Wizard of Oz*, or *Willy Wonka and the Chocolate Factory*. Each July, children from around the region converge on the theater for a Hampton summer tradition, a two-week culture camp in which youngsters are exposed to drama, music, and visual arts.

In 2009, with generous contributions from the Stanley family, onetime owners of the theater, the arts council was able to acquire the vacant 11,500-square-foot retail space adjacent to the theater. With support from donors and community, the T.G. and Ailie Stanley Cultural Arts Center was born. The Stanley Center has already been used to host several cultural and historical exhibits, and the possibilities for its future use are endless.

The quaint, small-town atmosphere and Southern flavor of the Lowcountry has attracted the attention of Hollywood, and one can find Hampton County backdrops on the big screen and the small screen alike. In 1982, *The Big Chill* was filmed in nearby Beaufort County, with one segment filmed at Central Baptist Church in Hampton County. In 1993, several scenes for *Forrest Gump* were filmed in Varnville and Hampton. Several other major motion pictures, and even a couple of B movies, have been shot in nearby scenic locales. Most recently, the town of Yemassee captured the attention of reality television viewers in the series *The Week the Women Went*.

Hampton County continues to utilize its historical theater, small-town charm, and beautiful Southern landscapes to attract visitors in person and on-screen. And this community continues to have a heart for the arts.

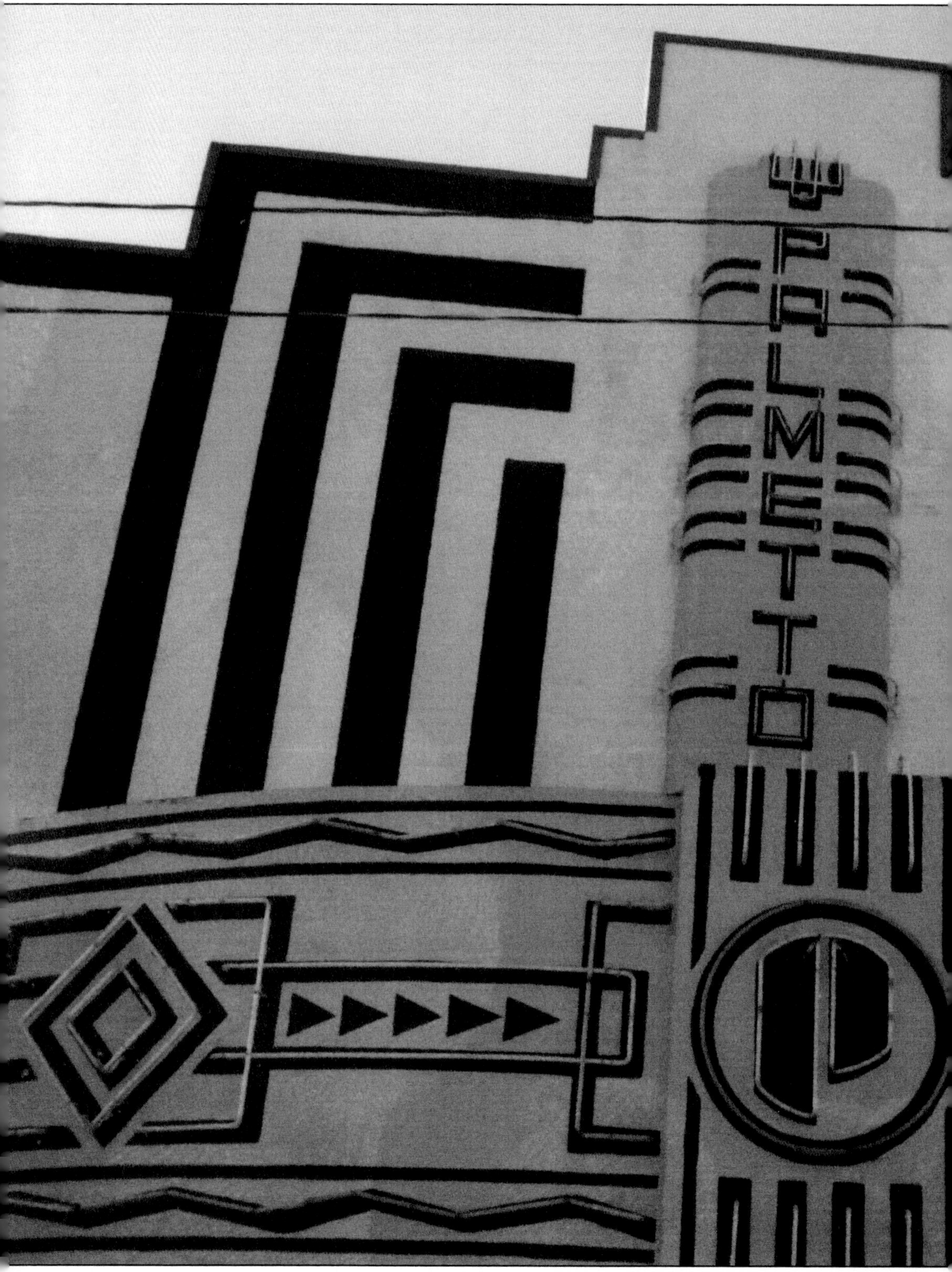
PALMETTO

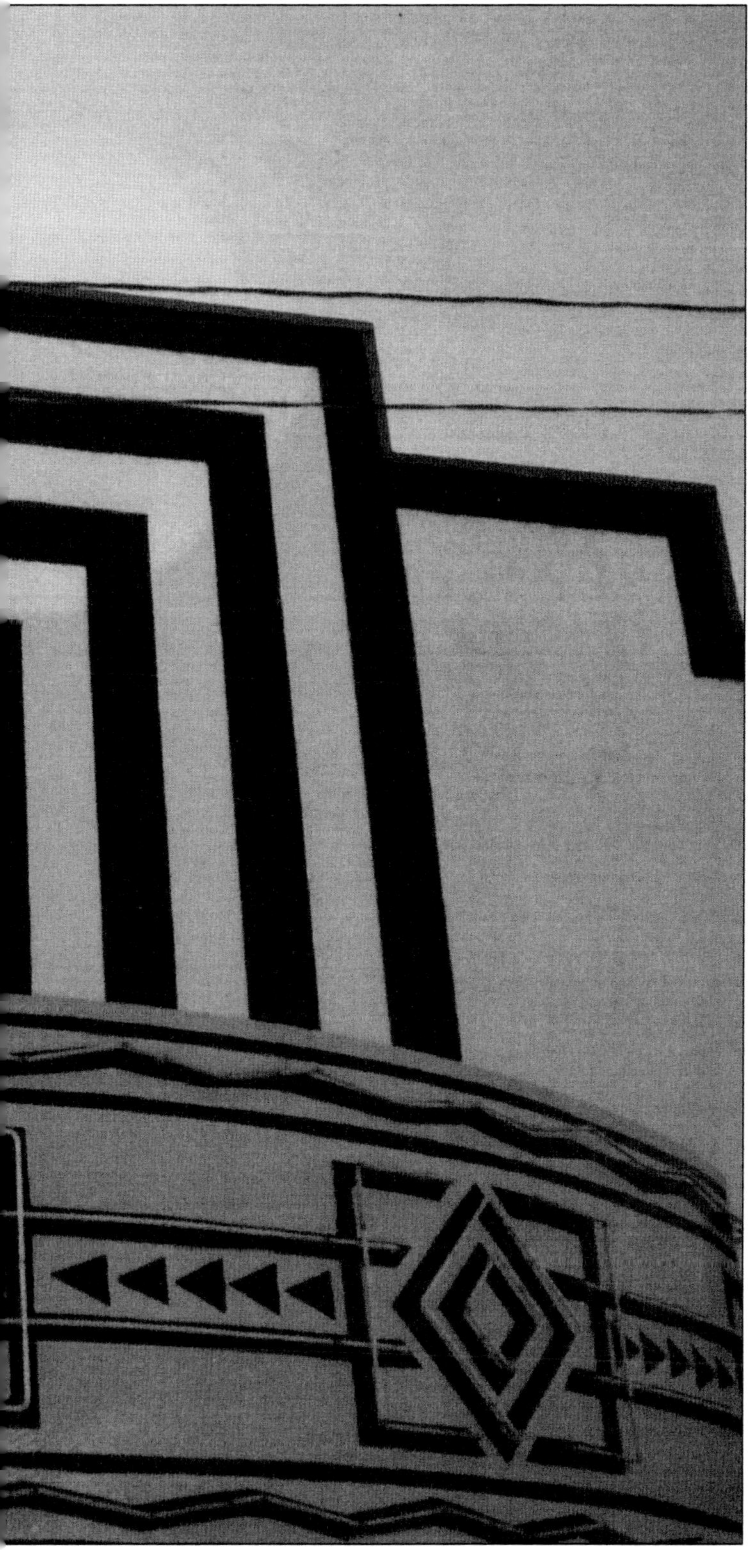

The prominent, ornate and projecting marquee of the Palmetto Theater has been a Lee Avenue landmark since 1946. Sen. George Warren himself welcomed the crowd to the show on the first night of operation. While not the first movie theater in Hampton County, the Palmetto was the only one to operate successfully on a long-term basis. Other theaters that once operated in the county include the Strand Theatre on East Carolina Avenue in Varnville, opened by William Harrell Rentz in 1919; the Hampton Theatre opened by Charles A. Harper Jr., of Estill, in 1943 in a garage building behind the old National Guard armory in Hampton across from the World War II prisoner-of-war camp; the Anne Theater in Estill, also owned by Harper; the Palmetto Drive-In Theater, more commonly known as the Hampton Drive-In, which was opened northeast of Hampton in May 1953 by Julius G. Scott and D.P. Richardson and operated primarily by the Clyde Jarrell family; and the Yemassee Drive-In, which was operated by the Green family. (Courtesy of HMVC.)

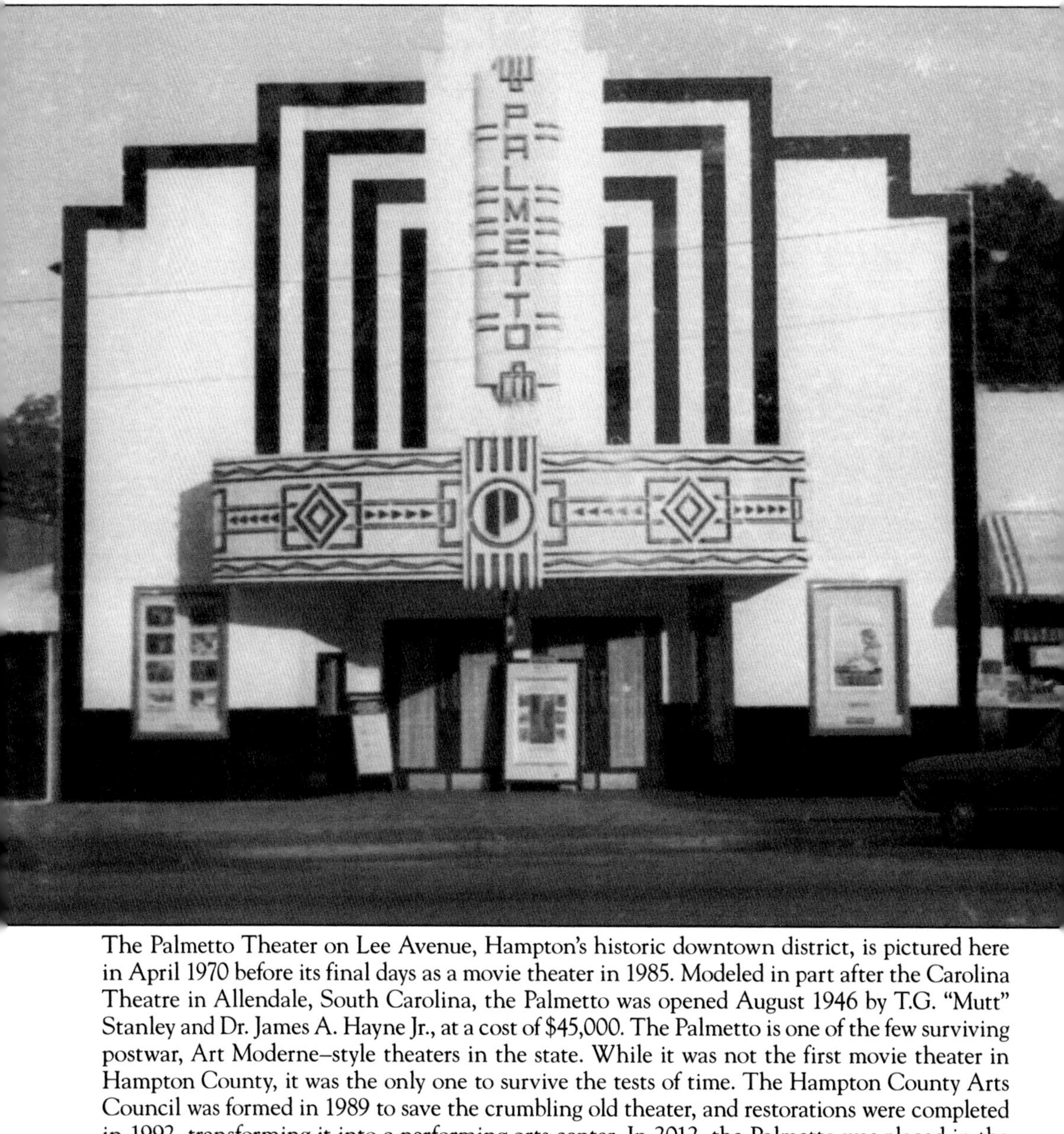


The Palmetto Theater on Lee Avenue, Hampton's historic downtown district, is pictured here in April 1970 before its final days as a movie theater in 1985. Modeled in part after the Carolina Theatre in Allendale, South Carolina, the Palmetto was opened August 1946 by T.G. "Mutt" Stanley and Dr. James A. Hayne Jr., at a cost of $45,000. The Palmetto is one of the few surviving postwar, Art Moderne–style theaters in the state. While it was not the first movie theater in Hampton County, it was the only one to survive the tests of time. The Hampton County Arts Council was formed in 1989 to save the crumbling old theater, and restorations were completed in 1992, transforming it into a performing arts center. In 2012, the Palmetto was placed in the National Register of Historic Places. (Courtesy of DM.)

The Palmetto Theater, which opened Monday, August 12, 1946, was the brainchild of T.G. "Mutt" Stanley (right), a onetime mayor pro tem of the town of Hampton, and Dr. James A. Hayne Jr., a local physician. The equally popular Theater Soda Shop was also opened in 1946 by Haskel Avant. Stanley and Haynes toured several other theaters around the state, and the Palmetto was heavily influenced by the Art Deco movement, which was popular in the 1930s. Hailed as an auspicious improvement for Hampton, the Palmetto offered several motion pictures, newsreels, and cartoons a week and, because it had a full stage, also hosted live performances during its early days that included Gene Mils and his Twilight Playboys, western star Lash LaRue, and Prince Tiny, the "Hollywood wonder horse." (Both, courtesy of Hampton Friends of the Arts, Inc.)

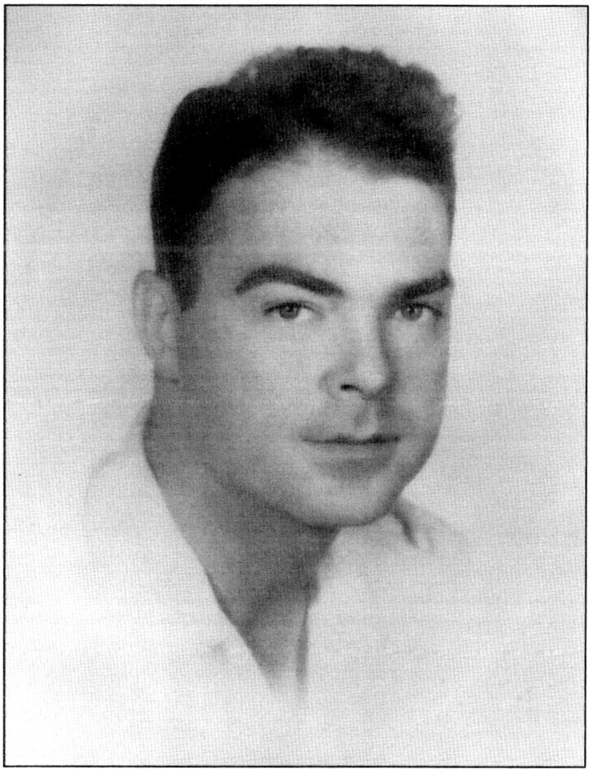

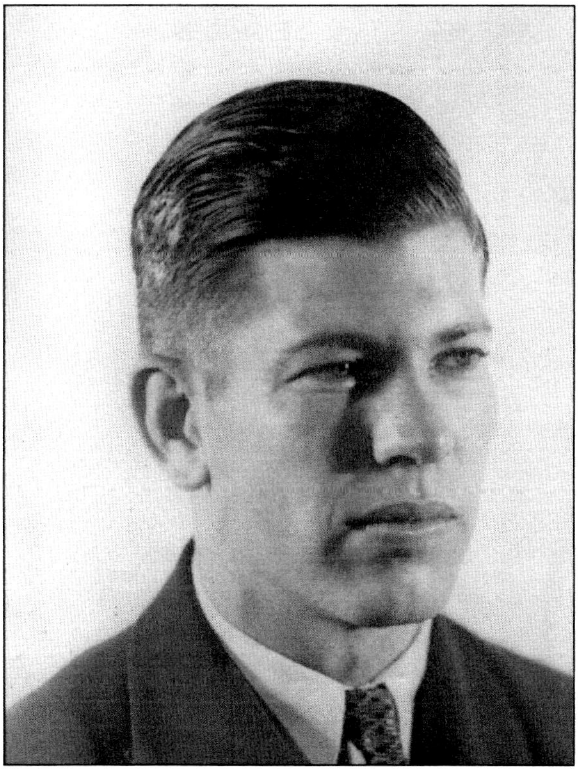

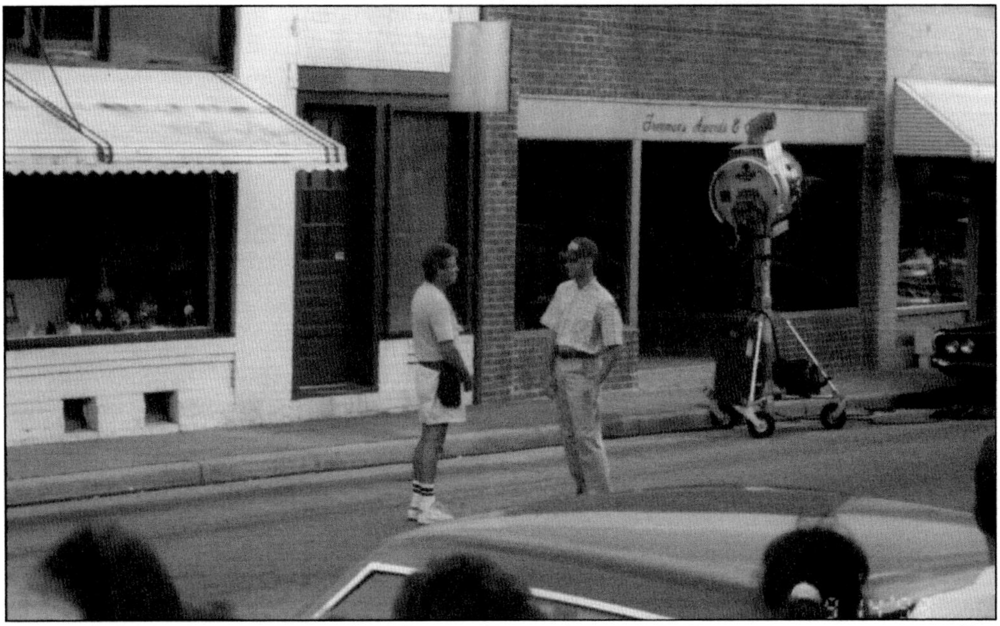

Nationally known actor Tom Hanks talks to a film producer while shooting a scene on Varnville's Main Street for the movie *Forrest Gump* on September 14, 1993. *Forrest Gump* producers were looking for a quaint, small Southern town to film a portion of the movie, including scenes of Forrest's childhood, and found the town of Varnville to be the perfect setting. (Courtesy of Marcia Wood.)

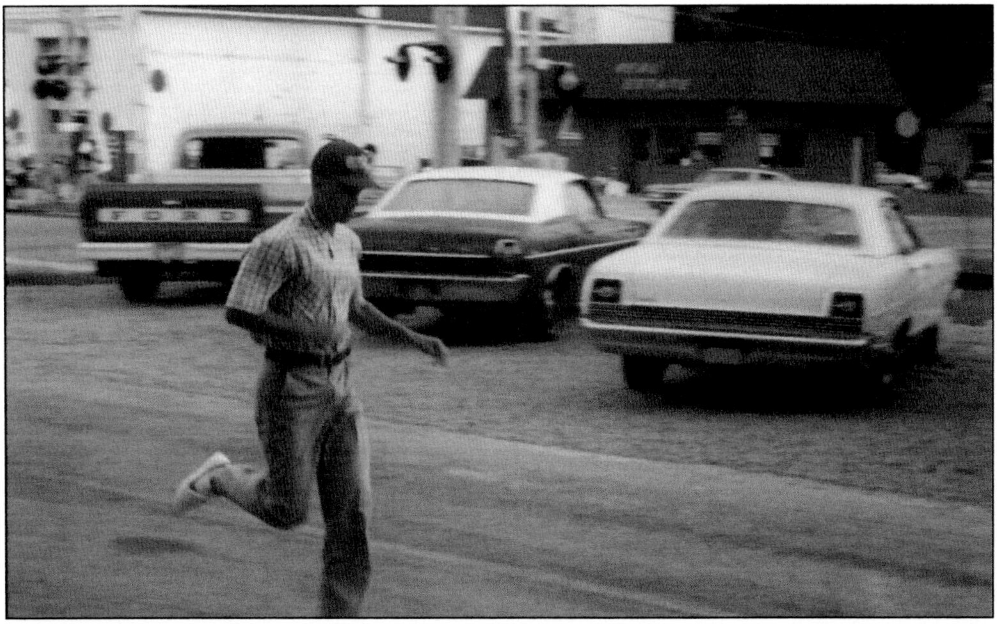


Tom Hanks runs through Varnville, as he does through much of the movie, during *Forrest Gump* filming in Hampton County on September 14, 1993. Based on the 1986 novel by Southern author Winston Groom, the Paramount Pictures film, which was released on July 6, 1994, and directed by Robert Zemeckis, quickly became an international blockbuster and earned almost $678 million at the box office. (Courtesy of Marcia Wood.)

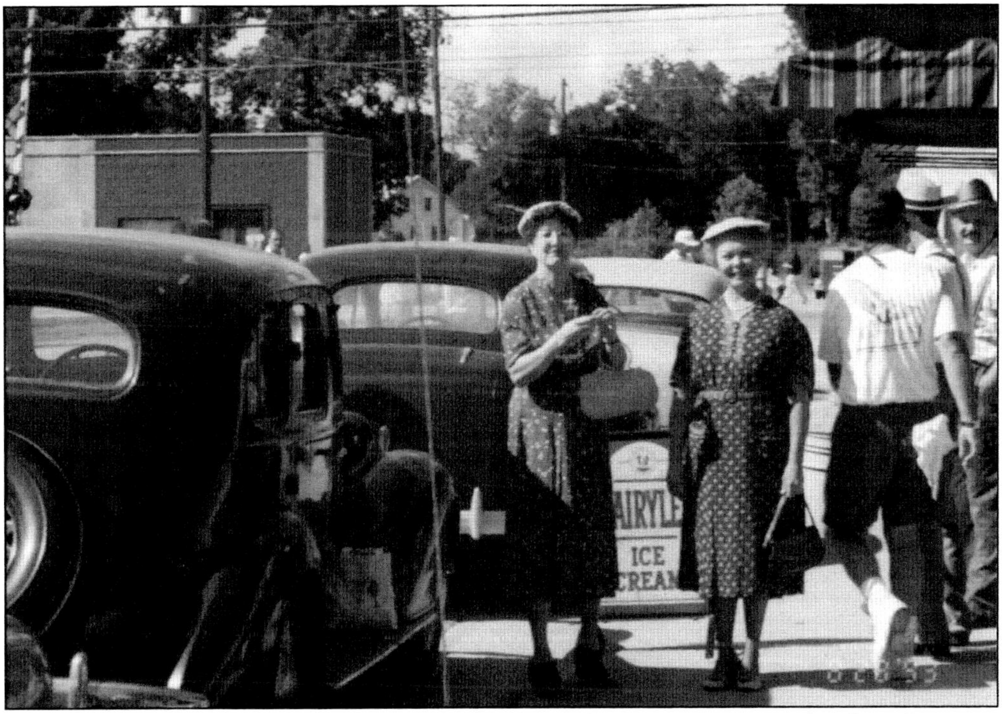


Adorned in period dress and surrounded by antique and vintage cars, many locals took part in the *Forrest Gump* filming as extras, including well-known retired English teacher Betty Ruth Crews (left), shown here during filming on August 28, 1993. Many locals enjoyed meeting the all-star cast that includes Hanks, Sally Field, Gary Sinise, Mykelti Williamson, and Robin Wright. (Courtesy of Marcia Wood.)

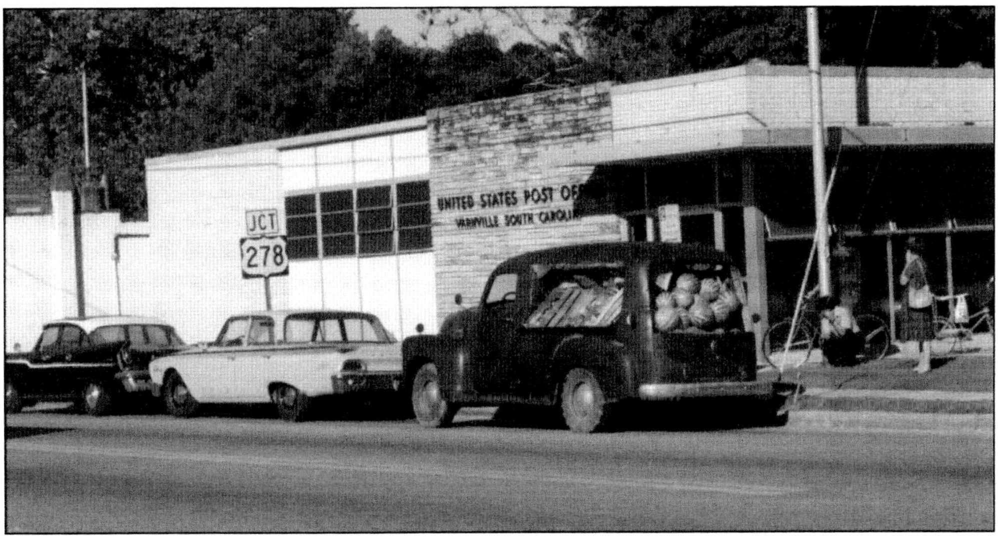


The streets of downtown Varnville traveled back in time in 1993 as the fictional town of Greenbow, Alabama, during the *Forrest Gump* filming. Old cars lined the street in front of the town's post office, and several Main Street buildings were remodeled to appear as they would have in the 1950s and 1960s. Other scenes of the film were shot near Yemassee, which is also in Hampton County. (Courtesy of Marcia Wood.)

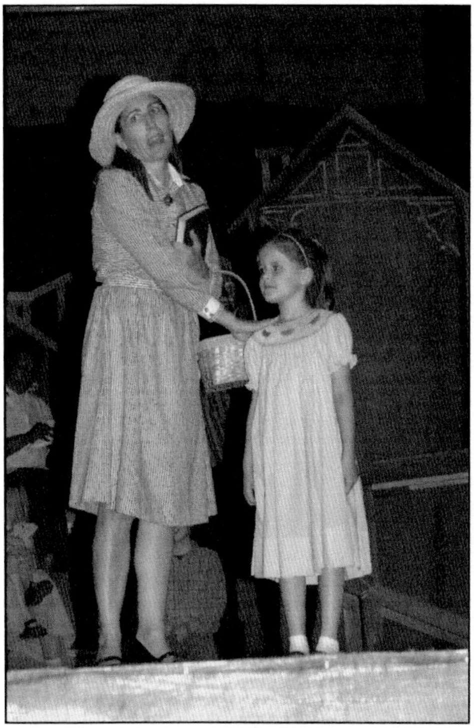

Lowcountry actress Terri Boone (left) leads a scene during the Salkehatchie Stew play *Weathering the Storm* in 2010. The Salkehatchie Stew project, founded by the University of South Carolina Salkehatchie Leadership Institute, is a five-county history and community folk-play project in which volunteers interview elders in Hampton County and surrounding areas to preserve their stories, and unique local history, while bringing them to life onstage. (Courtesy of HCG.)

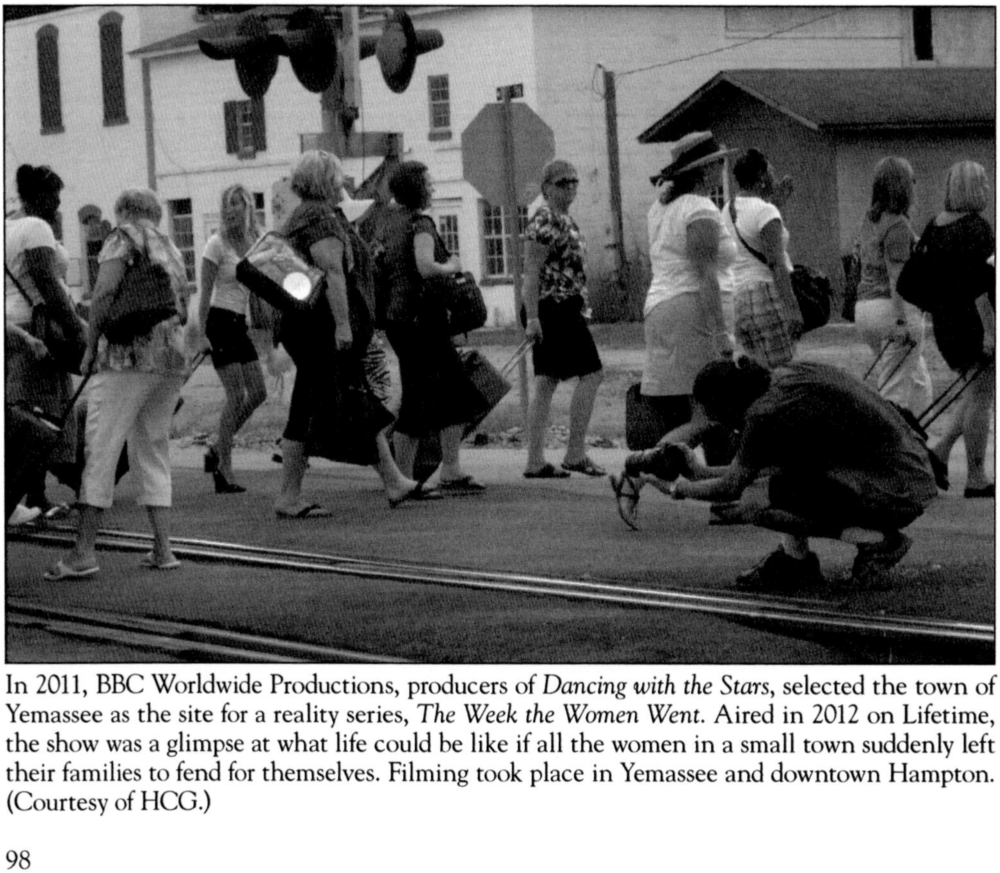

In 2011, BBC Worldwide Productions, producers of *Dancing with the Stars*, selected the town of Yemassee as the site for a reality series, *The Week the Women Went*. Aired in 2012 on Lifetime, the show was a glimpse at what life could be like if all the women in a small town suddenly left their families to fend for themselves. Filming took place in Yemassee and downtown Hampton. (Courtesy of HCG.)

# *Six*

# Faces and Places

One will find them in every community. They are the well-known people, the favorite stopping places, and the local landmarks and institutions that give any location its unique sense of place and character. These local institutions could include a 200-year-old church that one's family has attended for four generations; perhaps it is an old school that friends and family attended decades ago but still hold fond memories of; perhaps, to many locals, their local pharmacy can be an institution, when one considers that the family business has been serving the community in the same location for more than 80 years.

The Rivers family owned dry goods and grocery stores on old Lee Avenue, Hampton, and their name still shines through the aging Main Street storefronts. The Brunson family kept generations on the road in new cars, constructed numerous buildings large and small, and still runs the local hardware store. Cranel Herndon ran an international trucking business out of humble Hampton and enjoyed putting his trucks in the watermelon festival parade. When one thinks of drugstores, it may bring ice-cold soda pop from Vincent's soda fountain to mind, or drinking coffee with the gang at Stanley's Drugs. When in Hampton, one expects to pick up the latest copy of the *Hampton County Guardian*, the local newspaper that has been around for more than 135 years, or cruise in the car while listening to Tony Gross on WBHC radio.

When locals drive past the renovated Hampton County Courthouse, some may recall a funny story about Judge Eltzroth or "Buster" Murdaugh. In a trip down Lee Avenue, many stop and visit the late Reba Peeples' Frock Shop, and recall the time her lifelong friend Betty Ruth Crews stood on top of a school desk to make her students learn. And one may even run into the friendly local funeral home director, who has a sense of humor and likes to shake people's hand and ask, "How ya feeling?"

These are the faces and places that make Hampton County what it is.

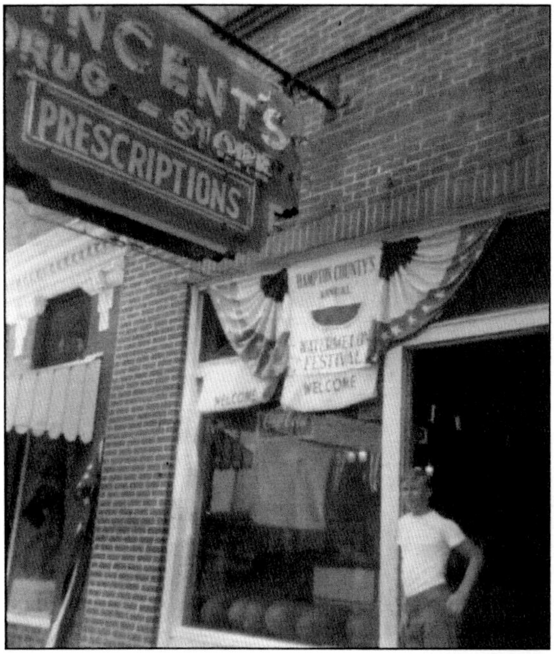


At left, Ralph Stanley relaxes in front of Hampton's Vincent's drugstore in 1955. A Lee Avenue landmark since it opened its doors as Hampton Drug Company around 1933, Vincent's has remained a family-owned business for more than 81 years, and it is still going strong today. Founded by Dr. Francis Vincent (below), the pharmacy is now owned and operated by his son Dr. Jimmy Vincent, who has been a pharmacist for more than 40 years. A second son, James, is also a pharmacist. In addition to supplying the medical needs of the community, Vincent's is known for its old-fashioned soda fountain, and for decades many youngsters enjoyed ice-cold cherry Cokes and fresh-squeezed orangeades or lemonades. Stepping through its doors is like stepping back in time. (Both, courtesy of Vincent's Drugs.)

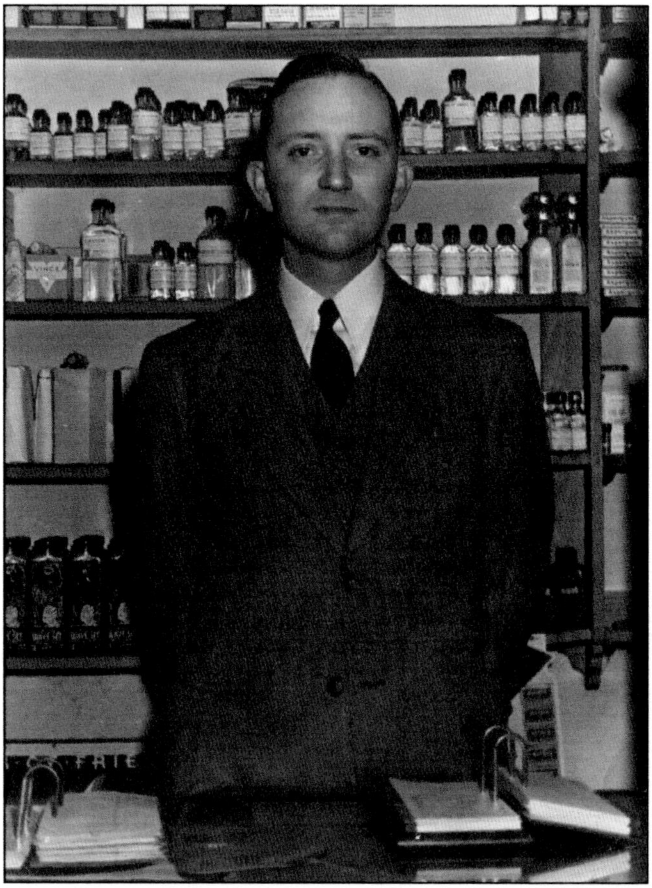

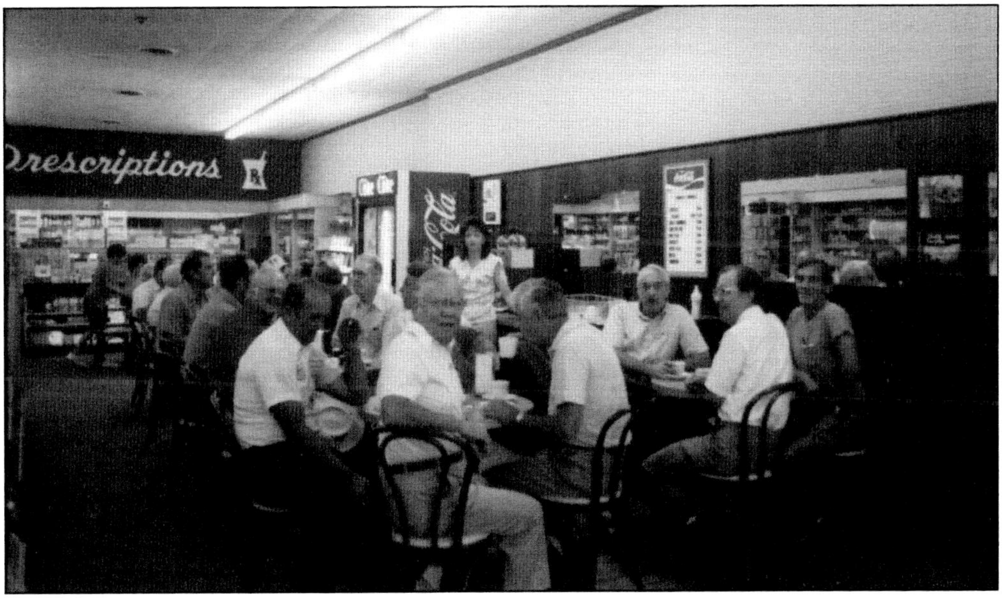

Stanley's Drug Store was a thriving business and a landmark at the corner of Lee Avenue and Mulberry Street for decades, until it closed in 1998. The two-generation business was owned and operated by the Stanley family, which included T.G. "Mutt" and Ailie Floyd Stanley, Allan Floyd "Bubba" Stanley, Thomas Griffin Stanley Jr., Phillip Hayne Stanley, Sally Stanley Dobson, and Barney McClure Stanley. But Stanley's was much more than just a place to pick up a prescription; it became known as a gathering place for freshly brewed coffee, news, and gossip by local retirees and businessmen alike. Pictured here in the 1980s are Stanley family members and staff with the unofficial Coffee Club of Stanley's Drug Store. Many jokes and juicy tidbits of news were shared and friendships made over a steaming cup of coffee. (Both, courtesy of Sally Dobson.)

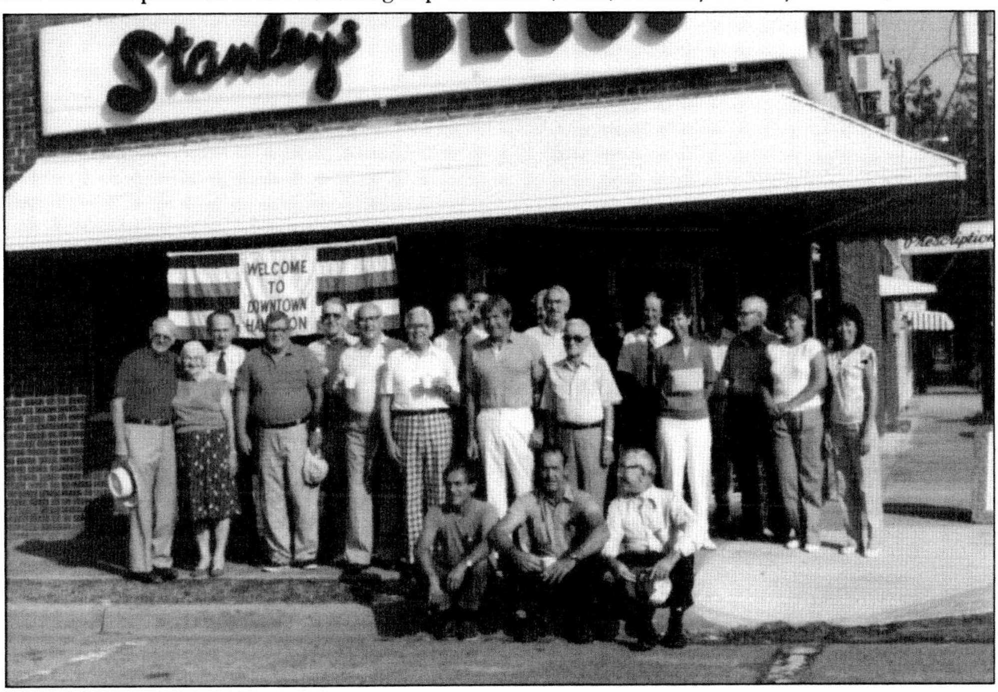

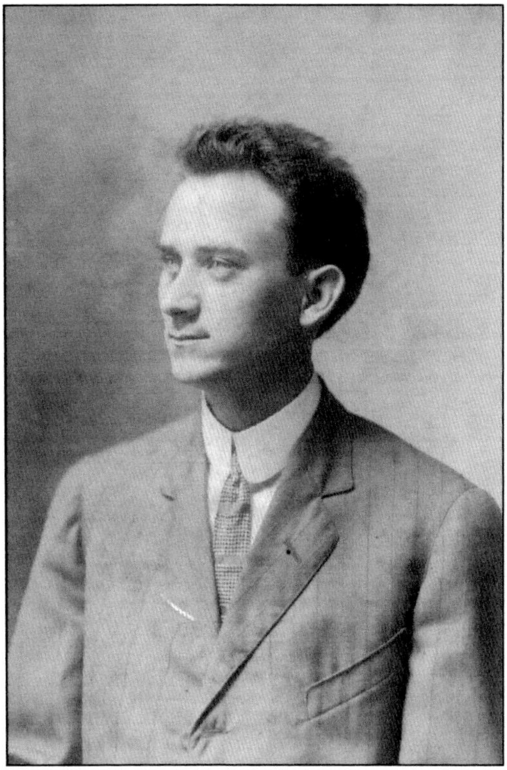

J. Frank Rivers (left) was one of the children of J.H. Rivers Sr. and one of the later owners in the family business, J.H. Rivers and Sons, located on Lee Avenue, Hampton. The original founders of the Rivers business dynasty were J.H. Rivers Sr., M.E. Rivers, and their siblings, and the original business was actually a commissary (below) on the family farm located on Highway 601 North between Hampton and Crocketville, a business which later moved into Hampton. As merchants, the Rivers family supplied Hampton County citizens throughout much of the 1900s with almost everything: dime-store goods, gasoline, groceries, livestock feed, and dry goods. (Both, courtesy of Anna Sue Rivers.)

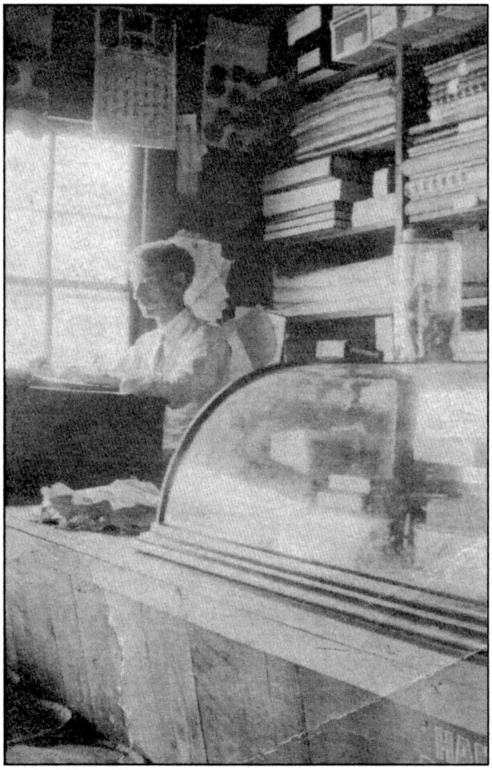

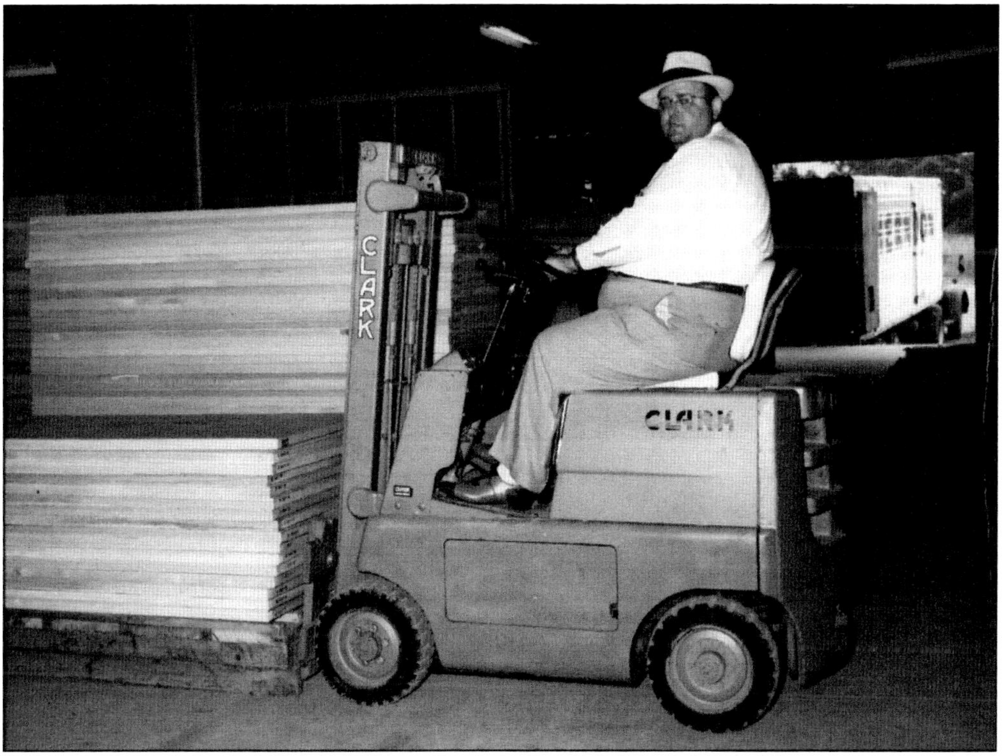


In 1937, Cranel B. Herndon (above) started peddling Colleton County farm produce in a secondhand truck that cost him $40. In just a few short years, this humble business had grown to become a major motor transport line that shipped everything from South Carolina produce to plywood and Micarta plastics from Hampton's Westinghouse plant to 23 states around the country. The Cranel B. Herndon Fast Motor Freight Service, which was located directly opposite the giant Westinghouse Micarta plant, was known as one of the largest hauler of plywood in the nation. A giant of a man at 6 feet tall and 300 pounds, Herndon was also known for his giant heart and as a big booster of his community. Herndon trucks were a common sight in many watermelon festival parades. (Both, courtesy of Libby Smith.)

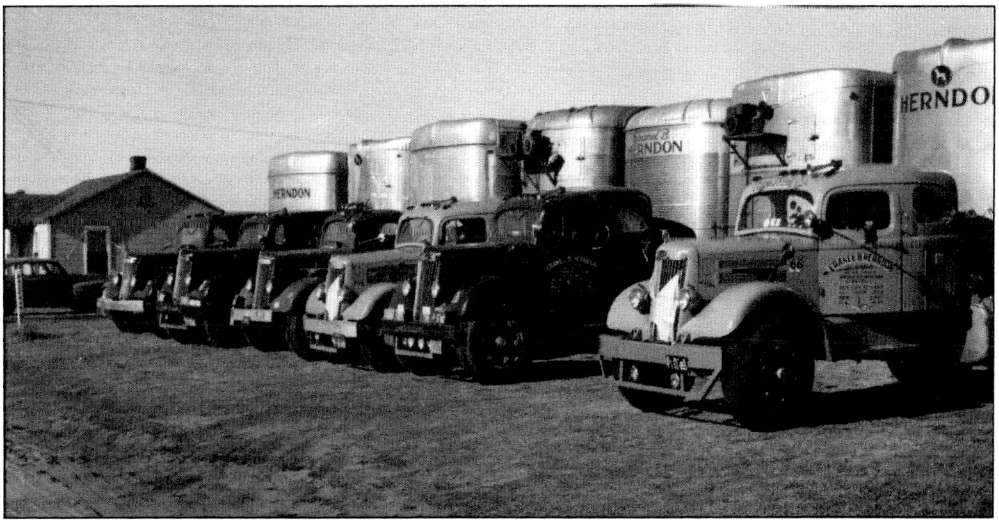

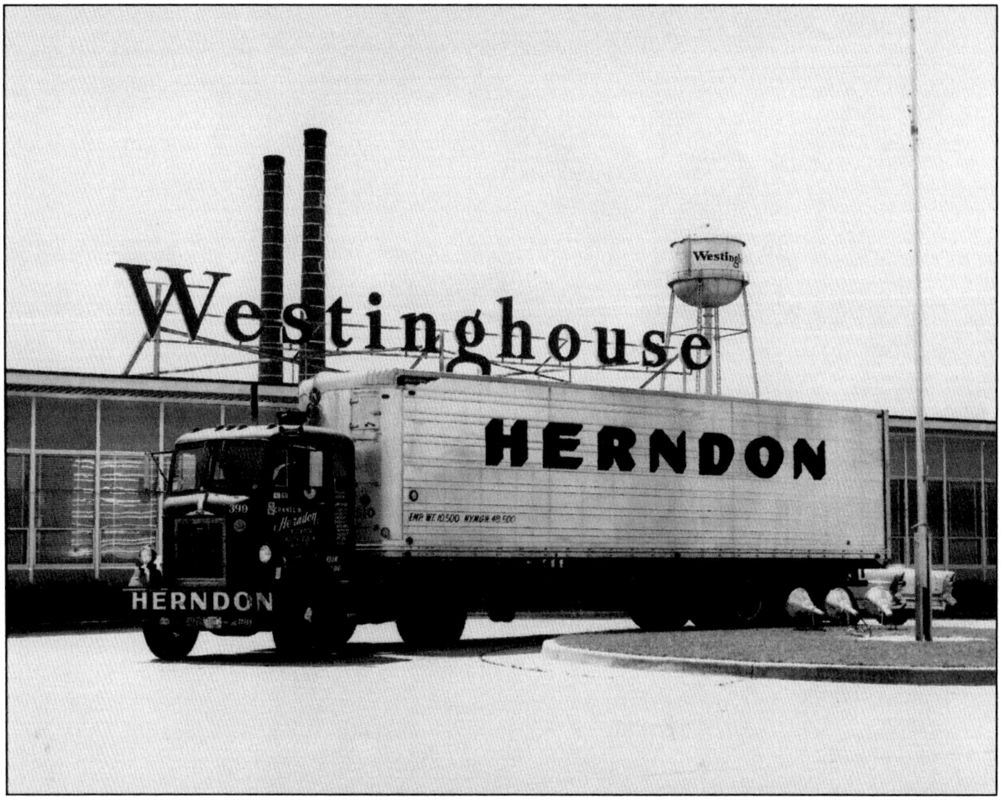


Pictured here are two of Hampton County's former economic giants: the Cranel B. Herndon Fast Motor Freight Service and Westinghouse Electric Corporation's Hampton Micarta Division. When Westinghouse came to Hampton County (as Plywoods-Plastics in the late 1930s), it gave life to many spin-off businesses that ranged from trucking to metal fabrication and building construction. For decades, these two giants helped thousands of Lowcountry families build better lives. (Courtesy of Libby Smith.)

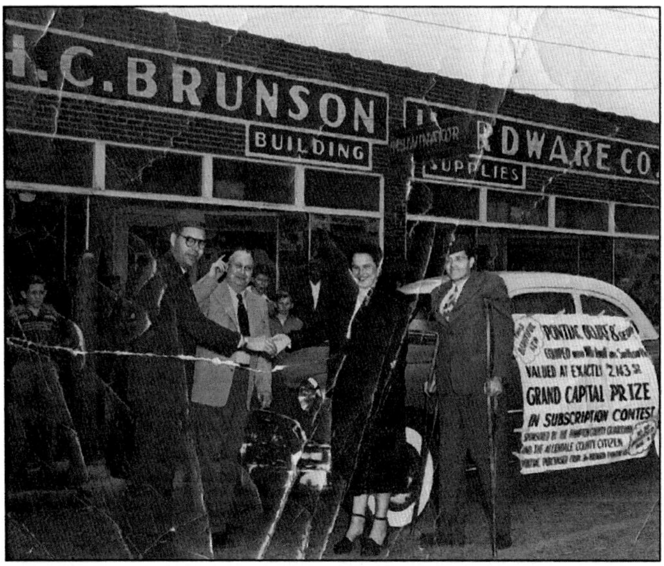


In 1948, Henry C. Brunson Sr. awards a contest winner at the former site of Brunson Hardware Company on Lee Avenue. Brunson overcame hardships early in life to start his first business, Brunson Automobile Sales, in 1940. He then established several more businesses in Hampton County, including Brunson Construction, Brunson Building Supply, a crate manufacturing facility, an auto parts store, a sawmill, and even a honey bee enterprise. (Courtesy of HCG.)

WBHC radio station owner Carl "Tony" Gross (right) presents a check to an unidentified Hampton Jaycees member. Gross, a native of La Follette, Tennessee, moved to South Carolina to work in radio in 1957, and in 1967 he came to Hampton, where he quickly became known for his generosity to community, customers, and employees. WBHC stands for "We're Building Hampton County." (Courtesy of Tony Gross.)

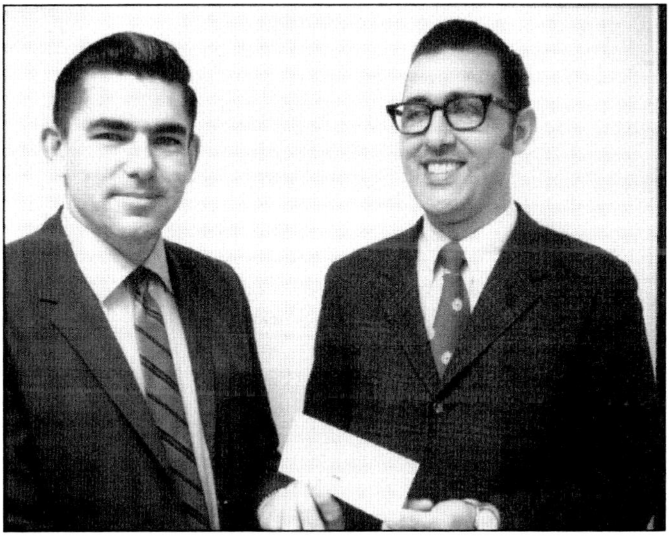

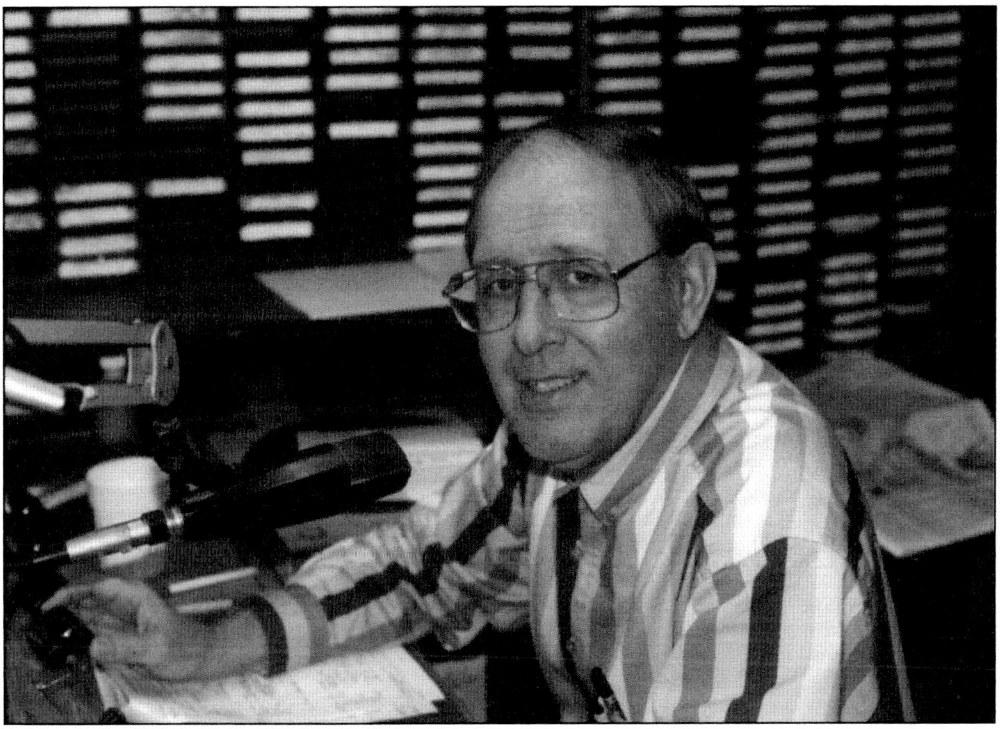

Tony Gross is pictured here on the air on January 21, 1997. Hampton County's WBHC-AM and -FM radio stations were founded by Joseph B. Wilder of Barnwell, South Carolina, and J.A. Gallimore, of Senaca, South Carolina, in September 1957. Gross became station manager in 1967 and purchased the station from Wilder in 1983. (Courtesy of Tony Gross.)

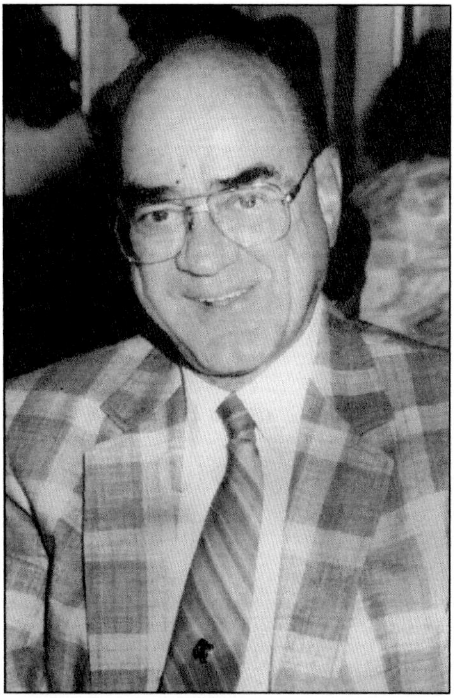

In 1952, Claire H. Detrick established C.H. Detrick and Company, the only accounting office in a 50-mile radius of the town of Hampton at that time. For more than 40 years, Detrick assisted people in South Carolina and parts of Georgia with tax-related issues. In 1987, the company was sold to Alice B. Hazel, certified public attorney. Detrick continued working until his health merited retirement in 1998. (Courtesy of Alice Hazel.)

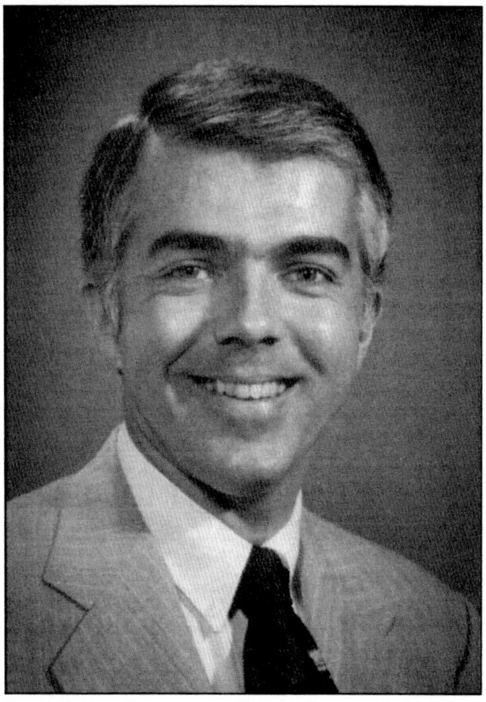

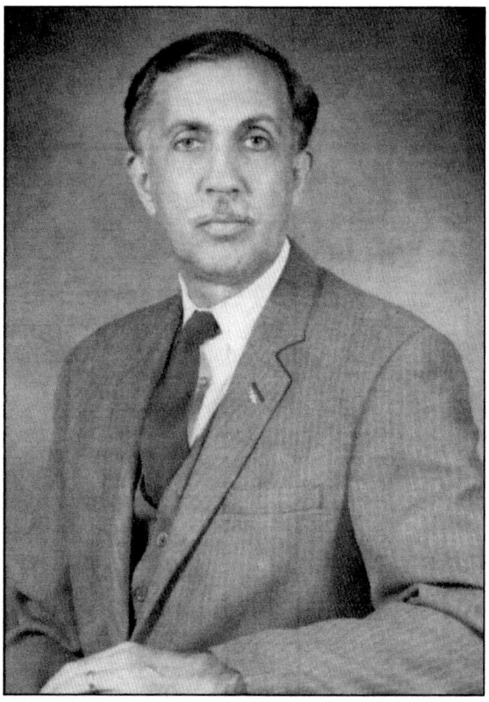

Raised on a farm in Colleton County, Gordon Rhoden (left) and John Rhoden came to Hampton County in the 1970s and found success with a lot of hard work and perseverance. The brothers not only operated a successful funeral home service established in the mid-1920s, but Gordon served a lengthy term as Hampton County coroner, and John served multiple terms as mayor of Hampton. (Courtesy of Peeples-Rhoden Funeral Home.)

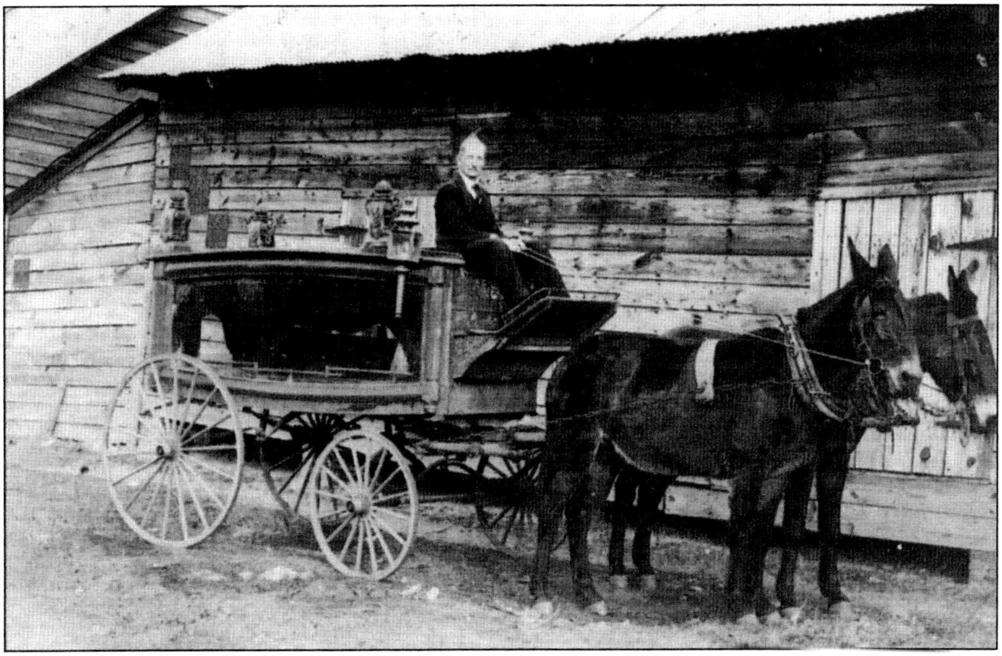

Above, Eugene M. Peeples, founder of a Hampton funeral home dynasty, is pictured on a mule-drawn hearse around 1920. Below, in 1933, motorized hearses are parked in front of Peeples's Hampton chapel. Established as Peeples Funeral Service about 1924, the business has grown and changed several times. After the death of its founder, Earl Peeples and Jimmy Holland operated it as Peeples-Holland Funeral Home until the untimely death of Holland in 1975, the year Gordon Rhoden came to Hampton to manage the firm. It later became Peeples-Rhoden Funeral Home, as it is known today. In 1978, John Rhoden joined his brother, Gordon, in the family business until John retired in 2004. (Both, courtesy of Peeples-Rhoden Funeral Home.)

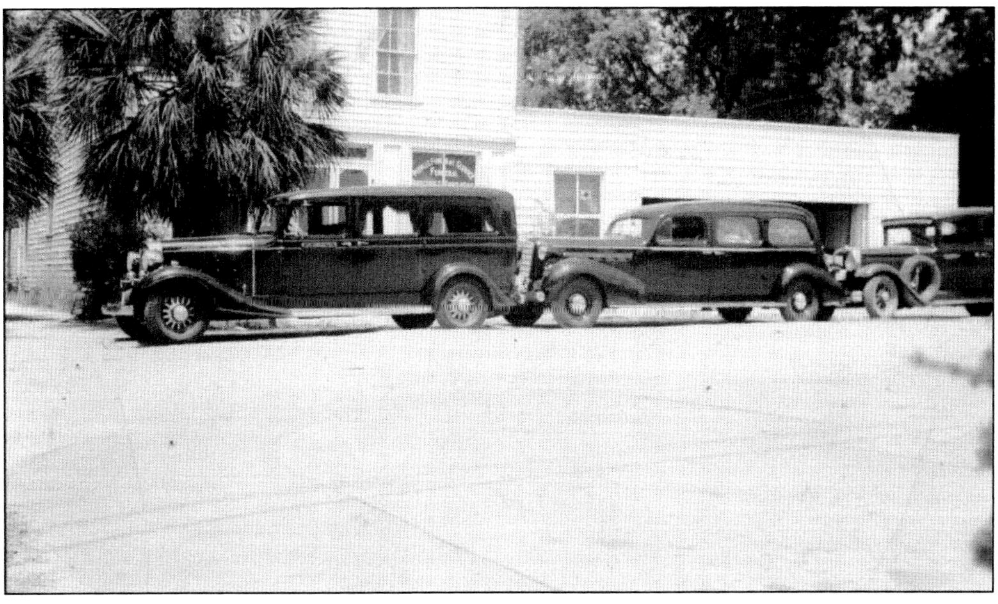

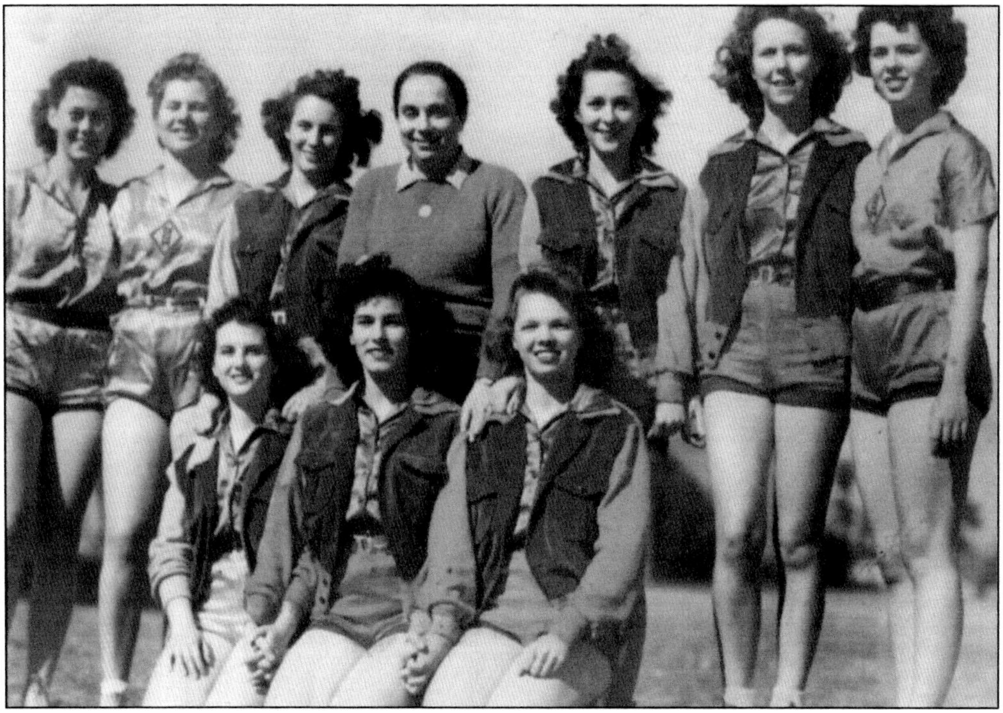

Marie Sullenger, pictured standing on the far right with her North Charleston High School basketball team in 1944, would later move to Hampton to become Marie Ellis, curator of the Hampton Museum and Visitors' Center. Marie married E.P. Ellis Jr., who opened Ellis Realty & Insurance Company in Hampton in 1946. Ellis Realty became a second-generation business and is still a business leader in Hampton County today. (Courtesy of Vivian Ellis.)

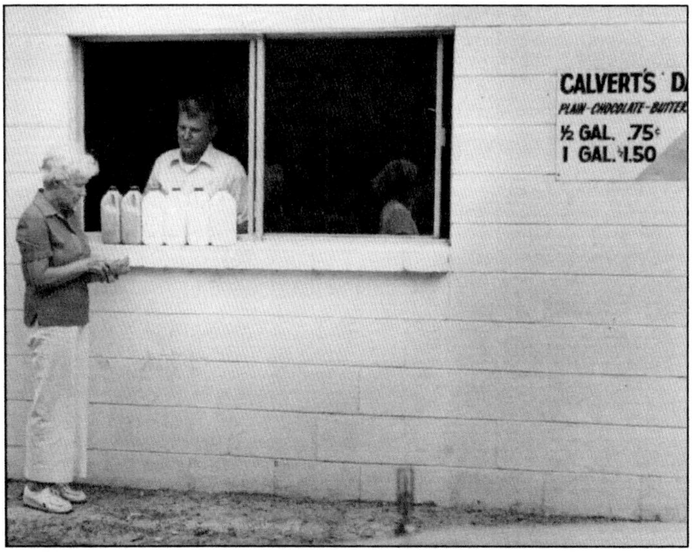


In this undated photograph, Ray Calvert waits on a customer, Mrs. Ralph Lewis, who drove regularly from Hilton Head to purchase milk from the Hampton-area dairy farm for herself and other residents of the island community. In September 1976, Calvert and his family invested $300,000 in the family farm and began pasteurizing their own milk and selling it around the county. (Courtesy of Myrtis Calvert.)

A legend in South Carolina's courtrooms, the Honorable Clyde Alfred Eltzroth (1916–2010) was the county tax collector from 1946 to 1953; practiced law with Murdaugh, Eltzroth, and Peters from 1952 to 1975; and was the resident judge of the 14th Judicial Circuit from 1975 until his retirement. He also represented Hampton County in the state legislature from 1961 to 1964 and was named Hampton County's Outstanding Citizen in 1975. (Courtesy of HMVC.)

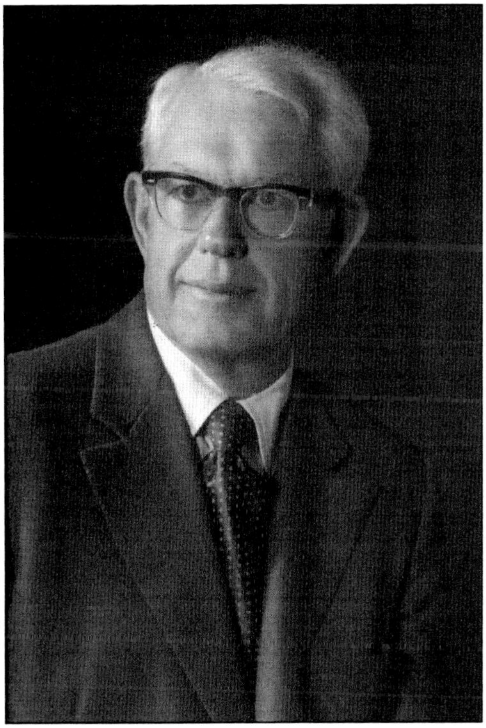

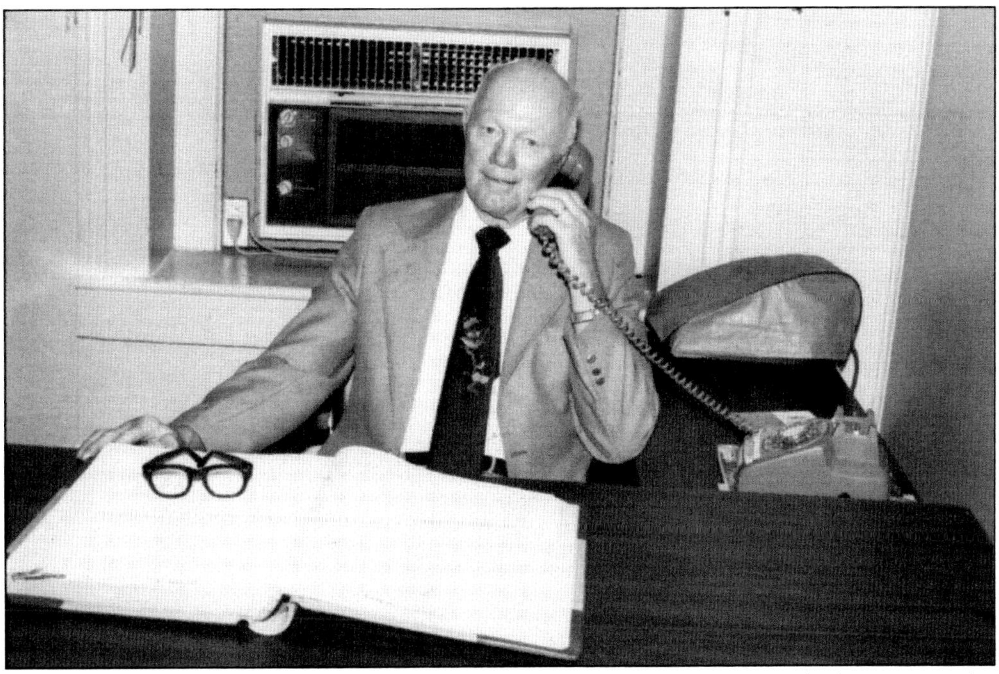

Col. Wilson Parker "Red" Tuten (1918–2007) served his country as a distinguished Air Force pilot and advisor for 30 years, was a World War II prisoner of war, and received a Purple Heart. He was elected county treasurer, an office that he held for more than 10 years. In 1995, to commemorate the 50th anniversary of World War II, he served as grand marshal of the watermelon festival. (Courtesy of HMVC.)

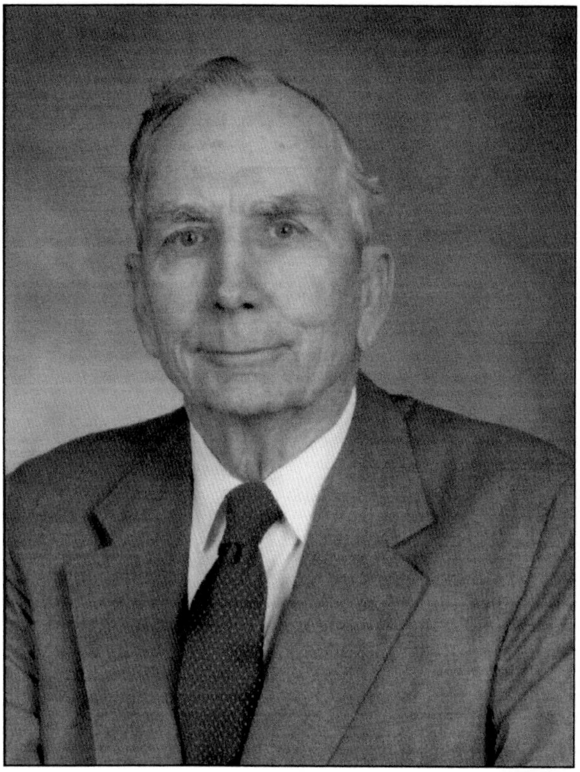

Stiles Mikell Harper (1910–2002), photographed here in 1985, was a pioneer in soybean processing and cofounder and president (1947–1976) of Harper & Bowers, Inc. and Southern Soya Corporation, the first solvent soybean processing mill in South Carolina. A statewide supporter of forestry and medicine, he was named South Carolina Tree Farmer of the Year in 1977, and in 1998 he was awarded the state's highest honor, the Order of the Palmetto. (Courtesy of HMVC.)

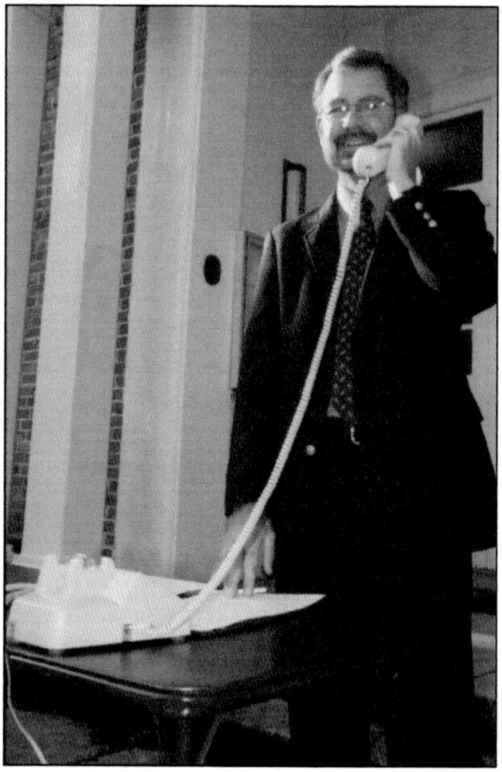

Brunson native William K. "Bill" Bowers, PhD, is a professor-turned-statesman. Bowers, a professor of business administration and accounting at the University of South Carolina, is also a Democratic member of the South Carolina House of Representatives, representing District 122. He was first elected to the chamber in 1996 and has served continuously. (Courtesy of HMVC.)

In 1910, Randolph Murdaugh opened a small law practice in Hampton that grew to become a legal giant in the Palmetto State. In 1920, Murdaugh was elected solicitor of the 14th Judicial Circuit and served until his death in a car accident in 1940. His son, Randolph Jr. "Buster", was then elected solicitor and served until 1987, the longest term of any solicitor in US history. (Courtesy of HCG.)

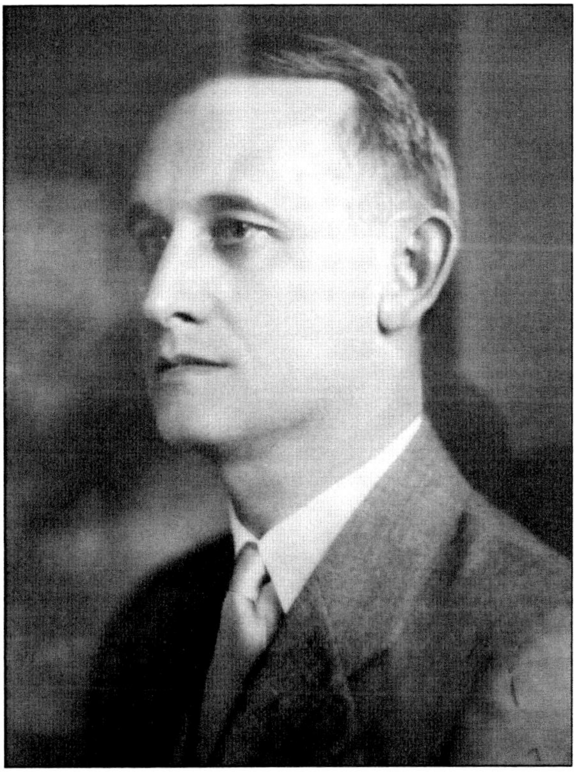

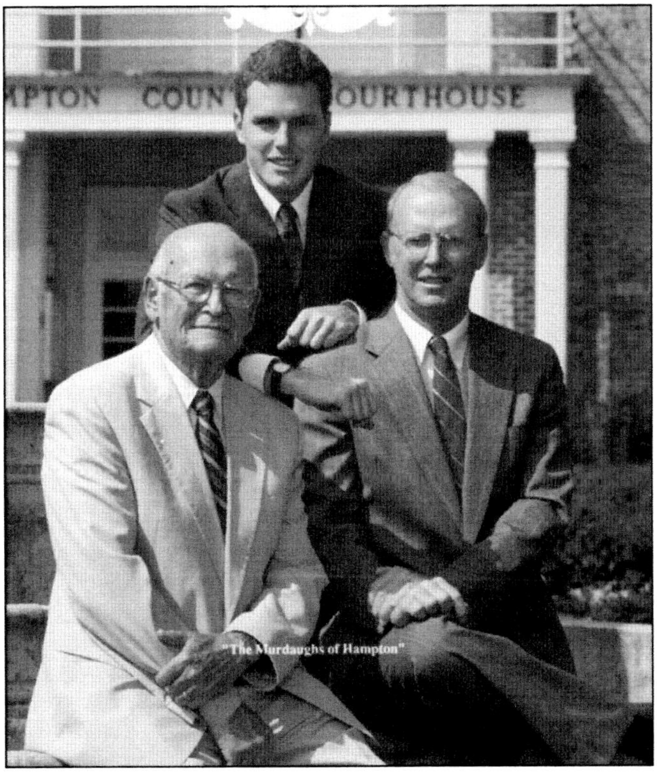


The Murdaughs of Hampton are featured in this 1989 edition of *Carolina Lawyer*, a publication of the University of South Carolina School of Law. In this four-generation law family, three Murdaughs have been solicitor for a total of 86 years. Pictured here in front of the Hampton County Courthouse are, from left to right, Randolph Murdaugh Jr., Randolph Murdaugh IV, and Randolph Murdaugh III. (Courtesy of HCG.)

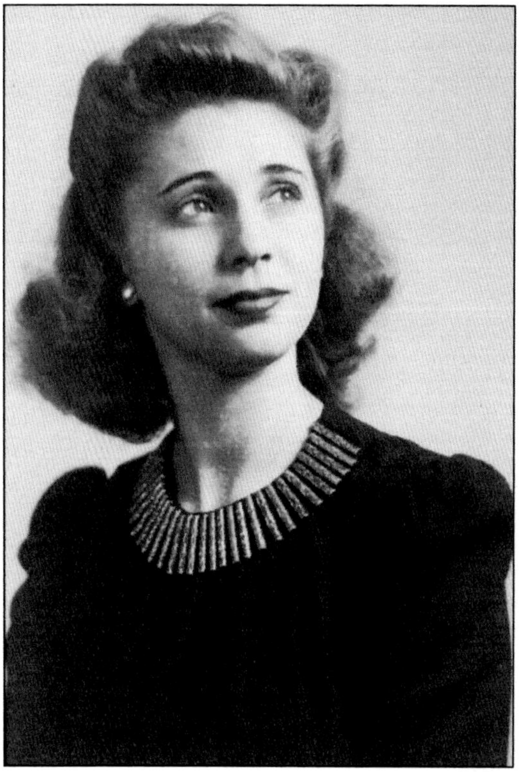

William and Reba Peeples (1924–2013) purchased the Frock Shop in May 1947, and Reba ran the Lee Avenue business for 66 years. Active in the community, she earned the chamber of commerce Business Person of the Year Award in 1990. She was also awarded the Friends of the Arts Award in 2006 and was the 2008 recipient of the Arnold Fields Arts and Culture Award. (Courtesy of Becky Young.)

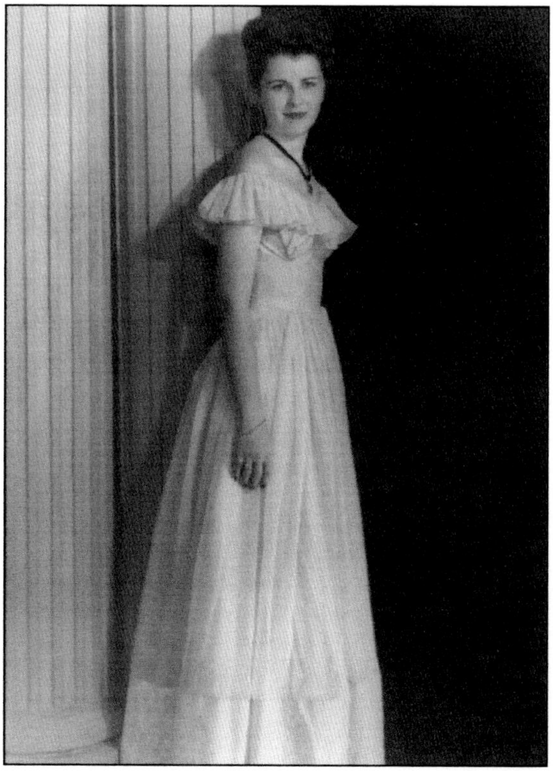

Marie Sullenger (Ellis) is pictured here in 1947 at Winthrop University. Marie later married Hampton realtor, insurance agent, and business owner E.P. Ellis Jr., and, after a career in public education, became the curator and driving force behind the formation of the Hampton Museum and Visitors' Center in the former Bank of Hampton building (1892–1926), which is in the National Register of Historic Places. (Courtesy of Vivian Ellis.)

Jacob and Anna Sue Rivers were photographed near a beloved holly tree at their residence two weeks after their marriage in 1947. A native of Estill who relocated across the swamp to Hampton, Anna Sue later became the first woman elected to the Hampton Town Council. While on the council, she was a strong supporter of museum curator Marie Ellis and the Hampton Museum and Visitors' Center. (Courtesy of Anna Sue Rivers.)

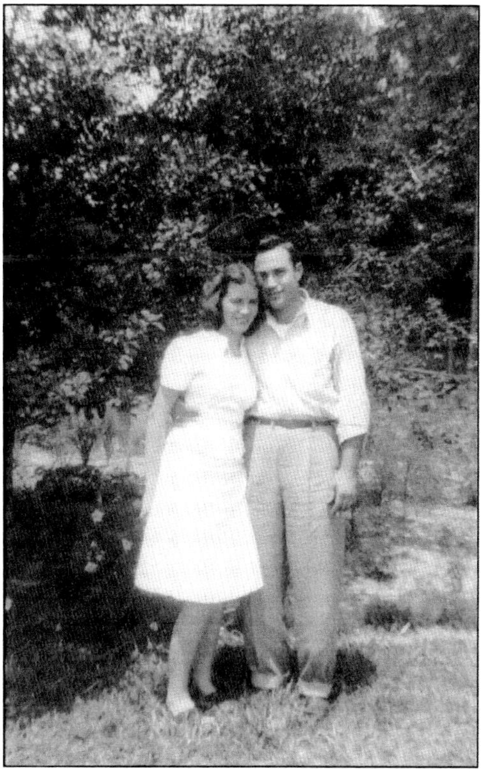

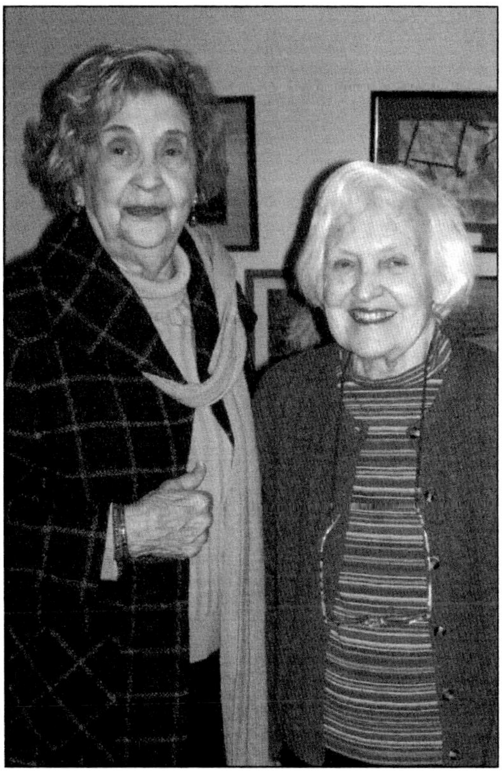

Martha Bee Anderson (1922–2009), pictured on the right with her friend Reba Peeples, was a beloved *Hampton County Guardian* writer from 1946 to 1993 and the eighth editor of the *Guardian*, from 1975 to 1981. Well known for her column Around the Clock, which ran continuously from 1947 to 1993, she also wrote for daily newspapers and was once invited to a White House press conference with Pres. Jimmy Carter. (Courtesy of Becky Young.)

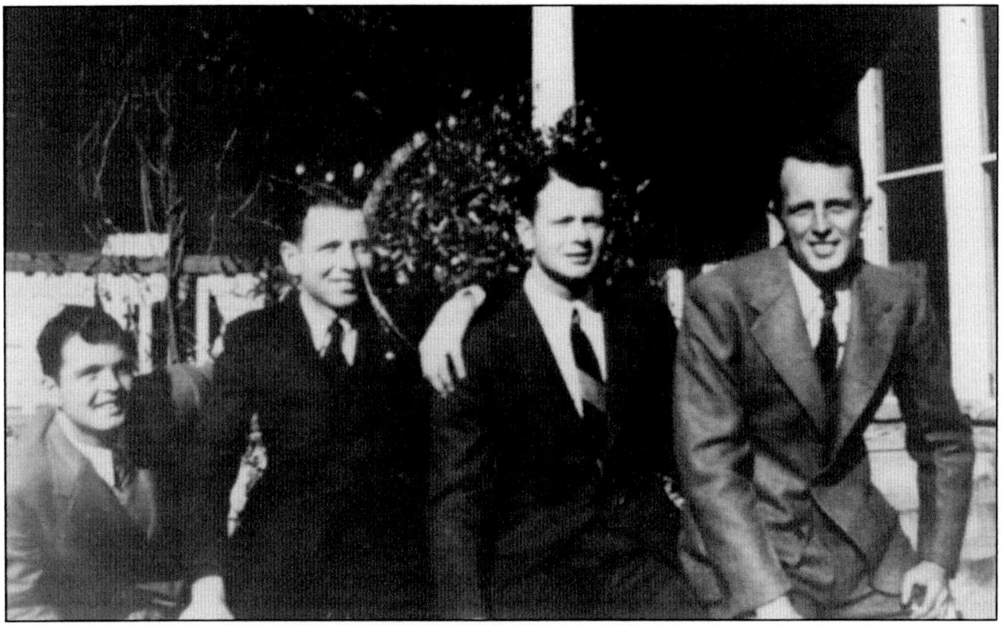

Residents of Estill and the surrounding area are familiar with the late Baker boys, pictured here from left to right around 1950—Broughton Baker, Clarke Baker, Maine Baker, and Bill Baker Jr. All four brothers served their country in World War II then returned home to become successful businessmen. Clarke was in dry goods, Bill sold furniture, Maine was in finance, and Broughton was a grocer. (Courtesy of Cecilia Baker McKenzie.)

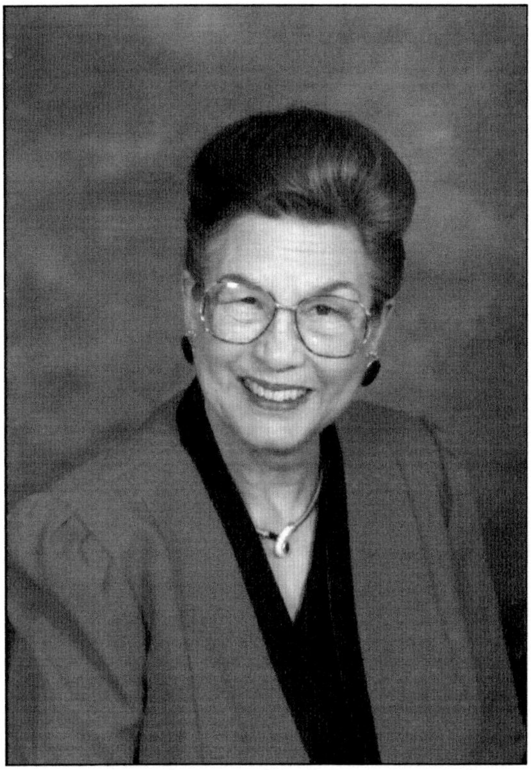

Mildred B. Rivers (1928–2003), wife of Hampton businessman Jacob Rivers, was a lifelong educator and historian in Hampton County. She was a meticulous researcher and archivist and published several historical works, including a book on the German prisoner-of-war camp in Hampton. She is credited as being the founder and first curator of the Hampton County Museum. The photograph was taken in 1998. (Courtesy of Beth Rivers.)

Isiah Rudy Loadholt, pictured here in the mid-1980s, was the 13th sheriff of Hampton County and the county's first African American sheriff. After a lengthy career as a police officer, Loadholt was first elected sheriff in 1983 and served until 1994. A plaque and exhibit in his honor were recently dedicated in the Hampton Old Colored School Museum. (Courtesy of Sheriff T.C. Smalls.)

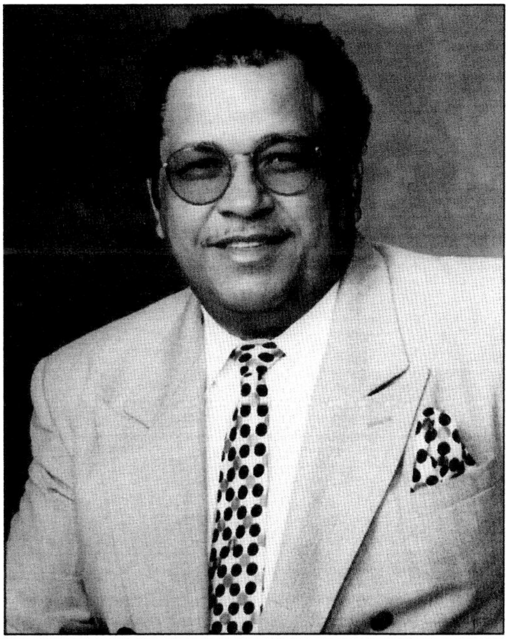

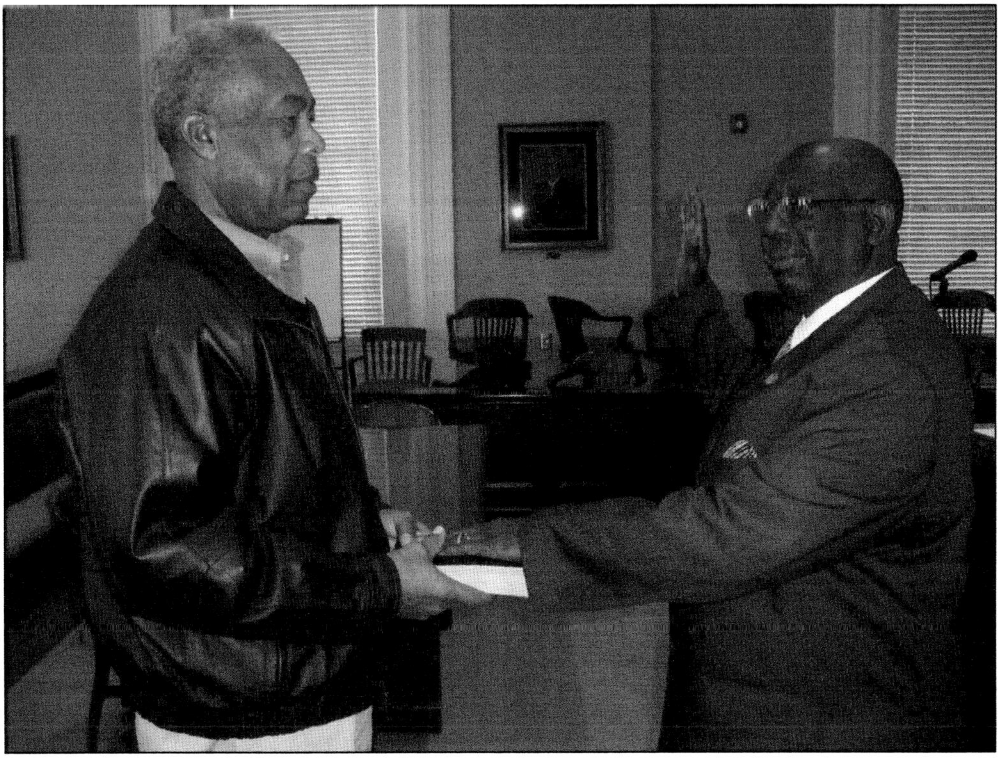

On December 29, 2010, Ernie J. Washington Sr. was sworn in as the first African American coroner of Hampton County at a ceremony in front of 14th Circuit Court judge Perry Buckner at the nearby Colleton County Courthouse. Holding the Bible for Washington is Kenneth Mears, retired South Carolina Law Enforcement Division agent. Washington was the 12th coroner for Hampton County, a position dating back to 1882. (Courtesy of HCG.)

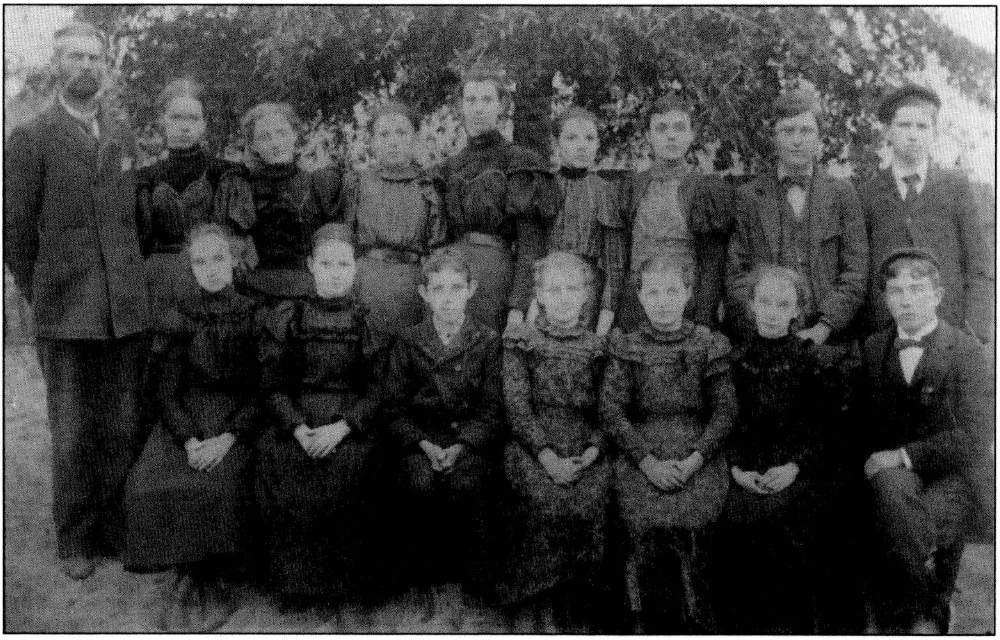

A group of Brunson School students and teachers is pictured here in the late 19th century. From left to right are (first row) Etta Williams, Bertha Ulmer, Charlie Fontaine, Etha Brunson, Dessie Brunson, Tiny Williams, and Arren Preacher; (second row) Dr. Macy (teacher), Theresa Lightsey, Carrie Lewis, Bertha Mole, Josie Fontaine, Pearl Youmans, Eva Hogarth, Julius Gray, and Martin Lightsey. (Courtesy of BMVC.)

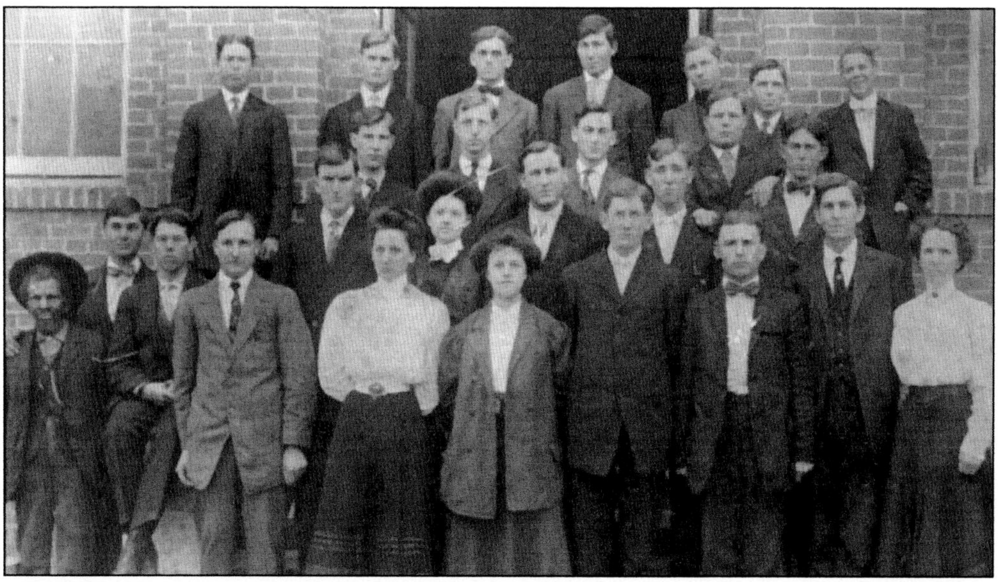

The 1909 Brunson special business class picture includes, from left to right, (first row) Andrew Stokes (janitor), Charlie J. Miley, unidentified , Roy Brant, Carrie Deer, Carrie Bell Robertson, Emory Davis, unidentified, J.C. Eagerton, and Mrs. Eagerton; (second row) George Gray, Viola Miley, unidentified, Mack Mixon, and Bob Mixon; (third row) ? Polk, Carl Kearse, Charlie Barnes, and Charlie Thames; (fourth row) Perry Mixon, ? McTeer, Herman Ficken, Dallas Deer, Claude Gooding, Dallas Smith, and Boyd Elkins. (Courtesy of BMVC.)

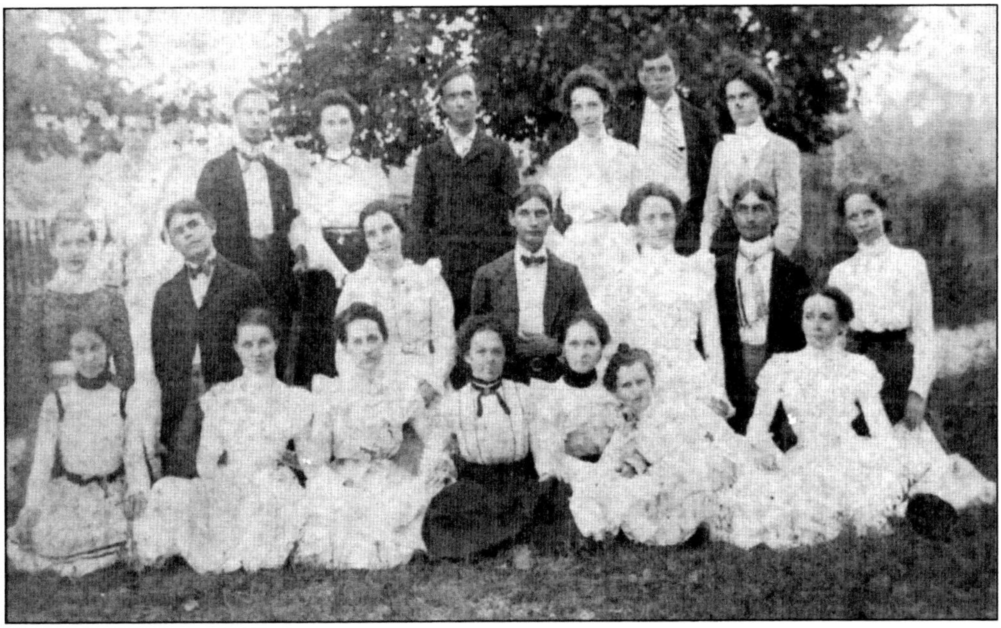

These Brunson young people pictured around 1900 include, from left to right, (first row) Mack Gooding, Dessie Brunson, Carrie Ulmer, Bonnie Lovett, Bertha Ulmer, Hattie Lightsey, and Alma Lewis; (second row) Etha Brunson, Cape Folk, Wilma Hines, Owen Barker, Carrie Lewis, Edgar Brunson, and Theresa Lightsey; (third row) Pearl Youmans, Zeke Addison, Emmie Gooding, Ed Owens, Gertrude Simpson, George Addison, and Hattie Gooding. (Courtesy of BMVC.)

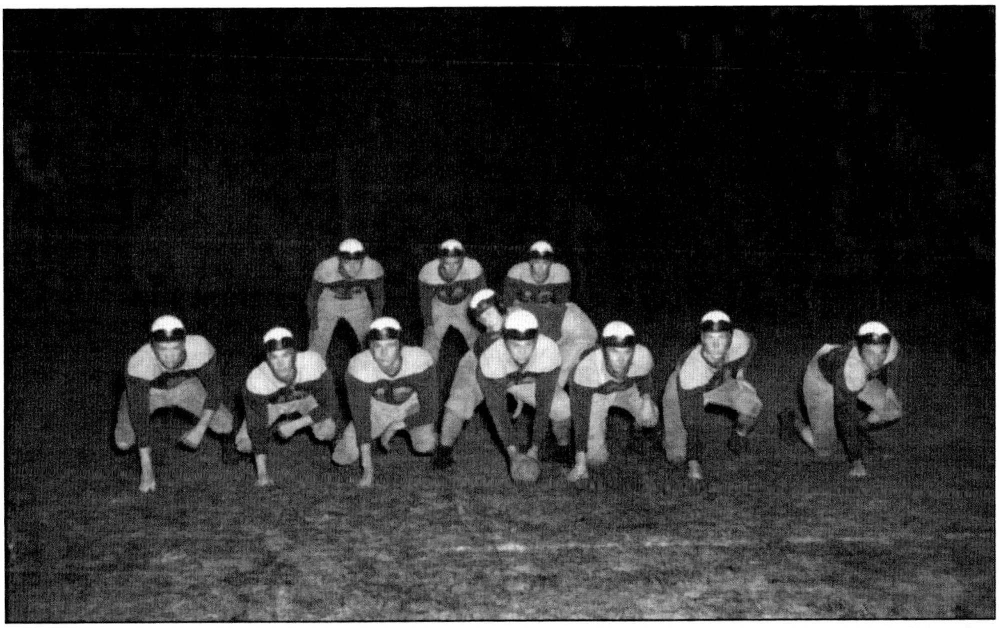

The Brunson High School and Fairfax High School consolidated football team posed for this photograph during the 1948–1949 season. That year, the two schools joined together to compete because there were not enough players at each school to form an 11-man team. Football was a more physical sport in those days; note the smaller protective pads and the absence of face masks. (Courtesy of BMVC.)

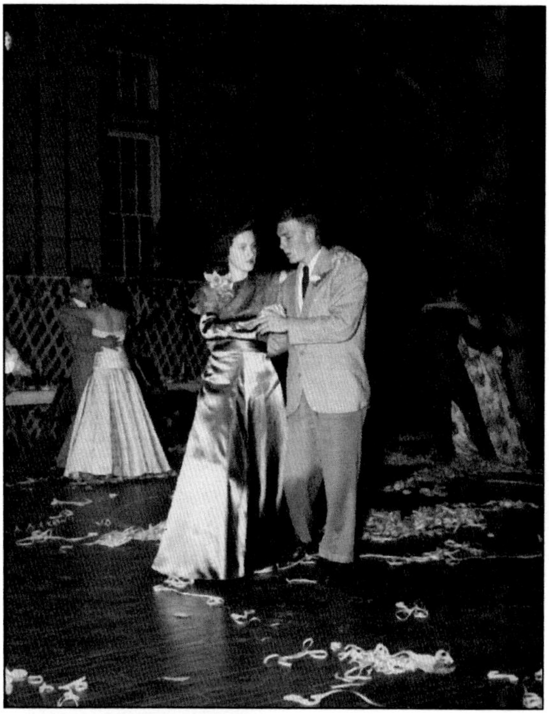

With the school's gymnasium decorated just for the occasion and littered with confetti, an unidentified couple twirls in a formal dance during the junior-senior prom at Brunson High School during the 1948–1949 school year. Education in Hampton County has changed greatly over the decades, but the prom has remained a tradition and a rite of passage into adulthood. (Courtesy of BMVC.)

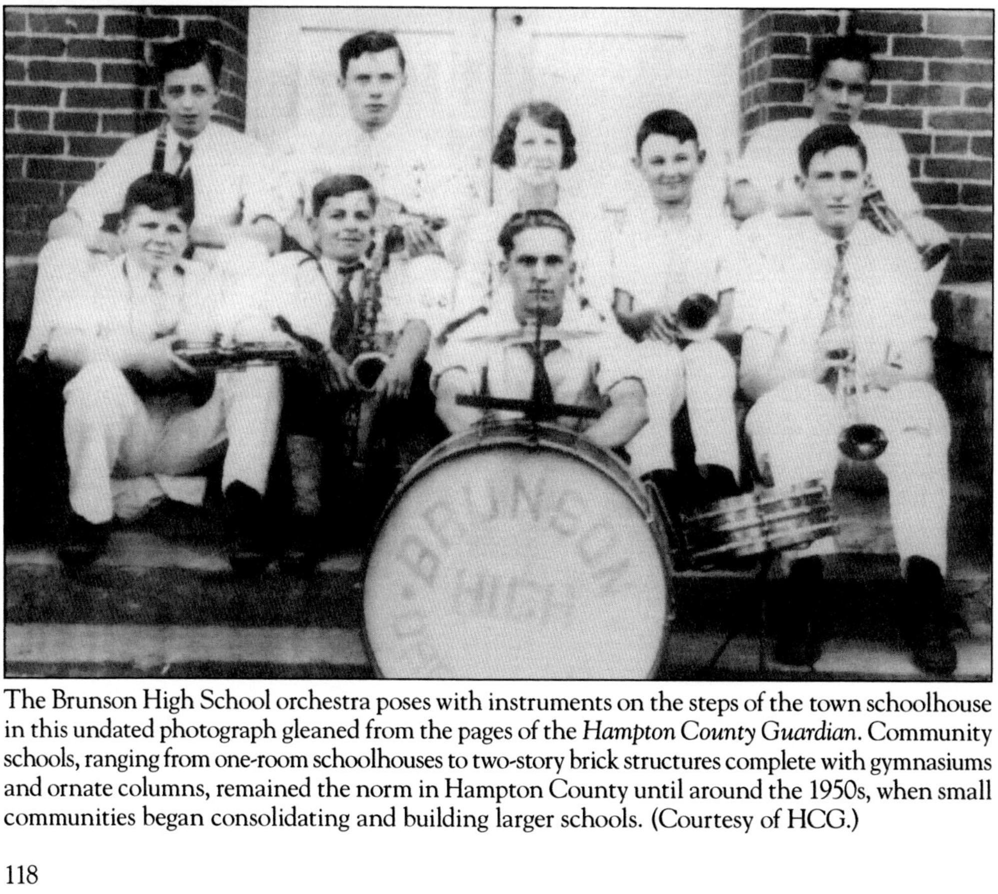


The Brunson High School orchestra poses with instruments on the steps of the town schoolhouse in this undated photograph gleaned from the pages of the *Hampton County Guardian*. Community schools, ranging from one-room schoolhouses to two-story brick structures complete with gymnasiums and ornate columns, remained the norm in Hampton County until around the 1950s, when small communities began consolidating and building larger schools. (Courtesy of HCG.)

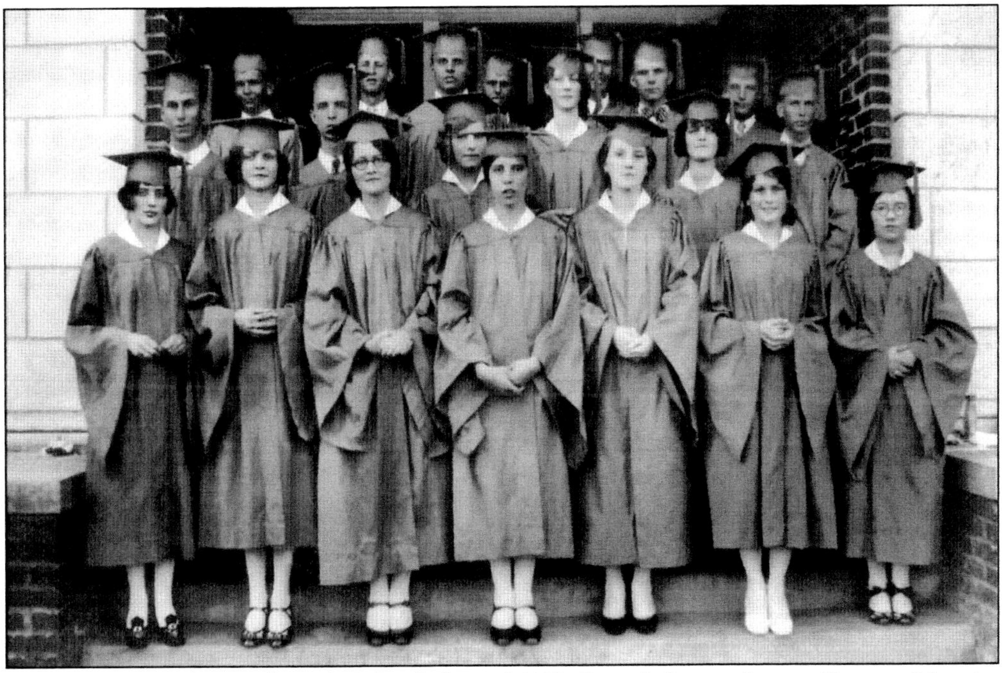

Pictured here is the Estill High School class of 1929. From left to right are (first row) Louise Rushing, Eunice Youmans, Clara Lee Peeples, Alice Fitts, Lucille Solomons, Laura Oswald, and Olive Solomons; (second row) Dudley Rouse, Ernest Ramsay, Sadie Smith, Thelma Herndon, and Lucille Laffitte; (third row) Wattie Peeples, Sigo Solomons, Robert Riley, Herbert Davis, Buster Hamilton, Howard Rhodes, J.T. Rouse, and John Barnes. (Courtesy of HCG.)

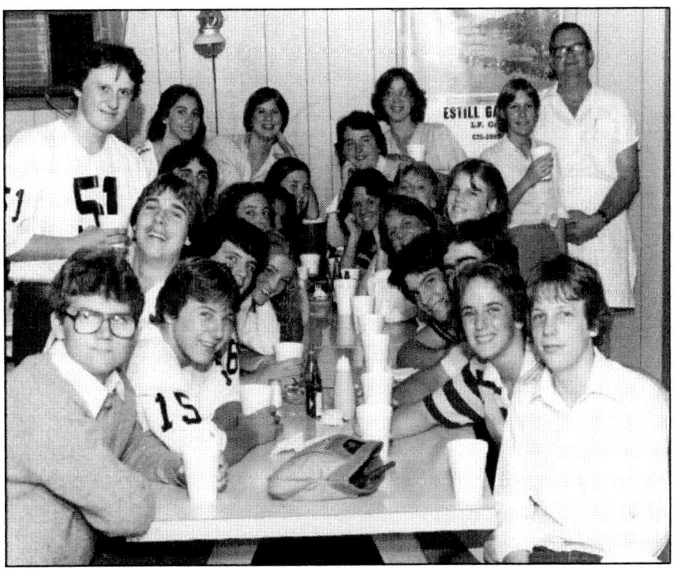

The Patrick Henry Academy class of 1980 relaxes with restaurant owner Lester DeLoach (back right) at nearby Lester's Barbecue. From the mid-1970s to the late-1980s, the Patrick Henry senior class had a tradition of taking senior leave on Thursdays and Fridays to enjoy lunch at this restaurant. Lester's was founded in the mid-1960s and is still operating as one of the oldest family restaurants in Hampton County. (Courtesy of HCG.)

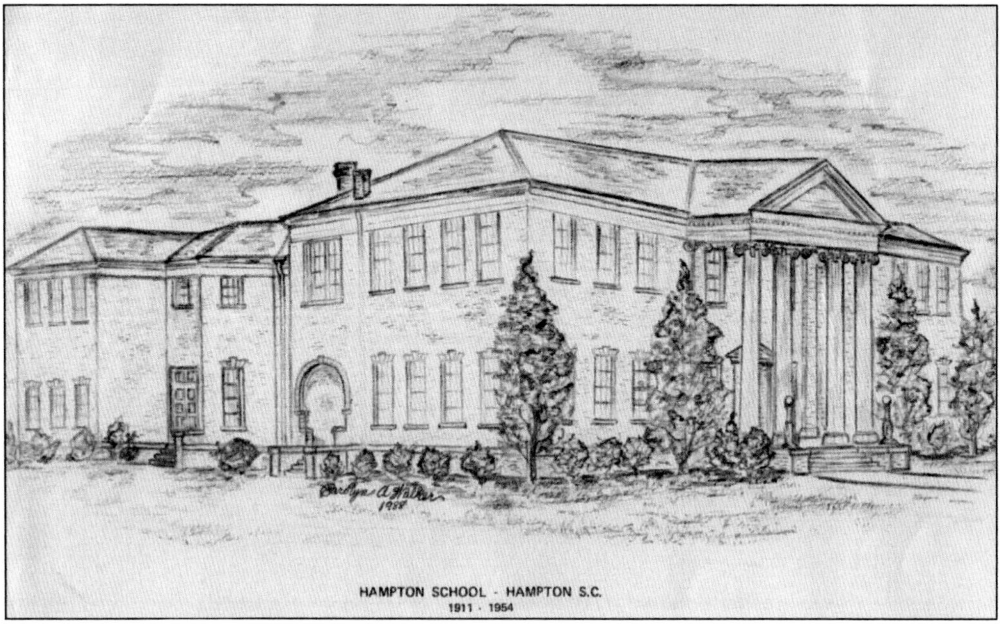


The glorious Greek Revival–influenced architecture of Hampton School, built in 1911 on Mulberry Street, can be clearly seen in this 1988 artist's rendering. The size and age range of its student body is evident in the undated group photograph. This building was demolished in 1954 when the current high school was built. The previous Hampton school building, and the first sizable one, was constructed in the late 1800s on land donated by Capt. Arnold Browning. The famous soon-to-be governor Wade Hampton gave a dedication speech to a waiting crowd from its second-story balcony. The current high school was then named in honor of Wade Hampton. A South Carolina Historical Society marker has since been erected on Mulberry Street at the site of this once-grand school. (Both, courtesy of HMVC.)

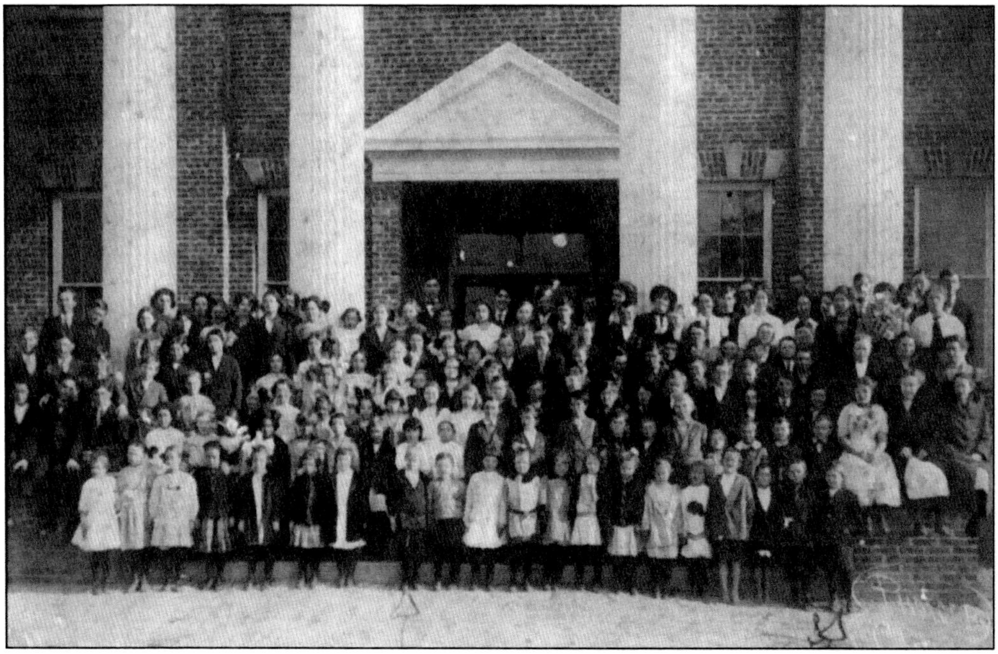

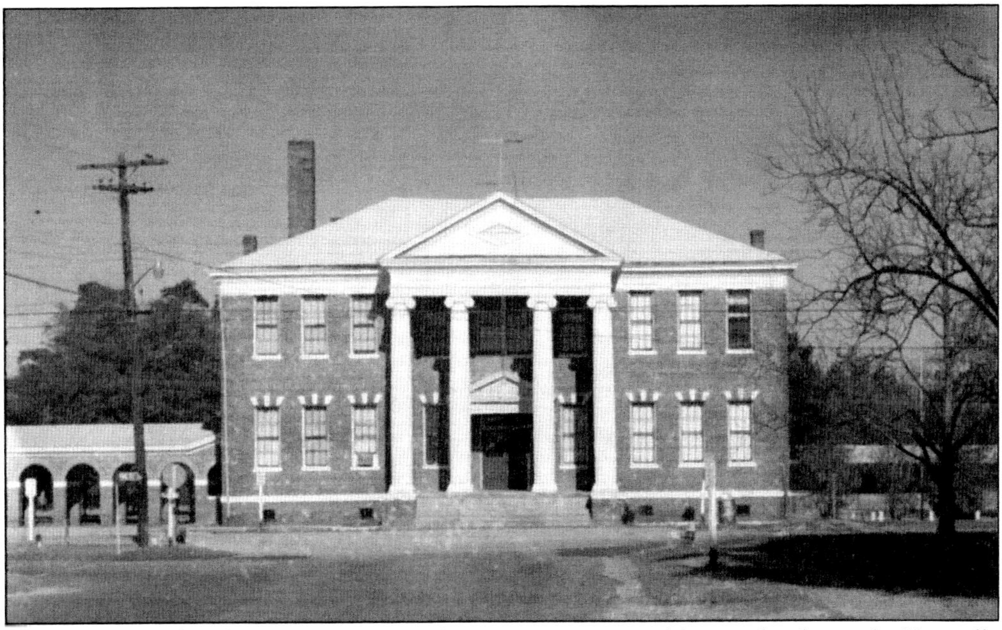

Following a fire that destroyed an early 20th-century, two-storied frame school near the Varnville Christian Church, the much grander Greek Revival Varnville School, featuring Ionic columns, was built in 1911 during the term of J.W. Rouse, Hampton County superintendent of education. Mostly replaced by modern construction, the school's gymnasium still stands and is currently used as the county recreation department. (Courtesy of HMVC.)

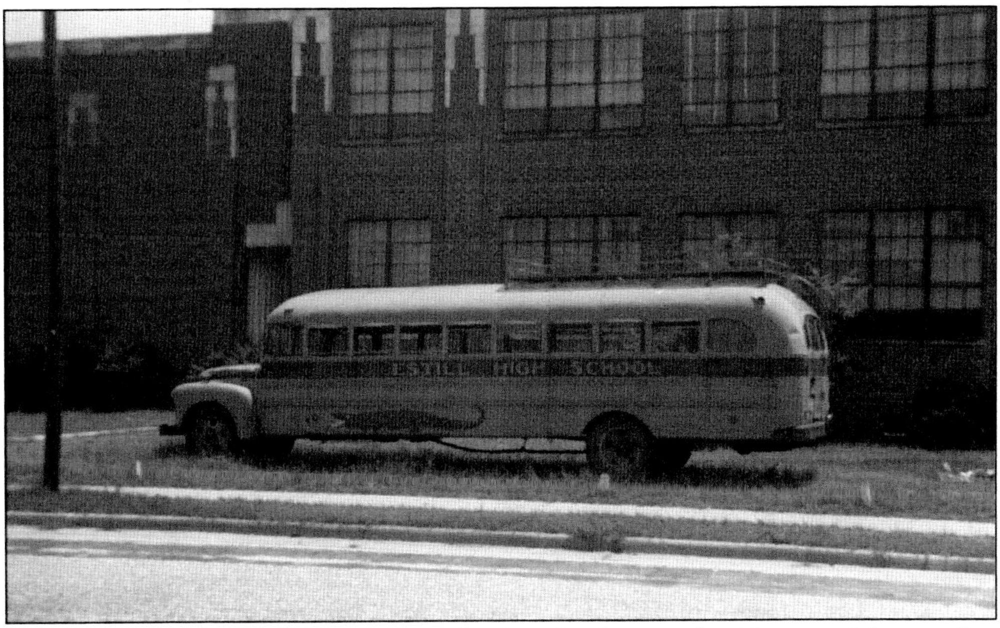


The Estill High School Alligator mascot rides the school activity bus like a watchdog standing guard over the students in this 1961 photograph. The high school building was constructed not long after the South District was formed in 1951, thus consolidating the smaller schools in Furman, Garnett, Luray, Scotia, and surrounding areas. This building still serves students as the Hampton School District 2's office and auditorium. (Courtesy of DM.)

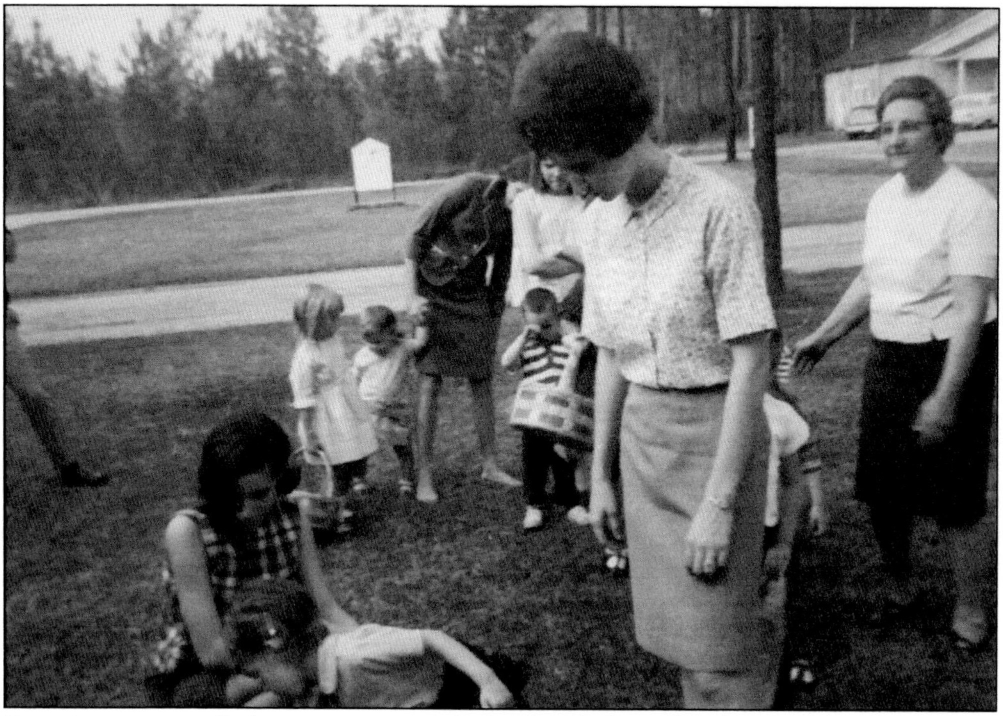

Sometimes one can find more action outside the church doors than between the pews. Above, mothers, grandmothers, and basket-toting children in various levels of excitement enjoy an Easter egg hunt on the church grounds on March 25, 1967. Below, the Nix reunion was immortalized in photographs on April 23, 1960. In Hampton County, the church was much more than the temple of the Holy Spirit and the house of the Lord; it was home to the family and community spirit as well, hosting everything from dinners on the grounds and reunions to softball games and sunrise services. In church, or out, family bonds and friendships grew stronger. (Both, courtesy of DM.)

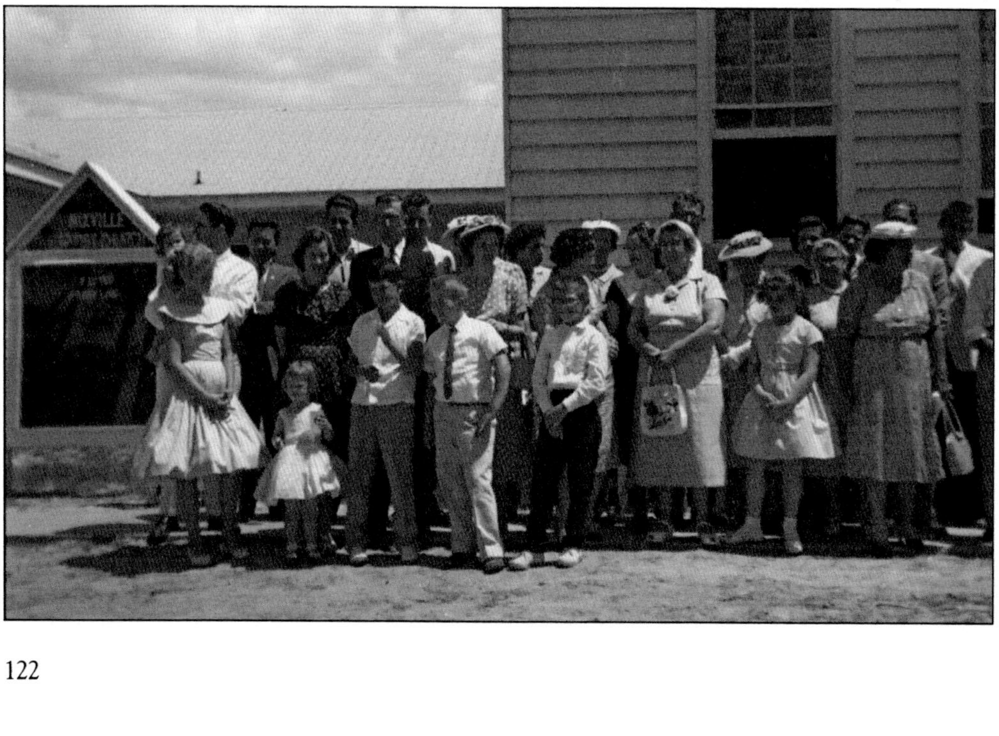

There is always a reason to celebrate in a Hampton County church. At right, a talented young musician strokes the ivories to lead the chorus during the Seckinger birthday party on March 10, 1968. Below, churchgoers adorned in 1770s-period dress hitched up the family horse and dusted off the old buggies for the Lawtonville Baptist Church Bicentennial Celebration in 1975. Pictured here, from left to right, are David McKenzie, David McKenzie Jr., Cecilia Baker McKenzie, Cecilia Williams Baker, and Eleanor Clarke Baker. Lawtonville Baptist was founded in 1775 and is still a thriving, living part of history in Estill today. (Right, courtesy of DM; below, courtesy of Cecilia Baker McKenzie.)

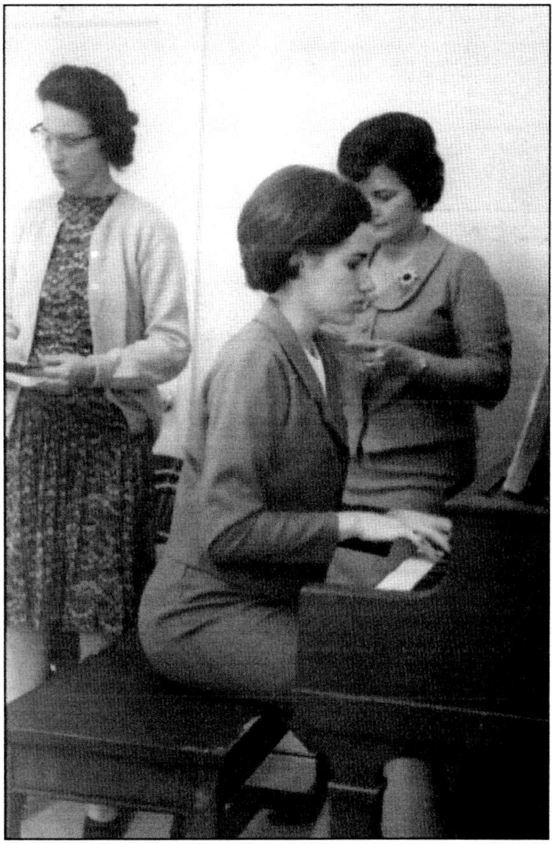

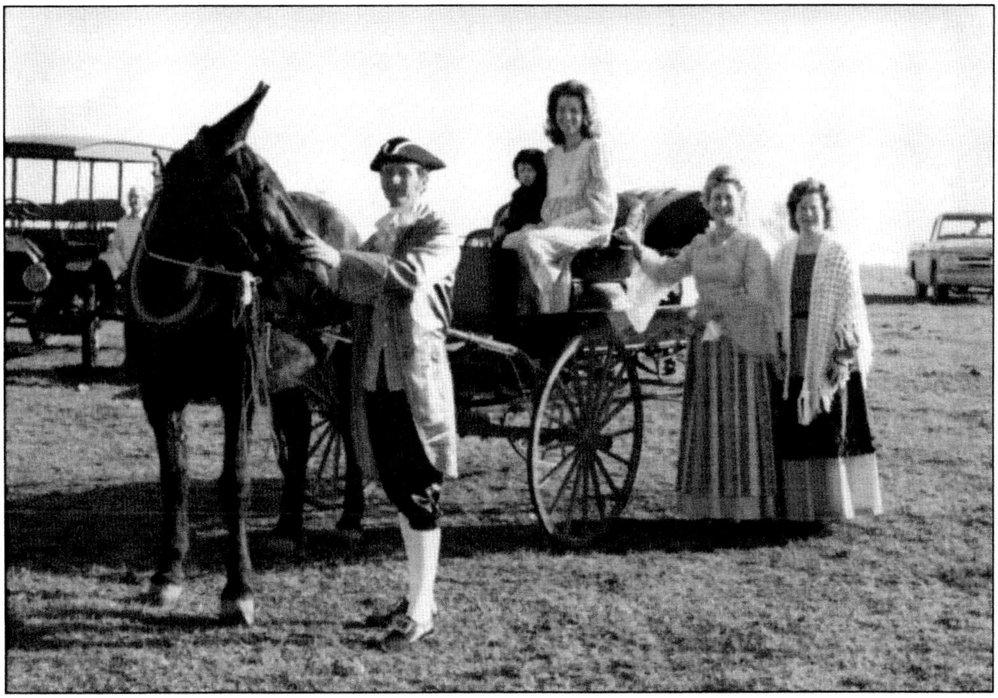

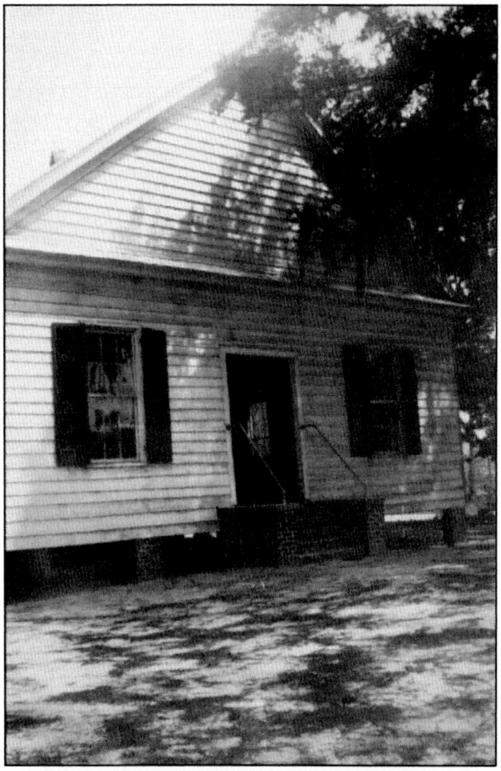

Steep Bottom Baptist Church was constituted on March 19, 1814, through the efforts of Rev. Hezekiah A. Boyd of Black Swamp Church and Rev. James Sweat. The original church building was burned by Gen. William T. Sherman's troops in February 1865. A replacement church sanctuary was completed in 1872 for the bargain price of $345, and it is still used today as a social hall. (Courtesy of Lettie Ginn.)

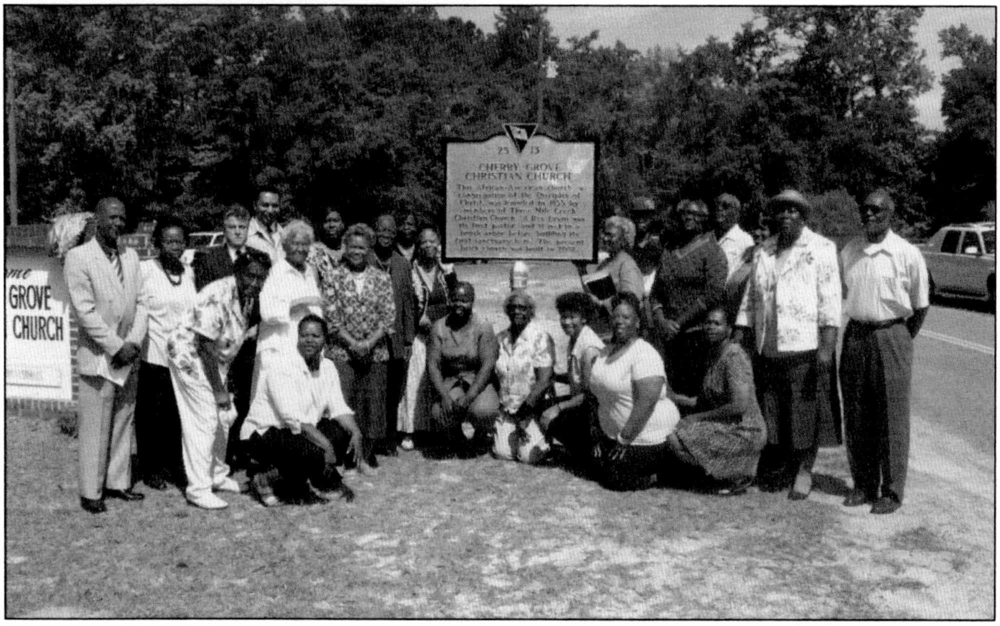


Greater Cherry Grove has not only survived the tests of time, it has grown and prospered over the past 155 years. The Greater Cherry Grove Christian Church was founded in 1855. Today, this African American church is one of the oldest Disciples of Christ churches in the state. In 2009, the South Carolina Department of Archives and History erected a marker at the church's original site. (Courtesy of Kim Doctor.)

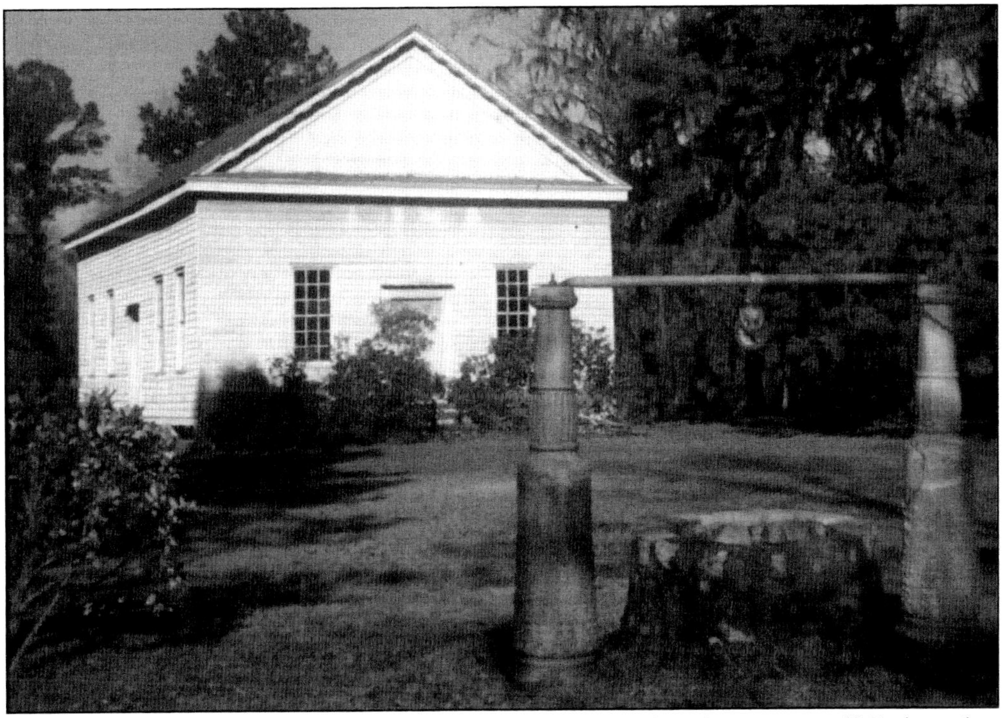

There are at least three churches in Hampton County that predate the county itself. Early settlers in Hampton County established churches not long after they built their own homes. Black Swamp Methodist Church, established in 1786, is pictured here in 1965. Among the earliest churches are Beech Branch Baptist Church, 1758; Pipe Creek Baptist (now Lawtonville Baptist), 1775; Prince Williams Primitive Baptist, 1812; Steep Bottom Baptist, 1814; Stony Creek Presbyterian at McPhersonville, 1832; Lebanon Methodist, 1834; and Efferson Missionary Baptist, 1850, believed to be the oldest African American church in the county. And from these churches, especially Steep Bottom Baptist, many younger churches branched out. (Both, courtesy of DM.)

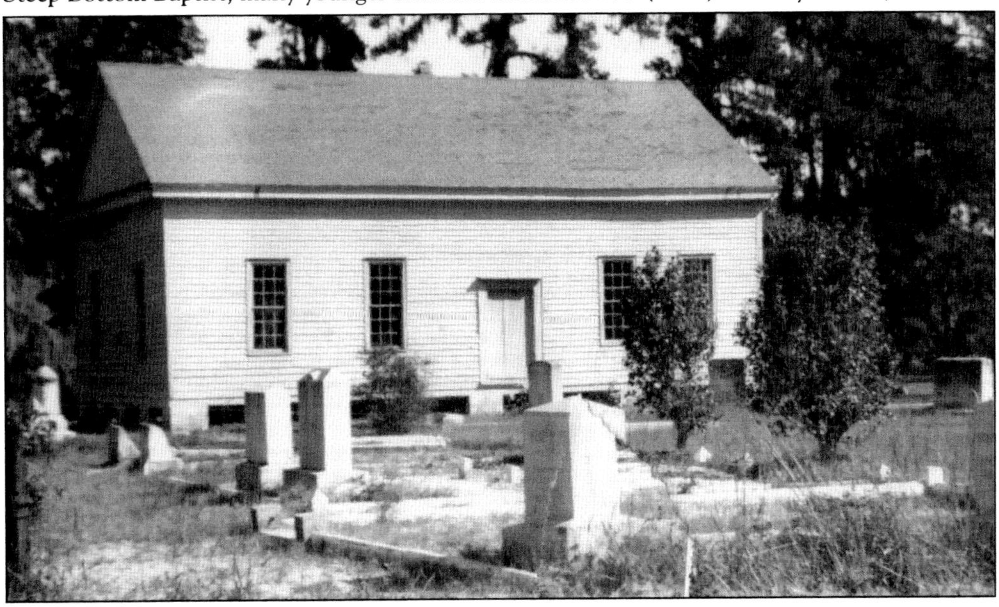

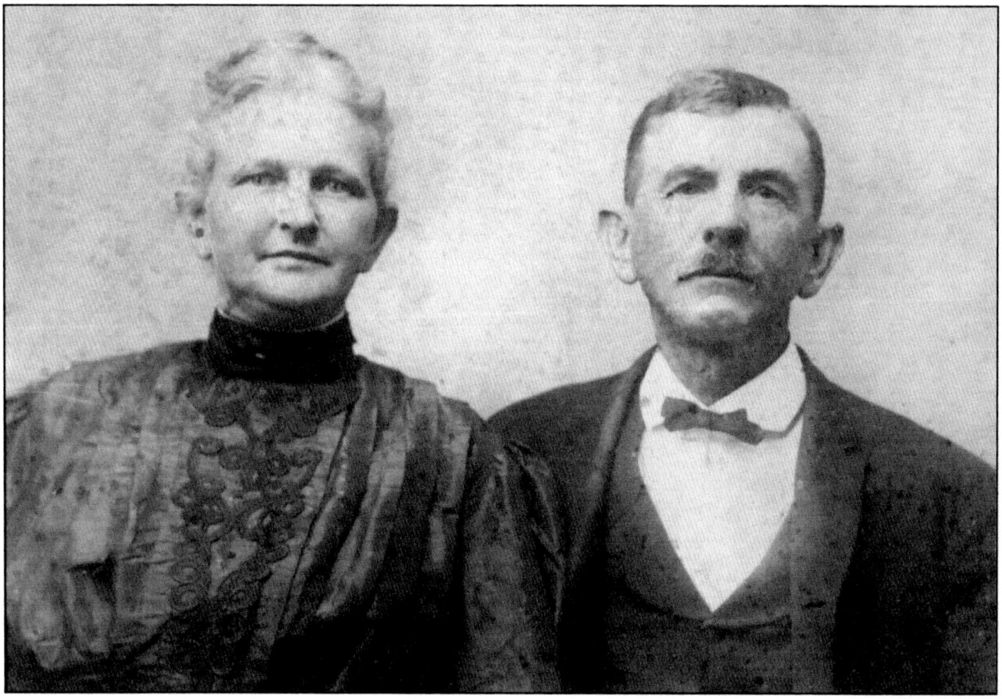

George Bender Clarke, pictured with his wife, Pauline Rhodes Clarke, was the builder who constructed the magnificently ornate Lawtonville Baptist Church sanctuary in 1911. Lawtonville Baptist, pictured below as it looked in 1965, predates the founding of the United States. This church was constituted in March 1775 while South Carolina was still a royal province of Great Britain. The first church building was erected near the village of Lawtonville and originally known as Pipe Creek Church of Regular Baptists. Although much of Lawtonville village was burned during the Civil War, the church survived because it was used as a hospital for Union soldiers. In 1884, the church changed to its current name and moved to its present site in Estill in 1911. It is listed in the National Register of Historic Places. (Above, courtesy of Cecilia Baker McKenzie; below, courtesy of DM.)

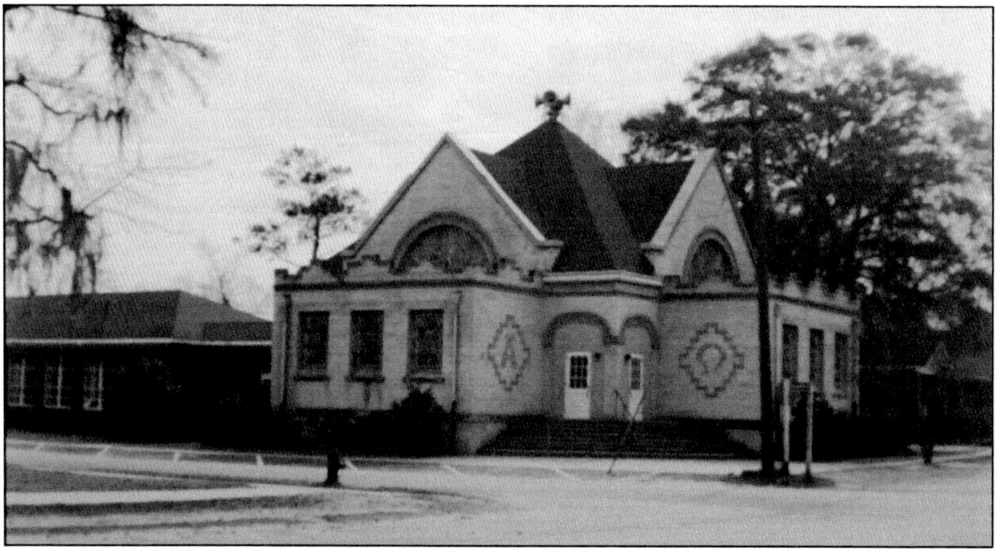

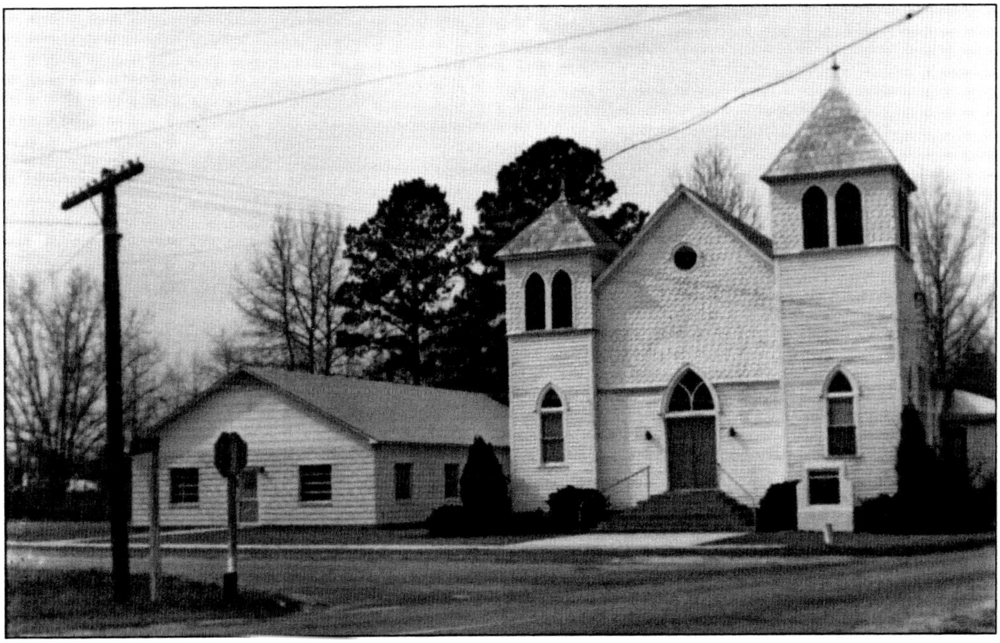

Its congregation may say that the road to redemption intersects with the highway of salvation at Estill Methodist Church, located at countryside junction near Estill and pictured above on February 6, 1968. With ivy climbing its chimney like a stairway to heaven and surrounded by lofty pine guardians, St. John's Methodist in Garnett is pictured below in 1970. There are an estimated 150 or more churches of almost every denomination scattered throughout Hampton County, and visitors or residents alike could say that there is more than one path to salvation for folks in these parts. One can find churches in the most rural, isolated farm communities, along busy main highways, and even in old storefront buildings. And as they say in many local churches when a worshiper agrees strongly with the Good Word—amen. (Both, courtesy of DM.)

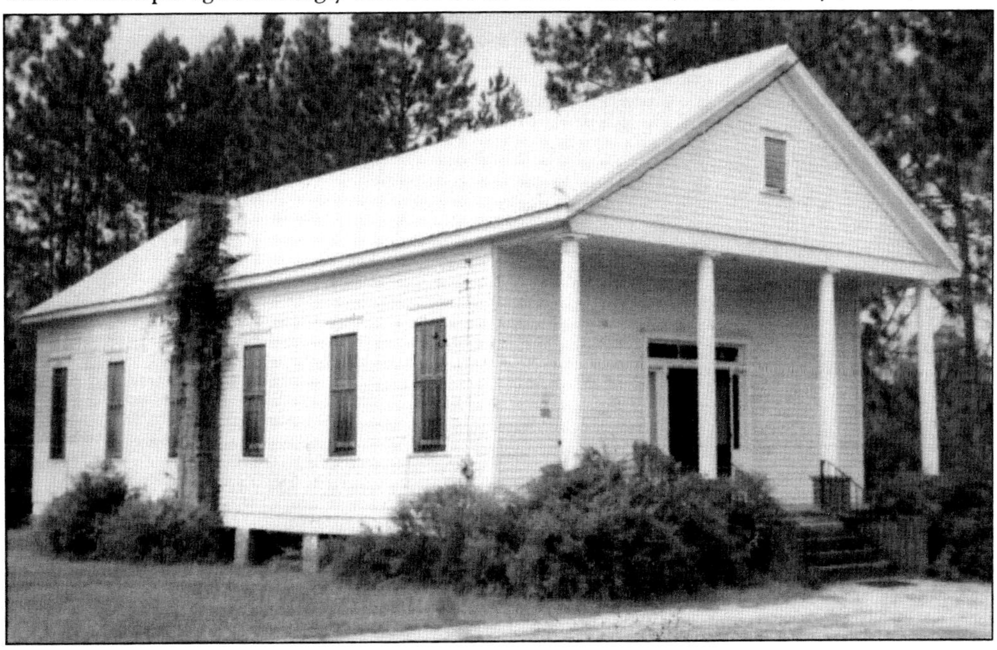